THE WORLD'S GREATEST SEA MYSTERIES

Michael and Mollie Hardwick

SAPERE
BOOKS

THE WORLD'S GREATEST SEA MYSTERIES

Published by Sapere Books.
20 Windermere Drive, Leeds, England, LS17 7UZ,
United Kingdom

saperebooks.com

ISBN: 978-1-80055-593-8.

TABLE OF CONTENTS

steam was not invincible. There are countless stories of such lost craft; of ships which survived although their crews had disappeared. The case of the *Mary Celeste* is not by any means the only one of its kind. Nor are these the only puzzles set by the sea. Of the many cries for help that have reached the shore in bottles, few have been proved to have come from the ships named. Men and women have disappeared without trace, though rumour and legend have never ceased to offer explanations — from the sad survivors of the *Grosvenor* East Indiaman to Commander Crabb in more recent times.

Sometimes the sea's mysteries are psychological, for men in a small community, alone together for months on end, behave inexplicably. What lay behind Drake's contradictory attitude to Thomas Doughty? Why did Benbow's captains commit virtual suicide by refusing to fight? What prompted the last voyage of "John Orth"? All these we discuss, leaving the reader to draw their own conclusions.

Sunken treasure is one of the sea's greatest lures, and has usually managed to keep its secret. The early divers who tried to salvage Shakespeare's

> *Wedges of gold, great anchors, heaps of pearl,*
> *Inestimable stones, unvalu'd jewels,*
> *All scattered in the bottom of the sea*

were no more baffled when they "woo'd the slimy bottom of the deep" than those working with modern equipment. The treasure-ship of Tobermory Bay and her golden store (if store there is) are still unsalvaged after almost four hundred years.

Of supernatural sea mysteries there is no end. Granted that the sailor is the most superstitious of men, and that one may take his yarns with (so to speak) a pinch of salt, many of them have a convincing ring, although in some, such as the case of

'Learn the secret of the sea?
Only those who brave its dangers
Comprehend its mystery!'

Michael and Mollie Hardwick
1967

1: A FROG HE WOULD A-SPYING GO

One Sunday in March, 1967, a little party from the Royal Air Force station, Thorney Island, which is at the head of Chichester harbour, Sussex, wandered along a beach close to the base, looking for shrimps. With Chief Technician Garth Slade and his two children were their friends, Sergeant Jeff Bull and his wife Margaret. It was Mrs. Bull who spotted what looked like an unusually large seashell, gleaming in the sand, which half buried it. One of the party prodded it with a stick. The shell moved, turned over — and revealed itself to be a human skull.

They wrapped the skull in a piece of cloth and took it back to the RAF guardroom, from where Chichester police were notified. The police collected the skull and took it to the Chichester pathologist, Dr. Donald King, who was able to tell them that it had been in the water about ten years and had suffered a slicing cut which had removed a considerable part of it.

The finding of human bones — skulls, even — while not an everyday occurrence is not an altogether rare event on the beaches of England's south coast. But within forty-eight hours of Mrs. Bull's find the Press agency wires were buzzing with it, and reporters from the national newspapers were making their own enquiries of the police, the pathologist, and everyone else concerned. This skull, it was believed, might well be very special indeed. It might provide the solution to the eleven-year-old mystery of the disappearance of Britain's most famous frogman, Commander Lionel Kenneth Philip ("Buster") Crabb, OBE, GM, RNVR.

Dental examination offers the best chance of identifying a skull whose ownership is suspected from other clues, and fortunately the Thorney Island skull had several of its upper teeth intact. Arrangements were made for it to be seen by a dentist who had attended Commander Crabb. While they awaited the outcome, journalists sent to their newspapers' libraries for the bulky packages of clippings about the Crabb case and proceeded to refresh their memories, ready to write a big story on the solution of the mystery.

Crabb, they reminded themselves, had been one of those men whose lives, though colourful and full of incident, are eclipsed by the sensational circumstances of their deaths. He had been far from unknown during his lifetime: some of the clippings dated back twenty years or more. Yet in the decade following his "death" in 1956 he had been the subject of hundreds of thousands of printed words in many languages, not to mention countless radio and television programmes of reconstruction and speculation. No wonder, for Crabb's story had become an accumulation of fact and fiction which had blended into a first-rate spy thriller, intensely mysterious, yet always capable of being solved.

Born in 1910, Lionel Crabb had made the sea his first career. He had served a Merchant Marine apprenticeship, but instead of sitting his second mate's examination had gone ashore in America to take a job with an oil company. It had led nowhere. In the years following, the little man with the sharp prominent nose and ready grin had moved restlessly from job to job, sometimes prospering, sometimes not. At one time he had thought of settling in China, at least for a while, but had abandoned the idea on finding himself unable to master the language. He repeated the attempt a few years later, but failed again.

He failed also to get into the Royal Naval Volunteer Reserve, both before the war and when it began, becoming instead a merchant seaman gunner on a tanker. At last the RNVR agreed to have him and he transferred to the Royal Naval Patrol Service, sailing in small civilian craft. He gained a commission, and then became a mine and bomb disposal officer, in which capacity he was posted to Gibraltar in 1942.

It was in the Mediterranean that he found his true calling. "Frogman" was a new term still, and certainly a new trade where the Royal Navy was concerned, though its Italian counterpart had a number of well-equipped and courageous men ready to ride into action beneath the sea's surface on piloted torpedoes and clamp mines of increasing destructiveness and complexity on to the hulls of Allied vessels. To counteract these attacks and protect several hundred ships at a time, ranging from large warships to rusty little merchantmen, Gibraltar possessed three launches, fitted with spotlights and small depth-charges, and two amateur divers equipped with Davis Submerged Escape Apparatus designed for submariners needing to escape to the surface after a disaster. Other equipment had been improvised by the divers. Rubber suits and flippers were unknown to them.

Making up in utter heedlessness of personal risk what they lacked in equipment, Crabb and a small band of colleagues saved tens of thousands of tons of shipping and thousands of lives during the remaining years of the war. He was awarded the George Medal and appointed to the Order of the British Empire and became a Lieutenant Commander.

At the end of the war he left Italy, where he had risen to command all anti-sabotage measures connected with shipping, and went to Haifa where Jewish terrorists were using some of the same methods as the Italians. Then in 1947 he was sent home to England, and in the following year found himself out of the Service and out of a job. Again, he tried several things before being offered a succession of civilian diving jobs by the Admiralty. He played a prominent part in the attempt to rescue trapped crew members of the submarine *Truculent* when she sank after a collision in the Thames estuary in 1950. He was recalled to naval service for a few years and reached the rank of Commander. He took part in the search for another submarine, the *Affray*; and twice he helped in attempts to find the sunken treasure galleon at Tobermory.[1] In March, 1955, he became to all intents and purposes a civilian for good.

Just to what extent Buster Crabb retained his association with his country's defence after this date has not been revealed. There is no doubt that he undertook various assignments within his own field at the Navy's request. He may have served also those nameless branches of the Security Services from time to time. It is not unlikely that he carried out the odd job on behalf of other Intelligence agencies friendly to Britain. Whether he was working for one of these, or for his own country, or purely for himself, on 19 April, 1956, is half of the mystery surrounding him. The other half is, what happened to him on that day, and where, if still in this world at all, is he now?

Very little is known: conjecture has amounted to enough words to fill several volumes.

April, 1956, was a momentous month for Britain and for hopes of world peace. Russia's President, Marshal Bulganin, and her Premier, Mr. Khrushchev, were paying an unprecedented visit to London, having landed at Portsmouth from the 12,000-ton cruiser *Ordzhonikidze*. This impressive warship, which had astonished the Western world by her great

---

[1] See Chapter 16.

speed and manoeuvrability, lay at anchor with her two attendant destroyers in Stokes Bay at the entrance to Portsmouth harbour.

On Tuesday, 17 April, Buster Crabb was seen in Portsmouth. He was a familiar figure there, the little man in the inevitable tweed suit and pork-pie hat with the romantic trappings of an eyeglass in the left waistcoat pocket and a silver-mounted ebony swordstick with its head in the form of a gold crab. Officers of HMS *Vernon*, the Royal Navy's underwater establishment at Portsmouth, seeing him in town would ritually ask him with an air of mock mystery, "Hullo, Crabbie. Something on?" And he would answer, "Just dropped in for a shave and a haircut". Everyone knew better than to enquire further.

This Tuesday he had a companion with him when he booked into the Sallyport Hotel in the High Street: a younger, fair-haired man who signed the register as "Matthew Smith". They had separate rooms. Crabb was out of the hotel all next day, from before breakfast until evening. The following day, the 19th, he left early again. "Matthew Smith" left later, paying the bill for them both and taking Crabb's baggage and swordstick with him.

Buster Crabb has never been seen since.

The disappearance of Commander Crabb might not have been noted as soon as it was had not his employer in a firm supplying equipment to Espresso bars tried to get in touch with him. On being told when he telephoned the Sallyport Hotel that Crabb had left, his employer managed to get in touch with an officer friend of Crabb's who promised to find out where he had gone. To the officer's surprise he could learn nothing, except that the head of Portsmouth CID had been to the hotel and removed four pages of the register, cautioning the hotelier and staff, in the name of the Official Secrets Act, not to discuss the case with anyone.

Another friend of Crabb's telephoned the Admiralty to ask for news of him. He was told simply that Crabb was dead.

Report and rumour sped swiftly through the naval establishments and quarters in Portsmouth and soon reached the National Press. Telephones at the Admiralty began to ring. Brief, unembroidered answers sufficed for a few days, but on 29 April the Admiralty ventured a short announcement:

> He is presumed to be dead as a result of trials with certain underwater apparatus. The location was in Stokes Bay, and it is nine days since the accident.

The combination of such reticence, the named location, the fact that the Russian warships had been anchored at Stokes Bay on the date indicated, and, not least, Crabb's record as a naval frogman could not fail to set the Press ablaze. But despite the most intensive foraging by dozens of newspapermen there proved to be very little fuel for kindling. Official circles were blandly and imperturbably saying nothing about the frogman's disappearance. Neither those reporters with special contacts in the Navy nor those flattering themselves that official evasion was bound eventually to collapse in the face of the public's determination to have the truth could be certain whether this was a case of known facts being concealed or of genuine mystification with a degree of embarrassment in it. Inevitably, in such circumstances, rumour raged.

Crabb, claimed one school of opinion, had been killed by the Russians while inspecting the hull of the cruiser *Ordzhonikidze* in order to find out for the Admiralty the secret of the warship's exceptional performance. His death had been brought about by some form of automatic anti-saboteur device in the hull itself which had either electrocuted him or had pinned him in a magnetic grip and held him until he drowned. More prosaically, some thought he had been seized by Russian frogmen sentries and drowned, or been shot from the cruiser's deck by a sentry who had seen him surface. Some of those who favoured the death theory claimed that his body would eventually come ashore or would be found at the bottom of the harbour. Others maintained that the Russians, embarrassed at having killed him, had taken the body on board the cruiser and would carry it away with them to dump well out at sea. A minority, however, contended that the body had already been recovered by Crabb's naval colleagues and had been buried at dead of night with full honours in an unmarked grave.

But for every one who subscribed to the belief that Crabb had met his death in one form or another there was another ready to declare equally emphatically that he still lived. The view from where most of these theorists were standing was as plain as any pikestaff: Crabb had been detected by the Russians, trapped either by their frogmen or by some anti-saboteur device, and taken aboard the cruiser. He would be taken back to Russia for interrogation by specialists about his last mission and Britain's underwater secrets in general, then either held prisoner for the rest of his life or simply liquidated.

Attending these principal theories of death or capture were many other ancillary beliefs: that Crabb's mission had been to discover whether the *Ordzhonikidze* had a nuclear bomb aboard her, for which purpose he would have been carrying a special detector instrument: that he had been acting not for Britain, but for some other interested power, such as America: that his mission, far from being offensive, had been to help safeguard the Russian warship from a sabotage attempt by anti-Soviet fanatics, and thus ward off a calamity which might precipitate a world war: or — tamely, by comparison with all this — he had dived from nothing more than personal curiosity.

Scraps of extra information began to emerge, though all served to intensify the mystery rather than dispel it. One reporter stated that he had been informed definitely by the Navy's underwater establishment that Crabb had not been working for them at the time of his disappearance. The Navy denied that any attempts had been made, or were to be made, to find a body in Portsmouth harbour. On the following day, however, another newspaper reported the Admiralty as admitting that Crabb had been working for them, but refusing to say in what branch or capacity. It emerged also in this story that one of his visits to Portsmouth some months earlier had coincided with the presence there of the cruiser *Sverdlov* and other Russian warships. Approaching the mystery from the Russian side, a reporter sought a statement from the Soviet Embassy and was told by a member of the naval staff that a frogman had been seen by a lookout aboard the *Ordzhonikidze*, but had remained on the surface for no more than a few seconds and had not been seen again. Any question of action being taken against the unknown swimmer was unthinkable, the spokesman added: the warship had been in a British port.

On Saturday, 28 April, "B. and K.", as Messrs. Bulganin and Khrushchev had come to be termed throughout the British Press, re-embarked and the Russian ships sailed. Whether they took Buster Crabb with them, alive or dead, none but the Russians knew. They certainly took with them a mystery which has yet to be solved.

The Press — and by now the story was receiving world-wide attention — kept up its efforts. One particularly intriguing new item of information came from a wartime colleague of Crabb's who revealed that he had intended to carry out his own search of Portsmouth harbour bed, but had been approached by an officer who had dissuaded him. The officer had gone on to say that the Official Secrets Act prevented him disclosing all he knew about the affair, but that he did know a great deal, part of which was that Crabb was definitely not in Portsmouth harbour. There were also reports that officers from HMS *Vernon*, too, had wanted to search for their old friend, but had been quietly warned off.

On 9 May, three weeks after Crabb had vanished, an attempt was made to bring the matter right into the open. In the House of Commons Mr. John Dugdale, Labour Member for West Bromwich, asked for the Admiralty's evidence of Crabb's death to be made public, together with the details of his disappearance and what efforts were being made to retrieve his body. The Prime Minister, Sir Anthony Eden, answered:

"It would not be in the public interest (*Opposition cries of Oh!*) to disclose the circumstances in which Commander Crabb is presumed to have met his death. While it is the practice for Ministers to accept responsibility, I think it is necessary, in the special circumstances of this case, to make it clear that what was done was done without the authority or the knowledge of Her Majesty's Ministers. Appropriate disciplinary steps are being taken."

Mr. Dugdale echoed the sentiments of a large part of the House when he described this as one of the most extraordinary statements ever made by a Prime Minister and a complete evasion of ministerial responsibility. The leader of the Opposition, Mr. Hugh Gaitskell, said:

"The Prime Minister will be aware that a great deal of information has already been published in the Press. Does he not think on reflection, in view of the amount of speculation which undoubtedly will continue in the absence of any information from the Government, that it really would be wiser in the general interest if a fuller explanation were given?"

(*Opposition cheers.*)

The Prime Minister responded:

"I can assure Mr. Gaitskell that there are certain issues which are the responsibility of the Prime Minister himself, and having given all reflection to all the information at our disposal I thought it my duty to give the answer I have, and I am afraid I must tell the House that I cannot vary from the answer."

In vain did the leader of the Opposition try to get him to elaborate. Equally fruitless was Mr. Emanuel Shinwell's attempt to persuade the Prime Minister to say precisely what he had meant by "appropriate disciplinary steps are being taken". Mr. Dugdale's bid to move the adjournment of the House, in view of the Government's refusal to state what it knew and had done about Commander Crabb, drew the Speaker's reply:

"When a Minister refuses to answer a question on the grounds of public interest it has been ruled in the past — and I adhere to it — that that is a matter which cannot be raised, and therefore I must decline the application."

Whatever had not been revealed in the way of details, it was now at least clear that a great deal was known somewhere. A further Parliamentary attempt to find out more was made five days later. Replying before a packed and hushed House, Sir Anthony Eden firmly declared that the circumstances of the case were such that no government in any country would say more than he was prepared to say. The national interest would not benefit from the discussion of certain matters of security. More particularly, the international interest had much to hope for from the new relationship with the Soviet leaders which their visit to Britain had inaugurated. Sir Anthony concluded:

"I intend to safeguard that possibility at all costs. I believe it is also in the minds of the Soviet leaders. It is for that reason that I deplore this debate and will say no more."

Something of what the Soviets were, indeed, thinking of the Crabb episode was now known. The Foreign Office had received a Note from the Soviet Embassy:

"During the stay of Soviet warships in Portsmouth, at 7.30 a.m. on 19 April seamen on board the Soviet ships observed a frogman floating between the Soviet destroyers. The frogman, who wore a black diving suit with flippers on his feet, was seen on the surface of the water for one to three minutes and then dived again…

"The commanding officer of the Soviet ships, Rear-Admiral Kotov, in a conversation with the Chief of Staff of the Portsmouth Naval Base, Rear-Admiral Burnett, draw his attention to the case. Rear-Admiral Burnett categorically rejected the possibility of the appearance of a frogman alongside the Soviet ships and stated that at the time indicated there were no operations in the port involving the use of frogmen…"

The Note then commented that reports in the British Press had since revealed that frogman activities had, in fact, been going on and that a Commander Crabb had met his death. In view of this discrepancy, would the Foreign Office kindly explain?

On 12 May *The Times* reported that, according to the Russian newspaper *Tass*, the Foreign Office had answered:

"As has already been publicly reported, Commander Crabb carried out frogman tests, and, as is assumed, lost his life during these tests. The frogman who, as reported in the Soviet

Note, was discovered from the Soviet ships swimming between the Soviet destroyers was to all appearances Commander Crabb. His presence in the vicinity of the destroyers occurred without any permission whatever and Her Majesty's Government express their regret for the incident."

Though newspapermen continued to dig for clues, little was forthcoming. Those who believed in Crabb's death, whether it had been caused accidentally or deliberately, seemed to be proved right when, in August, a skeleton was washed up near Portsmouth. But a pathologist was able to show that the bones had been in the sea for at least a year and possibly much longer: they could not be Crabb's. Those who had never doubted this verdict wagged their heads knowingly and pointed to a recent report, reprinted in the *Daily Telegraph* from the West German newspaper *Bild Zeitung*, to the effect that a French left-wing politician who had just returned from Moscow had disclosed that Crabb was in solitary confinement in Moscow's Lefortovo prison, and that he had been interrogated and had at length admitted that he had been investigating the *Ordzhonikidze*'s automatic steering mechanism when Russian frogmen had captured him. Having confessed, the report claimed, he had been offered a job in the Red Navy with the promise that he would not have to operate against Britain.

The *Daily Telegraph* had tried to authenticate this report from French Socialist sources, only to receive a denial that any information had been passed on about Crabb's being a prisoner in Moscow. Thus there seemed to be no more to the report than there had to the skeleton. But while a skeleton could be proved not to be Crabb's, there was nothing to show so positively that he was not a prisoner of the Soviets. In fact, a Reuter cable from Copenhagen in October quoted members of an anti-Communist movement as saying that Russian sailors who had visited Britain in the *Ordzhonikidze* had disclosed that on the cruiser's return voyage from England part of its hospital had been sealed off and guarded, with an occupant whom the sailors could not identify.

Through lack of facts the Crabb case faded from the newspapers, to return sporadically during the following months as new rumours arose. Then, on 9 June, 1957, came a sensation: the body of a man in frogman's clothing was fished out of Chichester harbour by anglers. It had neither head nor hands.

The discovery came just over a month after a Sunday newspaper story alleging that a "senior Whitehall official" had stated: "We are satisfied that Cdr. Crabb did not die when he went into the water in Portsmouth near the Russian warships… We have good reason to believe that he was taken aboard one of the ships and is now being held in Russia… I cannot disclose my proof for saying this, but it would not surprise me if Cdr. Crabb were to be produced at a Moscow press conference one of these days."

Instead, it seemed, the sea had produced Crabb's body. The frogman's suit it wore was an Italian two-piece type favoured by him in preference to the one-piece naval issue. The body had been found at a place to which currents might well have taken it if it had been drowned off Portsmouth. It had been in the water for some considerable time. From that point, however, identification became increasingly less certain. Crabb had been hammer-toed. While the upper part of the corpse was little more than a mass of bones, the lower part, which had evidently been afforded some protection from the "process, both mechanical and animal, of the sea" by the thick waistband, was in a fair state of preservation. The toes were certainly distorted, though not so distorted as Crabb's had been. Crabb had had a scar on one leg. The corpse had a scar, though not decidedly the same one. There were also rust marks on the legs, suggesting that the corpse had been caught up and held by some wire or metal during much of its period of immersion, which might well account for its not having come shorewards before.

The inquest conducted by the Chichester coroner resulted in an open verdict. It was impossible to say how the corpse had met its death. As to its identity, the coroner remarked: "We have all been warned from time to time in the legal profession about a chain being as strong as its weakest link, but there is also such a thing as a number of incidents which are minor indications building up to a conclusion, which I do not think can be resisted... Looking at the evidence in this case, I am quite satisfied that the remains which were found in Chichester harbour on 9 June were those of Cdr. Crabb..."

The body was buried at Portsmouth on 5 July. There was no official representative of the Royal Navy at the funeral.

Had the identification of the remains been just that little bit more positive, the Crabb case might have ended there in so far as his actual fate was concerned, though there would still have remained the considerable mystery of what he had been doing on that last dive, who he had been working for, and whether he had been killed at once, or captured, interrogated and later executed. But now the pot was kept boiling by a new disclosure: three days before the finding of the floating corpse three Russian submarines had passed through the English Channel on their way to Egypt. To many theorists this irresistibly suggested either of two things. Crabb had been in Russian hands. After interrogation he had been killed, and now his body had been put overboard from one of the submarines so that it would appear never to have left British waters. Alternatively, someone else's body, with its head and hands removed to make identification impossible, had been dressed in Crabb's suit and put in the water to float ashore in imitation of Britain's own masterly wartime hoax of "The man who never was" — in which case, it could be concluded that Crabb was still alive and in Russian captivity.

Three years passed, during which the name of Crabb occasionally appeared in Britain's newspapers, generally in connection with some fresh speculation or seeming hint from a foreign source. Then, in 1960, the well-known journalist, Mr. J. Bernard Hutton, published a book, *Frogman Extraordinary*,[2] setting out the entire story of the Crabb case from the Russian end.

After detailing all that was known and conjectured about the sequence of events from British sources, Mr. Bernard Hutton reproduced in its entirety a translation of a *dossier* compiled in Russia and circulated in various languages to Communist Secret Police chiefs in all the Iron Curtain countries, for the purpose of showing them "from the experiences of our best-trained Investigation Judges how to go about in seemingly hopeless cases and what methods and tactics to apply to break down the prisoner without the application of drugs, violence, or other such methods". The *dossier*, he stated, had been smuggled from behind the Iron Curtain by secret agents and had reached Britain in November, 1959. The information it contained had been most thoroughly checked and found to be absolutely genuine.

In the matter-of-fact phraseology of official reports, the *dossier* tells how Crabb's last diving mission was fated before it

[2] *Frogman Extraordinary*, published by Alvin Redman, also published in the USA as *Frogman Spy*.

began. An agent in Portsmouth had already warned the Soviet ships that he would be examining them, and he had been easily intercepted and captured. He had been kept under heavy sedation until the Soviet vessels were well clear of British waters, then transferred by helicopter to Russia. There he had been interrogated intensively, but had denied steadfastly that he had dived under the Soviet ships for any other reason than to satisfy his own curiosity. Reduced to a state of exhaustion by prolonged bouts of physical exercises, which he had borne with great courage, he had at length been switched to favoured-prisoner treatment and told that further interrogation would be unnecessary since the British Government's refusal to allow his case to be debated in Parliament, and their official disowning of him, were proof enough that he had been working officially for one Allied Power or another. Instead of being executed for spying, Crabb was being offered the chance to join the Red Navy as a frogman. He accepted, stipulating that he would not work against his own country.

The next move, the *dossier* went on, was to provide a corpse which the British would take to be Crabb's, thus ending all suspicion that he was alive and in captivity. A corpse had been duly procured and suspended in the sea, where it would remain until rendered unidentifiable. Crabb had been re-christened Lev Lvovich Korablov and set to work to learn Russian, working eight hours a day with a woman instructor. Within a month he was able to read newspapers with the aid of a dictionary and engage in everyday conversation. Less than two weeks later he was privileged to enjoy a day's sightseeing in Moscow. The report for that day reads, in part:

> During the car drive from Selskoye to Moscow, L. L. Korablov watched the landscape and the numerous blocks of flats and factories which were either completed or in the

course of erection with interest, and admitted that he was astonished to see such great building activity. When we reached Moscow, he frankly expressed surprise at the countless new buildings which had been erected after the war, and the dense motor traffic, and also the variety of goods which he noticed in the shop windows.

He appeared impressed when taken to the Lenin Mausoleum in Red Square, but he did not say anything. On passing a church and seeing that it was not closed, L. L. Korablov remarked that he had not thought Russians were allowed to visit churches. He was, however, most impressed when we took him to the reconstructed parts of Moscow and when he saw the airy thoroughfares with their high buildings. He did not conceal his amazement. It seems that best of all he likes the new Gorky Street.

He was equally impressed when we visited the G.U.M. store, when he found out for himself that large numbers of ordinary people not only buy articles of bare necessity but luxuries like television sets, radio receivers, electric irons, etc. He admitted that he had been under the impression that these things were only available in Russia to the better-paid circles, and said that, having seen the type of people who spent their money in the store, he now knows that every section of the population shops in the store.

He enjoyed food and drink in the Caucasian Restaurant and expressed his liking for the friendly service which the waiters gave. On several occasions he said that his first outing into freedom was like a lovely dream and that he expected to wake up at any moment and find himself back in reality.

During the whole day, only Russian was spoken and L. L. Korablov is well able to converse freely, though sometimes he is at a loss for a word and has to think to find the right expression.

The excursion to Moscow was a clear step forward to his being convinced that the Soviet people are not only prosperous but also contented. This opinion is based on the fact that L. L. Korablov repeatedly said that the faces of the people which crowd the streets, shops and restaurants are cheerful and that they look full of life.

To sum up the rest of the *dossier* briefly, Crabb duly entered the Red Navy, made rapid progress, becoming personally popular and professionally respected, gained a commission, and, as this remarkable document reaches its end, has become Lieutenant Lev Lvovich Korablov. The *dossier* also, incidentally, records the eventual transportation of the specially-prepared corpse to Britain by one of the three submarines en route to Egypt, and its casting adrift, after official Soviet circles had become alarmed by reports of the "senior Whitehall official's" statement that he believed Crabb to be alive.

In a letter to the present authors, Mr. Bernard Hutton reaffirms his absolute conviction of the genuineness of the details contained in this *dossier*. He speaks also of the receipt, since his book came out, of "further authenticated information from behind the Iron Curtain about Crabb-Korablov's activities as a frogman instructor at various commands of the Red Navy". He states that a few days before his book came out he received a photograph, too late to include in it, of a group of uniformed Red Navy officers on board a Soviet vessel, and showed it, without comment, to Crabb's divorced wife and to a wartime fellow-diver and close friend. Both identified one of the officers in the photograph as Buster Crabb. When shown the *dossier* text of Crabb's interrogations, both also remarked upon several outbursts attributed to him which were too typical to have been invented.

Certainly, the *dossier* fits the facts of the Crabb case as they are known in the Western world. The whole account, even if it possesses more of the qualities of a James Bond thriller than real life is wont to do, is convincing — except, for what the present authors' opinion is worth, in two respects. Crabb, a man of forty-six at the time and only just recovered from a deliberately induced state of complete exhaustion, is said to have progressed in less than six weeks from total ignorance of the Russian language to a point where he could read newspapers and converse freely throughout an entire day's sightseeing. This, surely, is a sheer impossibility, and two authorities to whom we put the question have confirmed as much, both maintaining that such proficiency could not be attained in less than a year, and would be unlikely at that. Could it be that parts, at least, of the *dossier* are, at worst, completely fabricated, or, at best, wishful thinking? The other passage which seems to us to belong to one or the other of these categories is the account of Crabb's reaction to his day out in Moscow. This crudely coloured account is quite at variance with the rest of the narrative, and simply does not bear the stamp of an official report. Was it, perhaps, slipped in for the benefit of those satellite officials who would read the *dossier* and might be thought to benefit from a touch of reassurance about the morale of the Muscovites? Or might it not be the one obvious error of judgment in an otherwise cleverly concocted narrative prepared expressly for the purpose of "leaking" to the West? In short, could someone in Moscow not resist the temptation to work in a page of propaganda at a convenient point?

We do not know how the *dossier* was obtained by Western agents, and we are unlikely to be told. Its authenticity might hang upon that. If it is authentic, does it necessarily tell the whole truth? Was the headless corpse really planted by the Russians — and were the remains those of an anonymous Russian or of Crabb himself? If Crabb is alive and serving in the Red Navy, what will become of him when he is too old to be of further value? Will "L. L. Korablov" retire on a pension to some Russian equivalent of Eastbourne or Worthing? Will he quietly disappear? Or will Commander Lionel Crabb be produced with a flourish and, perhaps, returned to the West?

In January, 1967, he was reported to be living in East Germany and training frogmen of the *Volksmarine*. This story was promptly denied by the East German Foreign Ministry, but Mr. Bernard Hutton, broadcasting on the BBC, said that he was convinced of its truth.

And so we return at last to the skull found on Thorney Island in March, 1967. When we left it, it was awaiting dental examination. This was duly carried out — to reveal that, since none of the remaining teeth had been filled, no possible identification could be made.

The Crabb file remains open, and we wonder what next? But we cannot resist scribbling a footnote before passing it on. If the Russians really did go to the lengths of producing a headless corpse so soon after disquieting comment had arisen in Britain in 1957, might they not have wished to scotch more recent talk of Crabb's presence in East Germany?

In other words, who arranged for an unidentifiable skull to be found one Sunday morning by a lady looking for shrimps?

2: THE MYSTERY CLOUD THAT KILLED

In the course of a single day in March, 1878, more than one thousand letters which had been accumulating at Portsmouth General Post Office were returned to their senders. All the letters had been posted in the Bermudas, and all too late for delivery, for each was marked "Sailed for England". They had been forwarded to Portsmouth, and now they went back again. This time they bore a new inscription: SHIP FOUNDERED.

The 368 men and boys to whom those letters would soon have been delivered would never read them now. They would never open or answer a letter again.

Over most of southern England, Sunday, 24 March, was a fragrant, calm spring day, as the training frigate HMS *Eurydice*, 921 tons, her scuppers open to let the balmy air ventilate her, moved serenely around Dunnose Head, Isle of Wight. It was afternoon, the traditional Sunday time of make-and-mend and recreation. Some of the boys who made up the main part of the vessel's complement were busy with needle and thread, or reading, or making models, writing more letters, skylarking: but most were lining the rails, gazing shoreward and talking of their expected landfall at the end of their first cruise away from their homeland. It was a beautiful day to be coming home: a perfect Sunday afternoon, redolent of all that characterized England. The sea was calm. No hazards lay in the trim frigate's path.

Yet, within a few minutes, *Eurydice* and all but two who had sailed in her were no more.

There are still people who remember their parents speaking of the horror of that day. The loss of a ship and all those in her is always a tragedy: this tragedy struck doubly at the sensibilities of the nation because of the seemingly supernatural mystery of its cause.

There was nothing old or unseaworthy about HMS *Eurydice* and her officers were efficient. She was in spruce condition, befitting one of the Navy's liveliest, handsomest 26-gun frigates. In 1877 she had returned to John White's yard at Cowes for conversion into one of several training ships capable of accommodating well over three hundred officers, men and boys. In November of that year she was commissioned in her new role, embarked her first complement and sailed from Portsmouth, commanded by Captain Hare from HMS *St. Vincent*. It was the unlucky 13th when she left harbour, but her four-month cruise to the Bermudas, accompanied by the brig *Martin* and, from Madeira, by HMS *Liberty*, was uneventful to a degree. The two accompanying vessels returned home together, leaving *Eurydice* to take aboard some seventy passengers and other supernumeraries before making the passage to Portsmouth alone.

She was sighted at last off the Isle of Wight on Sunday, 24 March, 1878, moving with her port quarter to the westerly breeze under plain sail — top-gallants and royals set, with lower and topmast studding-sails on the foremast and topmast studding-sail on the mainmast. Fine though she must have looked to Sunday afternoon strollers on the shore, the cliffs and green fields of home must have seemed far finer to nearly three hundred young men after four months away, not to mention to those longer-term exiles from Bermuda, civilians and soldiers, who lined the rails.

By nightfall they would be at Spithead. Some would go ashore and others would get their mail. In different conditions, they would not have felt so confident. The part of the Isle of Wight coastline they were passing, between Ventnor and Shanklin, could be a treacherous run. But not today. Not on this calm spring Sunday, with only one cloud in the sky…

But wasn't there something rather odd about that cloud? There was, indeed. The watchers on both ship and shore suddenly began to notice it. Although the breeze over land and sea was still only light, that single cloud seemed to be racing up from the north-west, its speed bearing no relationship to the wind. And what a cloud! It was cigar-shaped, cutting through the air with torpedo-like menace, making the bright sky on either side of it seem to glow in eerie contrast with its dense blackness.

That cloud had already made its impression on people farther away. It had sailed up from apparently nowhere, passing over Clifton, where carriages stopped in the middle of their Sunday morning drive across Brunel's famous suspension bridge to enable their passengers to alight and gaze up at it, and over Malvern, where some people left their dinner to step outside and watch the phenomenon. It had reached the vicinity of Dunnose Head a little after 3.30, which gave it in terms of distance and time a speed of more than thirty miles per hour. The cigar was estimated to be nearly twenty-five miles long and half a mile across.

And now something even more disturbing began to happen. Although the sky on either side remained bright, people over whom the cloud was passing felt a deep chill strike into them. A growling roar like prolonged thunder sounded and grew louder. The calm air became frenzied with tearing gusts of wind, enough to make people clutch at one another for support. Then there came a deluge of snow, falling so hard that it was blinding, so whipped by the wind that it stung like hail. The sky disappeared. The sea, before it, too, vanished in the swirling clouds of snow, was seen to be pressed flat, as though by some inexorable weight.

The storm lasted in all its violence for something like half an hour. Then, every bit as suddenly as it had begun, it ceased. The last of the cloud-torpedo passed over to reveal the sun. The air glistened enchantingly as light and moisture played together. People smiled reassurance at one another and stepped from hastily-taken cover.

When they looked seaward again, alarm returned. HMS *Eurydice* had disappeared.

It seemed ludicrous. There she had been before the sudden squall had blotted her out, moving sedately and calmly on her way. Now she was gone, although a heavily laden schooner which had been seen before, deep in the water, wallowing in the frigate's wake, was still on her course, plodding along as though nothing had happened.

But however phlegmatic her progress seemed from the shore, the schooner *Emma*, bound from Newcastle to Poole with coal, was about urgent business. When the squall had lifted, her master, Captain Langworthy Jenkin, had been quick to see wreckage and a flapping sail in the water ahead. He fancied he heard a cry. One of his crew was sent hastily into the rigging and shouted down at once that he could see a man floating in a cork jacket. Jenkin crammed on more sail and stood towards the struggling man. Having to tack once before he could reach him, he took the opportunity to lower boats. Four men were picked up, besides the one hauled aboard the ship. One was already dead.

As the *Emma* circled slowly about the spot, looking vainly for signs of life, the tops of *Eurydice*'s three masts rose slowly into view and stayed there. The stricken ship must have gone to the bottom nearly on her side and slowly righted herself to an even keel. But no movement was to be seen on the sea except a long line of debris drifting towards the horizon on an offshore surge of water caused by the storm.

Setting his colours to half-mast, Jenkin stood for Ventnor, working frantically all the way to restore the survivors' breathing. Two more had died before the Ventnor coastguard boat came alongside carrying a naval officer who at once recognized one of the dead men as Lieutenant Tabor, *Eurydice*'s first lieutenant, and the other as an officer of the Royal Engineers. The two remaining survivors were hastily taken ashore and restored. They proved to be an Able Seaman named Cuddiford from Plymouth and a nineteen-year-old ordinary hand, Sydney Fletcher, from Bristol.

They were the only survivors ever to be found from approximately 368 men and boys — the exact total has never been ascertained. Many of the others were washed ashore on the French coast, together with a great deal of wreckage, all swept across the Channel at great speed by the rush of sea which had overwhelmed the ship.

Perhaps because it was plain that Cuddiford had not long to live, the two men were subjected to the ordeal of making immediate statements at Admiralty House before the Commander-in-Chief, Portsmouth. This and other available evidence suggests what happened aboard HMS *Eurydice* on that terrible Sunday afternoon.

Seven bells — half-past three — had been sounded about twenty minutes ago and the afternoon watch were looking forward to relief in ten minutes' time as the frigate rounded

Dunnose Head, moving at a steady eight knots. Suddenly the strange, black cloud became visible and immediately the ship passed from calm into the path of a swiftly rising wind, accompanied by a rapid fall of the barometer. Captain Hare, reacting instantly to sudden danger, shouted to the men to "watch in" the royals — the topmost sails — and the lower stun'sails. As the men clambered into the rigging they heard the bosun piping all hands to their assistance, but before another moment had passed the full fury of that uncanny squall struck the ship, literally picking her up and flinging her down again pointing in another direction.

The stun'sails were already furled and Captain Hare roared to the hands high in the rigging to leave the royals alone and get down to safety. It was all there was time to do, apart from a brief, desperate attempt to let go the mainsail and the topsail halyards. The gunner's mate let go the topsail halyards, and a man named Bryant the main sheet. The water was already pouring over the lee netting on the starboard side, washing away the cutter. There was no time even to order the open ports to be shut, let alone to do it. The sea cascaded in, bowling over frantic men and boys as they struggled towards the hatchways. All below decks were drowned where they were.

Those on deck had more chance; but this was no ordinary shipwreck. A gigantic fist of wind smashed into *Eurydice*, beam on, sending her reeling over on to her side, flinging everyone and everything into the sea. Dozens were killed outright, smashed against wreckage, strangled in rigging, forced deep under the surface by the momentum. Others, dazedly treading water, were only momentarily luckier. The sea seemed to be freezing, numbing their limbs along with their senses. Then came the blinding rush of snow. It was too much even for the best swimmers. One by one they went down.

Cuddiford explained his survival:

I caught hold of the main truss, fell, and caught hold of the weather netting and got on the ship's side. We could see her keel. She righted a little before going down, bringing the mizen tops'l out of the water. She then went gradually over from for'rd, the greater part of the hands being at the fore part of the ship outside. She then turned over, bringing the port cutter bottom upwards. I and another, Richards, cut the foremost gripe, and then saw the Captain standing on the vessel's side near the quarter boat and the two doctors struggling in the water. I swam some distance, keeping over my head a lifebuoy which I found, and then picked up some piece of wreck, which I gave to some of the men in the water. I then came across the copper punt full of water. Five men were in it. The sea capsized the punt, and they all got onto the bottom. They asked me if there were any signs of help. I told them the best thing they could do was to keep their spirits up. One of them was just letting go his hold of the punt — I do not know his name. I next saw Mr. Brewer, the bosun, with a cork lifebelt on. He was struggling strongly. I then saw Fletcher in the water with a cork belt and breaker. I lost sight of him during the snow. About five minutes afterwards the weather cleared up. I saw Fletcher again, and we kept together. Then we saw land, but finding it too rough we turned our back to the land and saw a schooner. The schooner bore down on us, sent a boat and picked up two officers that I had not previously noticed with a wash-deck locker. A rope's end was thrown to me from the schooner, and I was then picked up. I judged that I was in the water an hour and twenty minutes.

During the whole of the day following the disaster the Commander-in-Chief, Portsmouth, Admiral Fanshawe, was in constant touch with the Admiralty. Telegrams poured in from all parts of the country, demanding details of the catastrophe, pleading for news of individual victims.

One telegram read:

> The Queen is deeply grieved to hear of the loss of the *Eurydice*. Her Majesty anxiously asks for further details.

In a telegram to the First Lord of the Admiralty, W. H. Smith, of newsagency and bookshop fame, Queen Victoria added:

> The Queen would ask Mr. Smith to make known her grief at the terrible calamity to the *Eurydice* and her heartfelt sympathy with the afflicted friends and relatives.

Smith forwarded the telegram to Portsmouth, where, with the other one, it was posted on the dockyard gate, outside which a dense crowd massed all day.

Rear-Admiral Foley, in charge of the dockyard, visited the wreck and examined what could be seen of her. All that Cuddiford had said seemed to be confirmed. *Eurydice* had gone down almost instantaneously in the midst of a seemingly inexplicable storm of near-hurricane ferocity.

When he returned to shore the Admiral found a request from the chief medical officer at Haslar Hospital, Portsmouth, for an appointment. When they met, the medical officer offered to fit up one of the alcoves in the hospital grounds for the reception of the bodies as they were recovered. The Admiral accepted and despatched an order to the dockyard for canvas and flags to be sent over to Haslar to await the arrival of the corpses. Very few were ever brought in. Five bodies came ashore on the Isle of Wight. Apart from the few which reached France, the rest lay deep in the Channel.

During the weeks which followed, divers and riggers worked steadily to cut away spars, sails and rigging. Meanwhile, formality required that Cuddiford, a dying man, and young Fletcher be arrested and tried by court martial, being the only persons who might conceivably represent any human error on the part of the ship's company. Their trial took place at Portsmouth, in HMS *Duke of Wellington*, with Admiral Fanshawe presiding. This new ordeal for the two men lasted several days, culminating in a verdict that, "Her Majesty's ship *Eurydice* foundered on the afternoon of Sunday, 24 March, 1878, by pressure of wind upon her sail during a sudden and exceptionally dense snow storm which overtook her when its approach was partially hidden by the proximity of the ship to high land."

The two seamen were given a complete discharge. It was all that could be done. No one could explain the mystery of that sinister torpedo of a cloud which had sailed out of the north-west on that balmy spring day.

First attempts to raise *Eurydice* met with failure. She lay in nearly ten fathoms and her keel and part of her hull had become firmly embedded in deep mud. The Admiralty ordered her to be stripped by divers where she lay, but Admiral Foley was determined to bring *Eurydice* into harbour. He had strong wire ropes attached to the inner sides of the ports, the other ends being made fast to four floating hulls stationed over and above the wreck. As the tide rose, the four hulls rose with it, lifting *Eurydice* bodily by the taut ropes. Steam-tugs then moved in and towed the lot of them to a bank under Culver cliff, leaving *Eurydice* there with one side and her upper deck above water at low tide. Owing to the fierce undercurrents off the Isle of Wight coast the divers could only work at slack tides and in perfect weather. The operation took months to bring to completion, being interrupted again and again by bad weather and rough sea, as if the elements which had sent the ship to the bottom so viciously were determined she should not rise again.

At length *Eurydice* was floated sufficiently to enable the tug *Grinder* to tow her into Portsmouth, with tugs supporting her on either side, their steam-pumps working constantly. Crowds watched as they brought her in, already half-dismantled. A great swathe of black crepe had been placed over her bows. Steamship whistles, sailing-ship sirens and foghorns and hooters on shore wailed in mourning as she was towed into the deep dock. Women wept and men bared their heads.

"As an example of perseverance and determination to succeed, the recovery of the ship is unique," the *United Service Gazette* declared. It was an academic exercise, though. Seemingly, she was brought into port so that man could wreak personal vengeance on her rather than leave her to the mercy of the sea. Almost as soon as she had ceased to move workmen swarmed aboard and began to tear her to pieces. By that evening she had been stripped right down to the copper. Within a few days what had once been "one of the finest of her class that ever floated" was no more than heaps of fouled timbers and battered copper.

Her figurehead and other material associated with her are in the Victory Museum, Portsmouth. Of course, commercially enterprising gentlemen cashed in on the disaster to the extent of buying some of her wood and metal and making them into souvenirs, which no doubt enjoyed a ready sale. While this chapter was being written an antique dealer offered the authors a tobacco jar made from *Eurydice*'s timber. We didn't buy it.

3: SPECTRES OF THE SEA

The sailor has always been the most superstitious of men. Isolated by great stretches of ocean for months at a time from his fellow-men ashore, he remains more unsophisticated than the soldier, even in these days of vastly improved communications. And, far more than the soldier or the landsman, he is a prey to the "skyey influences" of legend and hearsay. In the days before the blessing of electric light he lived through his night-watches in a world of illusory shadows and flickering lanterns, his eyes misled by sea mist and moon ray. Anything could happen at sea, however fearful or miraculous. Jack might be terrified, but he was never wholly surprised by phantom hulk, long-dead pirate, monster, mermaid, or (possibly most horrible of all) the apparition of a drowned messmate in his hammock. Whatever fears he suffered would all be repaid by the breathless interest of shore audiences when he spun his yarns in a Portsmouth tavern — perhaps adding a few colourful details which might earn him an extra pot of porter or pipeful of baccy from some sensation-hungry landlubber.

But even allowing for superstition and imagination, there are countless stories of strange appearances at sea which have been seen by whole crews at a time and by different ships on different occasions. Phantom sailors and the ghosts of their vessels seem to outlive land-wraiths, remaining as active in the days of steam as in those of sail. The theory has been advanced that the gradual fading of familiar spectres ashore — the ghostly nuns and headless monks of tradition — is due to the glare of electricity, in which the frail shadows cannot survive. On the dark surface of the sea conditions are more favourable.

This may explain the apparently endless voyage of the most famous of all sea-spectres, the *Flying Dutchman*. For some three hundred years Cornelius Vanderdecken has been afloat, ever since that day in the seventeenth century when he set sail for Holland from Batavia. Captain Vanderdecken had the reputation of being as merciless to his ship as he was to his men, pushing her on through storms and turbulent seas that would have deterred a more reasonable skipper. He had also a name for godlessness and blasphemy. On this particular fateful voyage his ship ran into violent headwinds when she reached the Cape of Good Hope. For nine weeks Vanderdecken and his weary crew urged her on, but in vain.

Understandably enough, Vanderdecken's patience gave way. He fell to his knees on the deck and cursed God, swearing a terrible oath that he would round the Cape if it took him till Judgment Day.

As if unseen powers had heard him the winds rose higher. Vanderdecken's shrieked curses rose above their howl as he tramped the deck, shouting snatches of a blasphemous song. Suddenly, from the blackness of the night, a brilliant light shone out and formed itself into a dazzling figure which floated down until it rested on the poop of the ship. The sailors knelt and prayed, some taking it for an angel, others for the Holy Ghost. But Vanderdecken stood his ground, not even bothering to remove his hat, and to the gentle salutation of the visitant replied with a volley of curses. The figure stood unmoved, and Vanderdecken then did something which paralysed his crew with horror. He drew his pistol and fired at the spirit, ordering it to leave his ship at once.

The bullet made no impression on it. Then it spoke.

"Captain Vanderdecken, you have taken an oath to sail until Judgment Day, if need be. For your blasphemies you shall do so. You shall neither eat, drink, nor sleep, or ever see your home port again, but sail the Seven Seas, a portent of disaster to all who see you. God is not mocked, Captain Vanderdecken!"

And so it is that ever since that night seamen have shuddered and crossed themselves at the sight of a phantom vessel rising from the waves, topmasts first, in the waters round Cape Horn and the Cape of Good Hope, or even farther south. Accounts of her appearance differ. Sometimes she seems like a ship of her own time, a Dutch merchantman, sometimes like a sloop or a schooner. The *Bacchante*, sailing in 1881 between Melbourne and Sydney, saw her as a brig. Aboard the *Bacchante* was a young man who was to be King George V, and he among others saw the sight as recorded in the ship's log:

> The *Flying Dutchman* crossed our bows. A strange red light, as of a phantom ship all aglow, in the midst of which light the masts, spars and sails of a brig two hundred yards distant stood up in strong relief ... on arriving there, no vestige nor any sign whatever of any material ship was to be seen either near or right away to the horizon, the night being clear and the sea calm. Thirteen persons altogether saw her.

One of those persons, the sailor who had first sighted her, fell from the fore top-mast crosstrees to his death on the deck, and at the next port the Admiral who had been aboard the *Bacchante* became fatally ill. The curse of the Dutchman still had power.

The phantom was said to have appeared in 1911 to a whaler, the *Orkney Belle*, off Reykjavik, her sails swelling in a non-existent breeze, her bows almost ramming the side of the real vessel. Then, from her depths, three bells sounded and, heeling to starboard, she drifted away. There is no record that disaster followed this appearance.

Another Dutchman who still wanders the seas is Captain Bernard Fokke, also of Vanderdecken's time. He was a brilliant navigator with a bad reputation, reputedly in league with the Devil. When his ship vanished it was said that he had been condemned by his Master to sail for ever. But a sight of him does not automatically bring misfortune. His legend and that of the two Waleran brothers of Falkenberg Castle in Lower Lorraine have become inextricably mixed with that of Vanderdecken.

The waters of the Solway sometimes carry ghostly longships, the dragon-prowed galleys of the days when Danish raiders were the terror of the seas. Two of these, which sank at their moorings taking all hands down with them, have been seen on light nights, and a venturesome little boat which went out to investigate them about the turn of the eighteenth century was caught up in the whirl of waters as the galleys sank from sight and vanished with them. Today nobody cares to take too close a look at those warrior-laden shapes, if they still appear.

Another ghost of the Solway is a shallop, sunk out of spite by a rival ferryman as it bore a young bride and bridegroom and their attendants across the bay. The man who wrecked it is still aboard, in skeleton form, and like Vanderdecken he brings ill-luck. A similar story is told of a ghostly bridal party seen off the Goodwin Sands.

The Gulf of St. Lawrence, between Quebec and Newfoundland, is said to be haunted by a British flagship, one of a fleet sent by Queen Anne against the French. She sank under the cliffs of Cap d'Espoir in Gaspe Bay, but every year, on the anniversary of the tragedy, can be seen as a bright vision

— her decks crowded with red-coated soldiers in mitre hats, her ports ablaze with light. In the bows stands an officer pointing landwards, one arm round the waist of a pretty girl. Then the lights fade, the vessel tosses, heels over and vanishes beneath the waves.

The coasts of New England are famous — or notorious — for ghost ships. The most terrifying is the phantom *Palatine*. When she is seen scudding down Long Island Sound it is a sign to prepare for storms — hardly surprising, in view of her story.

The *Palatine*, a Dutch trader, left Holland in 1752, with a load of emigrants bound for New England. She was not a happy ship. The Captain and crew were a drunken, brutal lot who terrorized and robbed their passengers and their heavy drinking was probably responsible for the ship grounding on Block Island, though the island was the headquarters of wreckers, who may well have lured the *Palatine* with false lights. As she lurched ashore, bands of these human vultures fell on her, seized all they could get in the way of valuables, flung overboard or knifed any passenger who tried to resist and raped or dragged away any women who happened to take their fancy. One woman remained, cowering below decks. Some stories call her a young mother whose baby had vanished in the pandemonium. She was driven from her hiding-place by a dreadful sound, the crackling of flames. The wreckers had fired the *Palatine*, having taken from her all they wanted. Now she was drifting out to sea with the wretched survivor aboard. The girl scrambled up to the deck and stood there shrieking for help, the flames mounting behind her. Then the masts crumpled, the decking fell in and the frantic figure vanished into the blazing inferno. Still, in those waters, the ship is seen, still the woman signals desperately for help and the *"Palatine* fire" lights up Block Island. But sceptics say that there may be a natural explanation of this light — perhaps phosphorescence.

Another burning ship is the *Packet Light*, wrecked, like Queen Anne's flagship, in the Gulf of St. Lawrence. She appears first in the form of a ball of fire.

Not all sea apparitions are bringers of bad luck. Some, like phantoms on land, seem sent to give help or well-meant warnings. Captain Rogers, of the *Society*, was lucky enough to receive such a warning in the year 1664. The *Society* was cruising along the east coast of America, bound for Virginia, apparently in no trouble. The Captain, thinking all was well, retired. He was deeply asleep when he was roused by a cold touch on his shoulder. "Turn out, Captain, and look about," said a voice. The Captain shook himself awake. There was nothing to be seen, but — a true sailor, ready to believe the unbelievable — he obediently went on deck and looked about. All seemed well, and he returned to his cot. A second time the touch and the warning came, and a second time he investigated, without result. The *Society* was about three hundred miles from land, he calculated, and could be in no danger of rocks or grounding. But a third warning came. This time the voice said clearly: "Go on deck and cast the lead." The Captain obeyed — and found to his horror only seven fathoms. Hurriedly he gave orders to anchor. When dawn came, it was seen that the *Society* lay close inshore, under the Capes of Virginia, instead of far out at sea. The ghostly visitant had saved her from certain destruction.

Another lucky skipper was Joshua Slocum. He was an old professional master mariner who had worked his way up from a deck hand to being master of his own small barque. But she had been wrecked and Slocum was reduced to working for two years in a Boston shipyard. Then, in 1892, the captain of a whaler made him a present of a little old sloop called the *Spray*. She was in poor shape after seven years lying beached, but Slocum vowed he was going to make her seaworthy. He personally felled a great oak tree to make her a new keel and ribs and worked for thirteen months until the *Spray* was as good as new, if not better. Slocum then methodically turned an old dory into a lifeboat, took aboard supplies and equipment and on 1 July, 1895, put out from Yarmouth, Massachusetts, to sail round the world.

It was a lonely venture, even for a man of Slocum's sturdy character. He comforted himself by shouting questions to an imaginary hand as to how the voyage was going, answering himself. "All right, sir; all right, sir!" There were human contacts, of course — notably on the island of Fayal, in the Azores, where Slocum was given a warm welcome, plenty of fruit and an enormous white cheese. A young woman proposed that for a small wage she should accompany him as domestic staff. Slocum politely declined the offer and sailed for Gibraltar.

So tempting was the food given to him by the people of Fayal that Slocum spent a whole day doing little else but eating it. Not surprisingly, the prolonged banquet of cheese and plums resulted in agonizing stomach cramps. As Slocum battled with his digestion, the wind began to freshen. Painfully he crawled up on deck and struggled to get reefs into his sails, doubling up in agony every few moments. Then, having lashed the helm, he somehow got back to his cabin, where he lay writhing on the floor, delirious with pain. At last he fainted.

When he recovered his senses, the *Spray* was tossing about like a cork. He knew that he would have to take the helm, though in his state it seemed impossible. Once again he struggled on deck. There, to his incredulous amazement, he saw at the helm a tall man, in clothing which seemed unfamiliar. Reassuringly, the stranger swept off his cap with a smile and, as though it were the most natural thing in the world, introduced himself as the pilot of the *Pinta* which had set sail from Spain to the New World as part of the fleet of Columbus — in August, 1492, almost *four* hundred years before Slocum had put to sea. Slocum was to return to his cabin and rest, he said, while he guided the *Spray*.

Too ill and bemused to think clearly or even consider all this particularly extraordinary, Slocum accepted the offer and asked his helper to stay aboard until next day. As the ghostly pilot returned to his duty he turned smilingly to Slocum, remarking that it was never wise to mix cheese and plums — or to eat white cheese at all without knowing its origin.

And the *Spray* sailed safely on to Gibraltar.

A similar experience befell Captain Johansen of Liverpool in 1900, but this time the vessel was sailing from Gibraltar to America. She was the *Lotta*, a small open sailing-boat, manned only by Johansen and his fourteen-year-old son. Their daring venture was rewarded by eight days of calm weather. On the morning of the eighth day both Johansens were basking in the sunshine, the boy asleep. Suddenly Captain Johansen heard a voice speaking — "making a remark" was his impression. He looked round, but saw nobody except the sleeping boy. It had been imagination, he decided. Then another voice spoke — and more voices, chattering away in a language he did not recognize. The boy woke, and listened with his father. Both were amazed, and neither could think of an explanation.

Two days after this strange event, a gale blew up while young Johansen was at the helm. "Let go the jib-sheet!" called his father. But the inexperienced boy let go of the tiller in order to obey. The boat at once began to turn beam-on to the sea. It was a moment of peril, until, as if waiting for their cue, a band of four shadowy men materialized. One grasped the tiller and wrenched the little boat back on course.

All night he steered her, a strange figure in rough, primitive clothing, with an iron prop where his left leg should have been. He and his companions talked continuously to the Johansens, who could not understand a word they said, and showed them great kindness and goodwill. Seeing the *Lotta* in safe hands, father and son slept. When the sun rose, the spectral crew had vanished. Next night they returned and seemed to signal other craft which the Johansens could not see. Concerned at the possible effect of their weight (if weight they had) in the bow of the tiny *Lotta*, Johansen sent the boy to tell them to move aft. As he moved towards them they vanished once more, and never returned.

Johansen was hard-headed, sober and sceptical. He recorded the occurrences of 30 and 31 August, 1900, as a matter of solid fact.

Nearer to our own time was the curious incident that befell a British submarine during the First World War. One of the most popular submarine commanders at a south-east coast depot was Ryan — not his real name, but that given by the recorder of the story in 1919. He was a cheerful, handsome man, distinctive in appearance, popular with everyone, and there was general mourning when his submarine failed to return from one of its routine patrols off the Dutch shoals. Either the Germans had sunk Ryan or an accident had happened, for he should have returned to base in three weeks and eight passed without news of him.

Another submarine set out on the same trail, moving on the surface of the sea by night, submerged by day because of the danger from German aircraft patrols. Proceeding slowly one sunny morning, she broke surface with her periscope. As the second officer scanned the sea around them he suddenly turned and cried: "By Jove! There's jolly old Ryan waving to us like mad from the water!"

The commander instantly gave orders for the submarine to be surfaced, life-lines to be thrown out, and all preparations made for the rescue of their friend who had been so miraculously preserved. Excitement reigned on deck as they drew near the place where he had been seen. But not a trace of him was visible, though only a few minutes had passed. Had he sunk? He had not looked like a drowning man — indeed, his face had been cheerful and smiling. Had the officer made a mistake? No, he could swear it was Ryan. Had he been thinking of Ryan at that moment, and translated his thought into a vision? Not in the least, he said.

The commander gave orders to press on; it was no use searching farther and exposing themselves to danger. Then, just ahead, an object was sighted. As they skirted it carefully they saw what it was — a pair of mines, right in the path the submarine would have taken, if Ryan — or his spirit — had not appeared and made her change course.

A less welcome return by a departed mess-mate was that of the paymaster of the *Monongahela*, a corvette of the United States Navy in the First World War. The red-bearded, one-eyed "Pay" was much liked and convivial; too much so, for it was his fondness for whisky which eventually caused his death. As he lay dying on board, he said to his brother officers: "Dear boys, you've been good to me, and I love you for it. I've loved the ship, too, and I can't bear to think of leaving it. I'll come back if I can, and you'll find me in my old cabin, No. 2 on the port side."

It is a measure of sailors' superstition that cabin No. 2 was allowed to remain vacant for three cruises. Then a young Assistant-Paymaster joined the ship, and being a man not given to fancies took possession of No. 2 and settled comfortably in it. The *Monongahela* was homeward bound from South American waters, after a peaceful cruise, when, one April night, awful screams brought everyone running to Cabin No. 2. Outside, on the floor, lay the Assistant-Paymaster, unconscious. They brought him round and asked what had caused his collapse. "A corpse in my berth," he managed to say. "One eye and a red beard. Horrible!" He had wakened feeling strangely cold. In the bed with him seemed to be something chilly and wet. With indescribable horror, he had pulled the bedclothes aside to reveal the awful dead thing, seaweed entangled in its straggling beard.

The ship's company crowded round and peered nervously into the cabin. The berth was empty — but the blankets were wet, and on them a few trails of barnacled seaweed.

One of the oddest things about such stories of sea apparitions is that it is always ordinary seamen or officers who come back, never the great naval commanders of the past. What has happened to the spirits of Nelson, Howe, Collingwood, Rodney, Benbow, Blake? Nelson's shade, we are told, used to be seen walking briskly across the quadrangle of Somerset House, to disappear into the Admiralty offices.

Yet it is strange that they have never been seen transfigured aboard Britain's fighting ships at times of peril, urging the sailors on to victory and glory. Only one among them is reputed to return — Sir Francis Drake — perhaps because his body never came home, but lies "slung atween the roundshot in Nombre Dios Bay", the blue Caribbean rolling eternally about his bones. His ghost is not seen, but the legend goes that when England is in danger his famous Drum of State will sound in warning. As he lay dying, he told those about him to bring it home to England and strike it when danger threatened. But it is said to have sounded sometimes of its own accord, summoning Drake to rise again and lead his Devon men against the Dons, or whoever the enemy happened to be at that time. The last occasion when it was heard, perhaps beating in triumph, was at the surrender of the German High Seas Fleet at Scapa Flow on 21 June, 1919.

There are tales, too, of Drake's haunting a fortress-like house on Dartmoor, and of the discovery under its lawn of the skeleton of a gigantic man with an Elizabethan watch by its side. Perhaps these were the remains of one of Drake's daring crews who sailed aboard the *Golden Hind*.

From the farthest shore of the Seven Seas to the galleon-haunted Goodwin Sands, phantom ships and their sailors float eternally, terrorizing or protecting the living. Are they really fog wreaths, shapes of illusion caused by changing light and poor visibility? Or the result of over-generous grog rations? Or, simply, what so many witnesses have believed them to be throughout the centuries?

4: WHERE IS THE *WARATAH*?

She was a fine ship, the *Waratah*, everybody agreed. Her birthplace had been Whiteinch in Scotland, her sponsors the firm of Barclay Curie. For those days she was almost a *Queen Mary* among liners, with a tonnage of 9,339 and a speed of thirteen knots. Sixteen lifeboats, 930 lifebelts, three rafts and a spare boat seemed to guarantee safety for passengers on her voyage between England and Australia. Her cabins were luxurious with a wealth of brass fittings and plush upholstery and she had a special system of fresh-water supply.

Nevertheless, when she was finished and they brought her from the Clyde to the Thames she seemed a bit uncertain in the water. The owners' representative, Mr. Lund, denied this. "The vessel behaved splendidly," he said. "She rolled very little and had only a slight list when broadside on to a gale." She was duly certified as an emigrant ship as well as a passenger steamer, and on 5 November, 1908 — perhaps not the most propitious of dates — she left on her maiden voyage for Australia. She carried 756 passengers and emigrants, plus her crew.

All went well on the outward and return voyages. There were slight cargo difficulties, a matter of balance, and a small fire occurred in a coal bunker. But Captain Ilbery was not worried. Nor were Lloyd's when they looked *Waratah* over before her second voyage. And so the calendar came round to 1909.

On her second trip, which began on 27 April, she was not by any means overloaded. There were 334 souls on board, all told. The homeward voyage saw her with 212 passengers and crew and a 6,500-ton cargo. Some of it she got rid of when she touched in at Durban on 25 July.

Next morning she steamed out of Port Natal, Durban, bound for her next stop, Cape Town, 800 miles away. She was one passenger the less. Claude G. Sawyer, an English businessman, remained behind, though he had no affairs in Durban and had paid his passage home. As he walked down the gangplank some of his fellow-passengers watched him go and significantly tapped their heads with their fingers. "Barmy, poor chap," they said.

For they had heard the reason for Mr. Sawyer's departure. He had had recurrent bad dreams. Night after night the vision that had come to him in his bunk had terrified him into wakefulness.

He saw himself leaning on the rail of the passenger deck, looking out to sea. Suddenly, from the waves, a figure rose, the figure of a knight in medieval armour streaked with blood as if he had fought in a terrible battle. Blood-soaked, too, was the cloth he held in one hand; the other hand brandished a sword.

The mouth of the dream-knight opened and shut and Sawyer knew it was trying to say something to him. All he could make out, by some sort of lip-reading, were the words "The *Waratah!* The *Waratah!*" Then the phantom sank below the waves.

In the cool light of day, Sawyer could make nothing of it. An armoured knight is the last apparition one expects to see rising from an ocean. A dreamer interested in the theories of Freud and Havelock Ellis might have treated it as a code message from the subconscious. Sawyer, however, was a man of old-fashioned outlook to whom a vision was a vision. He saw the blood-spattered knight not as a psychological symbol but as the manifestation of a man murdered long ago, perhaps thrown into the sea in those very waters, allowed to return and give him, Sawyer, a warning of disaster.

The passengers were amused, but Captain Ilbery was not pleased when the story reached his ears. An officer noted for diplomacy was detailed to hint to Mr. Sawyer that perhaps it was not a good thing to spread alarm and despondency aboard a liner. Sawyer said little. He just started packing. When he left the *Waratah* he had no regrets, except perhaps an apprehension that his wife in England would share the attitude of his fellow passengers. His telegram to her, announcing the change of plan, merely gave as a reason that he thought the *Waratah* was top-heavy. Perhaps he had heard other people say this. It was a criticism that had been made of her.

Top-heavy or not, she steamed happily on towards Cape Town. The day after she left Durban the tramp steamer *Clan MacIntyre* passed her, going in the opposite direction. They hailed each other cheerfully. In response to a polite inquiry, *Waratah* reported strong south-westerly to southerly winds between Sydney and Durban and wished *Clan MacIntyre* goodbye and good luck.

Next day *Clan MacIntyre*'s master thought she was going to need all her luck, for off the Cape of Good Hope she met a fearful storm, the worst her crew ever remembered. How was the *Waratah* faring, her master may have wondered. If she too had run into storms, at least she was big enough to survive them. The little *Clan MacIntyre* fought her way through the darkness and the tempest, and resumed her peaceful voyaging.

A Union Castle boat, the *Guelph*, had also seen the *Waratah* the day before, or thought she had, east of East London, and had identified herself in morse signals. The other ship replied, but her message was difficult to read except for the last three letters, "TAH". It meant nothing until the *Guelph* put into

Durban. But if indeed it had been a signal from the *Waratah*, she must have had some sort of trouble which slowed her up to have reached only the point at which the *Guelph* sighted her.

Cape Town was three days' sail from Durban. But on 29 July *Waratah* did not arrive there. Nobody worried much, even when she was a week overdue, except the insurance underwriters. Then concern began to grow in official circles, and the *Pandora* and *Forte* went out on Admiralty orders to search. They found nothing. The cruiser *Hermes* joined them. Theories and speculations flew about in London and Australia. On 10 August came a report that *Waratah* had been seen heading for Durban. It was false. No floating spar, no flotsam, nothing at all to suggest wreckage had been picked up. Could such a big liner have gone down without leaving a trace behind her? It would be as difficult as the total disappearance of an elephant in a London suburb.

Then the rumours started — the misleading reports which raise hope or the almost welcome end of hope in those who wait for news of missing ships. Two ships in the East London area, the *Insizwa* and the *Tottenham*, said they had seen bodies floating in the sea. Two men swore to the fact that one of them was that of a small girl in a sort of Red Riding Hood cloak. It was all so convincing that Captain Cox took the *Tottenham* back to see for himself.

There was no little dead girl, there were no corpses at all according to his findings. Cross-questioned, the men who thought they had seen her gave way and the one who had been most emphatic changed his story. Now he thought that what he had seen was a roll of printing paper with a red wrapper round it.

But the *Insizwa*'s captain thought differently. He was sure he had seen bodies and could describe what they were wearing.

He had not picked them up for fear of upsetting his female passengers. He, too, collapsed under close interrogation. Perhaps he had only seen blubber and other floating objects. More reports came in from ships that thought they had spotted the *Waratah*, but none was confirmed, and towards the end of August there was not much hope left. The search was called off. In Australia the services of intercession held in churches for the safety of the missing liner were discontinued. There is not much point in praying for help for those in peril on the sea when one is sure that they are beyond peril — beyond help.

The usual bottle-message joker was at work, but his fakes took in nobody. The ship had gone down, without a doubt, perhaps because of her rumoured top-heaviness or because she had unwisely loaded coal on her decks in Durban (though the captain of the *Clan MacIntyre* said this was not true). People remembered the uncertainty she had shown on her first trip south from the Clyde, though officers who had served in her firmly denied this. An expert on stability came back with a scathing opinion of the *Waratah*, and one of the officers who had vanished with her had been heard to make a sinister remark about her being likely to prove "a coffin for somebody". On the whole, the evidence was that she had been a poorly balanced vessel. Even Captain Ilbery seemed to have thought so. When Mr. Sawyer appeared at the inquiry and told the story of his ghastly dream he was no longer laughed at. After all, clairvoyants had been called in to try to discern the *Waratah*'s fate.

But never, in trance or in the cloudy depths of a crystal ball, did the last moments of the *Waratah* ever satisfactorily appear. The great liner and 211 people had vanished without trace, and this in the days of wireless communication and busy shipping lanes. It was a stranger disappearance than any of the earlier ones.

But rumours and legends fade with time. 1914 came and the First World War. Then peace, and the years between, and another war. This, too, was over and the second half of the twentieth century begun before the *Waratah* reappeared — to one man's thinking, at least.

A pilot of the South African Air Force was flying over a calm stretch of sea. Sunshine and blue skies did not predispose him to see visions. But, glancing downwards, he was amazed to see in the clear water the wreck of a great ship near in to the shore. He had read of the *Waratah* mystery and knew enough about her to recognize all that remained of her. He returned to his base, excitedly reported his find and went back to collect more details.

But the wreck was no longer there. The *Waratah* — if it had been she — had once more vanished.

Another report may carry some truth — that of an old man who had met an eyewitness of the liner's death. He had seen her go down, very near the shore, just about where the pilot saw the wreck. He was Jan Pretorius, an illicit diamond prospector, and at the time his trade had made it inadvisable to bring himself into the public eye by coming forward with evidence. So he kept quiet.

And that stately Edwardian lady, the *Waratah*, lies still in an unmarked grave.

5: THE GRAVE ON CAMPBELL ISLAND

Campbell Island, halfway between New Zealand and Australia, is a small and lonely place. Only forty-four square miles in area, it is just a speck in the great empty sea. It is nobody's dream isle. Its climate, for most of the year, is noted for bitter gales blowing from the Antarctic, icy blasts whistling up straight from the Pole, less than 4,000 miles away. Its inhabitants are mostly seals, penguins and sea-elephants.

But eleven men also live on Campbell Island. They are there in the cause of New Zealand's weather service. For years at a time each will live there, making observations and keeping records of the weather, such as it is. Their life is only a slight improvement on that of lighthouse-keepers.

The landscape and vegetation of Campbell Island are no more lush than one would expect to find in such a spot. Softness and colour are missing. But, among the dry, starved grass, one patch of colour there is — a rich pinky purple, such as glows on mountainsides in autumn. It is, indeed, heather. Near it, an almost vanished footpath leads to what was once a hut, something which served as a cottage. And if you stroll on Campbell Island in search of human interest there is something else to search for: a grave, now obliterated, but certainly there a century ago. To this lost mound of earth a legend clings. Whalers and other sailor-men who knew of it used to say that there lay a "lost lady of old years" who had come mysteriously from the sea to this lonely resting place. She was, they claimed, the daughter of Prince Charles Edward Stuart, Bonnie Prince Charlie, and his mistress, Meg Wilkinshaw.

The story goes that long after the tragedy of 1745 was over, the Jacobite cause destroyed and the Prince a meaningless figure in European politics, Miss Wilkinshaw was suspected of spying for King George's government. She had joined the Prince in his French exile, and there a daughter was born to them. They returned to Scotland, and after Meg's death Jacobite suspicions were transferred to the daughter. To put her out of the way of doing harm to the Cause it was decided to ship her overseas, as far away as possible. So a Captain William Stewart (he was the discoverer of Stewart Island, off the New Zealand mainland) was engaged to abduct her. Somehow the operation was bungled and Stewart had to abandon it. Instead, another man carried out the tricky job. No details are given of how it was done.

Many years afterwards — in the late sixties of last century — Campbell Island had an historically minded visitor. He was an official of the New Zealand provincial government, and he was deeply interested in the legend. He it was who connected up the clues of the ruined cottage, the footpath, the heather and the grave. It was said that the girl had planted the heather in memory of her native country. Even in that arid place "still the blood was warm, the heart was Highland", like that of Stevenson's Hebridean exiles. And so Bonnie Prince Charlie's daughter lived and died alone, and only the heather remains as her memorial.

This story, which was first committed to print in 1892, is a most charming and romantic one. Stevenson himself, if he ever heard it in his South Sea paradise, must have rejoiced in it. Up to a point it still persists. Unfortunately for romance, it cannot be true, so far as the known facts are concerned.

Prince Charlie had indeed a mistress named Clementina Walkinshaw whom he met in Scotland during the 'Forty-Five.

63

She was certainly suspected of espionage, because her sister Catherine was attached to the Hanoverian Court, and it was thought that Clementina was likely to pass on to her any information she might pick up about further Jacobite attempts to invade England. No action was taken against her beyond the attempts of exiled chieftains to persuade the Prince to give her up.

She followed the Prince to France in 1752, just as the legend says. There they led a cat-and-dog life, for he was no longer the radiant young leader, but a sour, disappointed man, the dark side of the Stuart character uppermost in him. The birth of their daughter, Charlotte, in 1753, reconciled them temporarily, for Charles loved her dearly. He nicknamed her "Pouponne", or Baby Doll. Clementina, worn out at last by his tempers and drunkenness, fled to a convent, taking the child with her, and no appeals from Charles would persuade her to go back to him.

For many years father and daughter were separated. Then, in 1784, when Charles was old and dying, he begged Charlotte to come to him in Rome. She obeyed. She was now aged thirty-one, a gentle, cheerful creature who was to be her father's comfort and refuge during the last months of his life. He legitimized her and created her Countess of Albany — the only honour a poor uncrowned king could bestow. She nursed him to the end, which came in 1788, and herself died in the following year at Bologna.

These facts dispose firmly of the Campbell Island legend — so far as it goes. But is the legend rooted in slightly different facts? "No smoke without fire" is a truism which has proved itself over and over again. The possibility exists that the exile of Campbell Island was indeed a Stuart on the wrong side of the blanket.

Charles, in spite of his beauty, gallantry, and subsequent reputation, was not a man for the ladies. He was very much a man's man, a soldier and a sport. When he was a boy his father had described him as "very innocent and extreme backward" with regard to sex. It was said of him that during that short triumphant reign of his in Edinburgh he would rather share the rough life of his troops under the stars, discussing military strategy and sharing a friendly bottle, than dance with the charming ladies of Edinburgh at Holyroodhouse, and when reproached for neglecting Edinburgh's beauties he pointed to a whiskered Highland sentinel and said, "These are my beauties". His aloofness, as might have been expected, made him all the more attractive to women. They pursued him determinedly, and one of the few who caught him was Clementina. A patriotic girl called Jenny Cameron was also said to have attracted his interest. In France before Clementina arrived he had at least two mistresses, Mme de Talmond and Mme d'Aiguillon.

After his death the legends began. In the nineteenth century, two brothers of striking appearance, magnificently kilted, proclaimed themselves to be the Sobieski Stuarts, grandsons of Charles and his wife, Louise of Stolberg. Their claim was never substantiated, but they aroused a lot of interest and some belief.

Another highly circumstantial story was told of a son born to Charles and Louise in 1773.

In the Highlands there was a tale of a lovely girl known as Flora "a Phrionnsa" — the Prince's Flora, not to be confused with Flora Macdonald. She, they said, was his daughter by a Highland lass he met during his wanderings.

In recent times an English innkeeper claimed direct descent from the Bonnie Prince. And most curious of all, in relation to

Campbell Island, there is another grave at Finsthwaite, on the shores of Lake Windermere in the English Lake District, which by some is firmly believed to be that of a daughter of his by Clementina, and therefore Charlotte's younger sister. Travelling under one of his many aliases, Charles was reputed to have arrived there in the 1760s with the child who died and was buried there. But the mystery of that grave is another story.

It seems likely, then, that one or two other illegitimate children of the Prince were about in the second half of the eighteenth century. The Stuarts were noted for their fertility, particularly outside marriage. Even with the bar sinister in their shield, they represented a potential menace to the Hanoverian throne potential Young Pretenders of a new generation. There might well be a certain amount of secrecy about their bringing-up.

Another possibility exists. The life of Charlotte, Countess of Albany, was always thought to be an open book, until the late Henrietta Tayler, an historian with an inquiring mind, began to investigate. She found that there were many uncut pages in that book with some astonishing information in them, as she told one of the present authors some years ago.

Far from being the spinster companion of her mother, leading a conventional life, Miss Tayler discovered Charlotte to have been the secret mistress of a French bishop. From carefully-worded letters, using code names, it appeared that she had had at least two children by him, and Clementina continued to bring them up when Charlotte had left for Rome. Their fate is completely unknown. They may have been put into convents or monasteries, depending on their sex, or have remained in the world under false names. If one was a daughter, she may somehow, for some strange reason, have travelled to Campbell Island.

The Stuarts were a doomed family. No venture of theirs prospered for long in politics, war or love. And in the eighteenth century to be an illegitimate Stuart was no passport to a happy life. With such a heritage of tragedy and no official name or status, a woman on her own might have ended anywhere. Fate might even have planted her in an Australian convict settlement — the place from which many people think that the woman of Campbell Island came.

A more down-to-earth theory — that she was a "whaler's trollop", a loose companion of whalers and sealers — is based on the readiness of convict women to get away from settlements by any means. The captains of whaling or sealing vessels would take aboard women who were desperate enough to go with them on lonely voyages, and where such women finished up is anybody's guess. Some, no doubt, were left on South Pacific islands when they were no longer useful aboard.

It is a reasonable enough explanation for the cottage and the grave, even the heather. Some colour is given to it by the story of one such woman — Elizabeth Farr, who sailed in the brig *Perseverance* with its master, Captain Hasselburg, in 1810.

Hasselburg it was who discovered Campbell Island while on a sealing expedition. It was rich in seals, so rich that he left some of his men there to do a year's hunting and collect many barrels of seal oil. On 1 November, 1810, he returned to pick up the hunters and the oil. The *Perseverance* lay at anchor. Hasselburg, three men, a Maori boy and Elizabeth Farr set off shorewards in the jolly-boat, leaving the rest of the crew aboard. It was bitterly cold and Hasselburg wore heavy waders and clothing, topped with a thick Flushing boat cloak.

Three hours later shouts from the shore brought another boat from the *Perseverance* to investigate. They found two dripping hunters and the boy who told them that the oil-loading had been done without mishap, but that when the jolly-boat left on its return journey it had capsized and three of the party had been drowned — a seaman, Captain Hasselburg and Elizabeth.

The survivors said they had reached shore safely and loaded all the barrels of oil aboard without any trouble. On the return trip they had been beating to windward when a sudden squall hit them. Before they could take in sail their boat had heeled over and had gone down within seconds. The seamen and the Maori had managed to reach the shore. Bloodworth, the carpenter, evidently made of stronger stuff, stayed behind to help the others. Before he could get to Captain Hasselburg, though, the master's clumsy, saturated clothes had dragged him under. The other drowning man had also gone down for ever. His body and the master's were never found.

Elizabeth remained afloat, making slowly for the shore, when the carpenter reached her. He clutched her by the arm and supported her the rest of the way, but it was too late. If he had known anything of artificial respiration he might still have saved her. Her breathing stopped. The carpenter left her under a bush and trudged off to search for the other men.

They are said to have buried the woman, but whether in a grave among other graves is not recorded. If they did, then the unknown woman of Campbell Island may well have been Mrs. Farr, a poor convict, put into the earth without ceremony or memorial. But there is absolutely no proof that she ever was buried on the island, and if she was there seems no particular reason why her grave should have been pointed out fifty years later when the New Zealand official came.

If the occupant of the grave had been a daughter of kings, however unfortunate, with something of the Stuart charm about her, some fading light of romance, she would have been long remembered. If she took after Charles, she may well have found comfort in the bottle during her last years and talked wildly as he did of old days and long-dead glories.

Perhaps the strange tale has some truth in it after all and under the arid ground of Campbell Island lies a lost princess. It would be fitting enough ending for the notorious ill-luck of the Stuarts, of whom Voltaire wrote: "If anything could justify those who believe in a fatality which nothing can escape, it would be that continuous series of misfortunes which befell the House of Stuart during three hundred years." And Prince Charlie himself was asked: "What has your family done, sir, to draw down the vengeance of Heaven on every branch of it?"

6: THE *MARY CELESTE*

When any mention is made of sea mysteries one name before all others springs to mind. That name is *Mary Celeste*. Everyone has heard of her, and however often her story has been told this book would not be complete without it.

She was a brigantine of 282 tons, and she sailed from New York Harbour on 7 November, 1872, with a cargo of 1,700 barrels of alcohol for fortifying wines, destined for Genoa. Her master, Benjamin Briggs, took along with him his wife and small daughter of about two years of age, two mates and five seamen.

A month later, on 5 December, the barque *Dei Gratia* of Nova Scotia was about 300 miles from her destination, Gibraltar. She, too, had sailed from New York. It was a fine afternoon with a light breeze blowing when the lookout man sighted a brig with only her jib and foresail set. This was curious in conditions which would have justified full canvas. No answer came to the *Dei Gratia*'s signal to the brig which was reeling about as though nobody was steering her.

Captain Moorhouse, of the *Dei Gratia*, sent a party of men aboard to investigate. On the way they scrutinized the decks, but could see no sign of life. Now her name could be read: *Mary Celeste*. They boarded her. Sure enough, the deck was deserted.

"One of her boats has gone," observed the mate. The other still hung from its davits. The wheel was not lashed but spinning free. The boarding party went below to investigate the cabin and fo'csle. Both were empty: but here accounts become contradictory. The most popular (and interesting) version has it that in the cabin the table was laid for a meal and three cups of tea, still warm, stood on it as well as a boiled egg with the top cut off and an unfinished plate of porridge. Beside the place which was presumably Mrs. Briggs's was an uncorked bottle of cough medicine. None of it was spilt, an indication that there had been no rough seas since the cork had been removed. The moneychest (always kept in the captain's care) did not appear to have been plundered and two watches were found. In the crew's quarters were pipes and tobacco. In the galley, says this version, the range had been raked out recently and was warm, like the tea. Later, and probably more accurate, chroniclers deny this. But they agree that seamen's clothes were found hanging up to dry and that the chronometer and the ship's papers were missing, except the log, in which the last entry was dated ten days before, and said that all was well. The ship's position had then been 36° latitude north and 27° longitude west. Compasses had also been left.

There were signs of feminine occupation in the cabin — a sewing machine, a thimble, and a cotton-reel, and on the table a child's pinafore. A harmonium, some religious music and books completed the domestic picture. On top of a locker was the first and only living thing the investigators found, a fat cat, sound asleep, and quite unmoved by whatever had been happening around it. In the cabin was also a distinctly sinister discovery, a bloodstained cutlass.

Returning to the deck, the *Dei Gratia* men made some more odd discoveries. One hatch cover was overturned, but the cargo was untouched. There was a deep, new cut in the starboard rail with some darkish stains near it. And on both sides of the bow a narrow six-foot niche had been carved.

Captain Moorhouse, whose primary interest lay in the financial side of the business, towed his prize into Gibraltar

71

and made a salvage claim for her. At the inquiry the mysterious aspects of the find were discussed in detail. Nobody could account for the disappearance of the crew or imagine how the ship had got from the last position named in her log, about 500 miles away to the spot where she was found without being steered there. And if her crew had been aboard during those ten days, why was the log blank for the period? Nobody knew. They merely granted Captain Moorhouse and his men £1,700 salvage money.

The *Mary Celeste* was now handed back to her owner, Mr. J. H. Winchester, Captain Winchester, as he sometimes liked to be called, with the following report:

Gibraltar, 2 January, 1873.
The American brig, *Mary Celeste* of New York, was brought into this port by the British barque *Dei Gratia*. *Mary Celeste* picked up on high seas on 5 December, abandoned. Brig in perfect condition but was taken possession of by Admiralty Court as a derelict. Fate of crew unknown.

Winchester had an ingenious theory. The barrels filled with alcohol had generated gas which had exploded and blown one of the hatch covers off. Scared by the explosion, the crew had escaped in the missing boat.

But the boat and its occupants were never found, so this theory could never be proved. Other solutions to the mystery followed thick and fast. The *Mary Celeste* had been assaulted by an enormous sea-beast, perhaps a giant cuttlefish. The crew had fought the creature with an axe, hence the mark on the rail and the bloodstains. But no cuttlefish, however large, could have eaten both the missing boat and the missing crew, and the stains on the deck turned out to have been made by wine.

Then, of course, there were pirates to be thought of. Perhaps they had attacked the *Mary Celeste* and sheered off when the *Dei Gratia* appeared. But the *Dei Gratia* had seen no other vessel. Had there, then, been an epidemic of cholera or some such disease, which had forced the ship's company, or those who had not yet fallen ill, to take to the boat? Some substance was given to this by a grim discovery in the following May. Spanish fishermen, out in their boats, encountered two floating, odoriferous objects. They proved to be rafts, laden with rotting bodies, and one of the corpses was wrapped in an American flag. But no connection between this unpleasant find and the *Mary Celeste* was ever established.

The official record of the mystery, in the Department of State, read as follows:

> Document 136, from U.S. Consul Johnson, dated Gibraltar, 7 January, 1873. "Result of analysis adverse to blood existing on sword and woodwork belonging to the brig *Mary Celeste*."
>
> Document 137, from the same, dated 20 January, 1873. "Principal owner of brig *Mary Celeste* arrived from New York to claim brig from Admiralty Court. Nothing heard of missing crew. Chronometer and ship's papers not to be found on board the brig."
>
> Document 138 "Brig *Mary Celeste* restored to her original owner 12 February, 1873."
>
> Document 139. "Brig *Mary Celeste* cleared for Naples under command of Captain John Hutchins, sent out by owner from New York for the purpose. Forwarded to Mrs. Bilson, of New York, effects of Henry Bilson, missing mate of brig *Mary Celeste*. The brig's last voyage."

This last document is puzzling. The mate of the *Mary Celeste* was called Richardson.

Gradually the theories died away, and the theorists found something else on which to exercise their detective faculties. In 1883 young Dr. Arthur Conan Doyle had electrified the world with a story called "J. Habakuk Jephson's Statement", published in the *Cornhill Magazine*. It purported to be the true confessions of a survivor of the *Mary Celeste* (Dr. Conan Doyle called her the *Marie Celeste*, and in doing so started a popular misapprehension). J. Habakuk Jephson represented himself as a doctor of medicine of the University of Harvard who had sailed on the ill-fated ship. He had carried with him a talisman, a present from an old black woman, which saved his life when all the rest of the ship's company had been destroyed by the sinister Goring. This wildly romantic tale by an author then unknown was pure fiction — invented names for the crew were given and many other details were inaccurate — but incredulous readers accepted it as fact. At last Solly Flood, Advocate-General at Gibraltar and Queen Victoria's representative at the Supreme Court of the Admiralty, issued a statement to the newspapers that J. Habakuk Jephson's reminiscences were a complete fabrication.

It was a splendid piece of publicity for a budding author.

Dr. Conan Doyle had become Sir Arthur, and a famous man, when in 1913 a group of other interested literary men put their heads together in an attempt to solve what was by now a classic puzzle. All were novelists. Barry Pain, humorist and airman-to-be, rejected supernatural theories as being too easy.

"Looking, then, for a natural explanation, it is clear that the crew and passengers of the brig did not leave her of their own free will or in pursuance of any plan of their own. What, then, was their motive for leaving? Clearly it was fear. If they had been lured away by any kind of attraction, they would at least have finished breakfast first and taken with them some of their personal belongings. They had to go at once — on the moment — and they went because they were afraid."

Working on this premise, he pointed out that they must have left in some boat other than that belonging to the brig. (He ignored the fact that one of her boats was missing.) The fear, therefore, arrived with that boat. What was in it? The most likely answer is — gunmen. Somewhere nearby a ship engaged in shady dealings, piracy or smuggling perhaps, had lost some of her crew by illness or accident. She needed more hands. She dared not approach a port and draw attention to herself, therefore hands must be recruited by violent means. A jolly-boat was sent out with some plausible excuse for making contact with the *Mary Celeste*. Then, having got aboard her, the thugs drove all the men into the boat in relays at gunpoint. One of the raiders took a fancy to the chronometer and stole it. Mrs. Briggs and the child "could not be neglected", said Mr. Pain, leaving their fate a blank.

Morley Roberts, who had been a great traveller and sailed before the mast, said he had been brooding on the mystery for thirty years, but still confessed himself baffled. On the whole he was inclined to think it was a put-up job, with financial gain at the back of it.

Horace Annesley Vachell thought that "some absolutely un-foreseen phenomenon" must have made everybody on the *Mary Celeste* jump overboard to their deaths, something like an explosion beneath the sea which generated a lethal gas-cloud into which the brig sailed. The effect of this was to madden those aboard and cause them to leap desperately over the rails, the captain and mate retaining enough sanity to grab the chronometer and ship's papers first. But this theory, Mr. Vachell admitted, was based on a complete ignorance of the properties of gases. The next four years, 1914–1918, no doubt enlightened him somewhat.

Arthur Morrison, a novelist fascinated by London's dockland and one of the earliest writers of detective fiction (his Martin Hewitt, Investigator, followed very closely in the footsteps of Sherlock Holmes), treated the whole question fictionally, in a horrific yarn. Joseph Hallers, A.B., his protagonist, was a follower of Swedenborg. To him the spirit was all, the flesh sinful rubbish. So, one by one, he disposed of the crew and the captain's family, mainly by means of poisoned coffee, remaining himself to dance and gibber triumphantly on deck before leaping overboard with the chronometer (symbol of Time) in his arms.

A few months after these theories had been aired, the *Strand* magazine, which had acted as their forum, published a remarkable development in the mystery. This they described as "no less than the discovery of what appears to be a perfectly genuine account of the disaster, left by a survivor!" A highly respectable correspondent, A. Howard Linford, headmaster of Peterborough Lodge, a preparatory school in Hampstead, had written to say that he had just remembered that he had a personal connection with the *Mary Celeste* riddle. An old servant, Abel Fosdyk, when at the point of death had committed to Mr. Linford's charge three boxes containing a quantity of papers, and had said that they concerned the *Mary Celeste*. The name, at the time, meant nothing to Mr. Linford, whose preoccupation with his duties must have limited his general reading. These boxes, when opened, proved to contain Fosdyk's diary for the past thirty years, and "a set of shrewd observations on all that passed". With the documents was the photograph of a tiny girl in an Alice-in-Wonderland dress. The caption, in faded pencil writing, read "Baby at the age of two years". This was said to be a portrait of Captain Briggs's daughter, given to Fosdyk by Mrs. Briggs.

The *Strand* published the manuscript, and with it a facsimile of a passage of Fosdyk's handwriting. It may be relevant to observe at this point that the writing is rounded, small, slightly backward-slanting, suggestive of a child's or a woman's, absolutely unlike the forward-sloping copybook hand which was universally taught in Victorian schools and lacking the *f*-like letter *s* still characteristic until quite late in the nineteenth century. The present authors have compared it with that of a man born in 1839 — roughly of the same generation as Fosdyk — and it is different in every respect. This strongly suggests that the manuscript itself was not all it purported to be. It is highly literate for a fo'csle hand with a strong flavour of the sentimental-cum-flowery style popular in 1913. And a sailor-man does *not* say "we heaved to".

The narrative describes life on the *Mary Celeste*, an unusually comfortable vessel, the charms of "Baby", as little Miss Briggs was always called by all aboard her father's ship, and the personal characteristics of some of Fosdyk's mates — Joe, the carpenter, Robin, Fred, Ginger Odell, Ned Clark, two Williamsons, and stowaway. No names corresponding to these appear in the official list of the *Mary Celeste*'s crew, nor, indeed, does that of Fosdyk. A sort of barricade had been rigged up to stop the child climbing on to the bowsprit and was known as "Baby's quarterdeck", the narrative went on. Captain Briggs appeared to be heading for a nervous breakdown, which was no doubt the reason why he challenged the mate, Harry, to a swimming match round the ship to prove that a man can swim fully dressed. (The mate's real name, according to official records, was Albert.) The entire ship's company watched this from "Baby's quarterdeck" — thirteen, or was it fourteen, of them? — and, not surprisingly, it gave way and they fell into the sea. Fosdyk's account of his own subsequent miraculous escape from drowning is of no great interest as the whole story is obviously a complete fabrication. It seems that somebody had been leading Mr. Linford up the garden — or the quarterdeck.

The next version was published in January, 1914, in the *Liverpool Weekly Post*. It told how Mr. R. C. Greenhough, an officer in the Mercantile Marine, had in 1905 been an apprentice in the barque *Ardorinha*, bound for Chile. He and some other young men were sent out to one of the St. Paul Islands to collect sand. They took the opportunity to do some exploring and under a rock found what all boys dream of finding on an island, a skeleton. Even better, by its side was a bottle containing manuscripts.

"Buried treasure! Hooray!" was the boys' first thought. But the reality was disappointing. The paper in the bottle was damp, rotting, and difficult to read — particularly as it was in German. Greenhough, a determined youth, kept the bottle and its contents and later had the document translated.

The dead man's testimony was that he had captained a ship which was mixed up with something shady, perhaps smuggling. On the last voyage disaster had struck. Poison had got into the ship's food supplies or been put there and three of the crew had died in two days so that the vessel became undermanned. The captain knew he must get help from another ship in order to reach Gibraltar and recruit men to replace the dead ones. But there was the danger that the English authorities there might investigate his cargo (whatever that may have been), entailing prison and the loss of what he carried. His desperate journal went on:

Managed to get steam to give steerage way. I headed for Lisbon. Early morning sighted small brig becalmed. Mate said: "Take her crew." It was the devil's voice. Went aboard. Captain asked why we came. His wife and child were with him. It was hard. It would have been easy without the woman. But the mate got behind the captain, he and two others threw him. His wife fainted. Then we pointed pistols. Crew went into boat quietly. One man shot. He fell into the sea. We left no one on board. The brig was called *Marie Celeste*. Would to God I had never seen her! Then the child would be yet alive. I cannot forget the child.

Here is a good, meaty story. But what happened to Captain Briggs and his crew in the end? And why did the *Dei Gratia* not see all this going on, the day being so clear? It was the old pirate theory over again and could all too easily be demolished.

The year 1917 brought hints from a mysterious person called Chuppy, or Chippy, Russell, who was also, it seemed, Jack Dossel, bo'sun of the *Mary Celeste*. He lived in Shrewsbury and worked as a sort of unlicensed chemist. They do not appear to have illuminated the darkness at all. In 1924 came a confused tale sent to the *Daily Express* by Captain H. Lucy, who had learned it from yet another "bo'sun", a man called Briggs, whom he had met somewhere in the South Seas. The fact that this man's name was the same as that of the *Mary Celeste*'s captain immediately suggests to the sceptical mind that poverty of imagination often shown by simple-hearted storytellers.

"Briggs" alleged that the *Mary Celeste* had come alongside a derelict, which he, the mate, and four of the crew boarded. Their instinct had led them to a good thing, for she carried a chest with £3,500 in it in gold and silver coins. Captain Briggs seized on this, kept £1,200 as personal prize-money, and handed out the rest to his crew. As they were only fifty miles from the Gulf of Cadiz, the best thing would be, he said, to scuttle their own ship, take the derelict's boats and sail to Cadiz with their loot. The nearness of another vessel caused them to leave the *Mary Celeste* afloat — it would have looked too suspicious to have been seen scuttling her — but they carried out the rest of the plan.

None of this ties up with what is known of Captain Briggs's character, or with the fact that he owned a third share in the *Mary Celeste*'s cargo — much too valuable to be sacrificed for just over a thousand pounds of looted money. We may dismiss "Bo'sun Briggs" as a South Seas romancer.

An entire book was written on the now historical mystery in 1929. This was *The Great "Mary Celeste" Hoax: A famous sea mystery exposed*, and was by Laurence J. Keating.

The facts on which this book was based, said Keating, had been drawn from John Pemberton, the ship's cook, one of the seven men whom he knew to have survived. Pemberton's narrative involved Mrs. Briggs, who had been a negative or non-existent figure in most previous accounts. She, he said, had a piano in the cabin. (Early reports had mentioned this as being a harmonium, a smaller and altogether more likely instrument.) Her constant playing and singing had irritated the mate, Hullock, and when during a storm the piano fell over and crushed Mrs. Briggs beneath it, her frantic husband accused Hullock of having murdered her. He then went mad, and, like Sir Joseph Porter in *HMS Pinafore*, "threatened a court-martial" as well as the possibility of setting fire to the ship. It must have been a relief to all when he disappeared, presumably because he had jumped overboard.

Now Hullock began to throw his weight about. Fights broke out, and one of the crew, Venholdt, was killed. Pemberton, the cook, took over as captain. Off the Azores Hullock and two others deserted — one of them Jack "Chippy" Dossel. This left Pemberton and three more of the crew aboard the *Mary Celeste*. At this point the *Dei Gratia* hove in sight, and here the plot thickens.

According to Pemberton, the *Mary Celeste* and the *Dei Gratia* had lain alongside each other in New York harbour and Captain Moorhouse had concocted a cunning plan. He would capture the *Mary Celeste* at an opportune moment and collect her salvage money — as, in fact, he did.

The whole story is, of course, wildly impossible. It provides a neat explanation for the puzzle of the *Mary Celeste* being empty of life when found. If, Pemberton stated, Captain Moorhouse was lying, then she was *not* empty of life and the mystery is considerably reduced.

But Captain Moorhouse was known to be an honest and cautious man. And the whole story falls down on a matter of solid fact. We know the names of the *Mary Celeste*'s crew and Pemberton, Hullock and Venholdt were not amongst them. The name of the real cook was Edward Herd.

Since then various frankly speculative versions of the story have been put about. Other deserted ships have been found, but the *Mary Celeste* has always held the public imagination more than any of them. In 1924, J. G. Lockhart, in his book *Mysteries of the Sea*, reverted to Arthur Morrison's religious maniac theory, but in his version it was Captain Briggs who went over the edge of reason and destroyed his sinful companions, including his wife and daughter. There is no contemporary evidence that Captain Briggs was anything but a well-balanced and sensible man.

None of the explanations put forward satisfactorily covers all the various puzzles, though one or more may be accounted for by each theorist. The unfinished meal, the missing chronometer and papers, the marks on the starboard-rail and the bow, the bloodstained cutlass, the missing boat, the displaced hatch cover — there are so many questions, so few satisfactory answers.

A new theory appeared while this chapter was being written, and we were able to discuss it with its author, Sir William Charles Crocker, a distinguished man of law with an immense experience of insurance claims, which interested him in the *Mary Celeste*. In his book *Far from Humdrum* (Hutchinson) he demolishes the tale of the ship having been found undamaged, and with the remains of meals and the evidence of recent life aboard her, attributing these details to the imagination of F. Solly Flood, Attorney-General for Gibraltar, who took a leading part in the original hearing of the *Dei Gratia's* salvage claim. The abandonment of the vessel he believes was caused by Captain Briggs's fear of an explosion from a mixture of alcohol vapour, a possibility when the alcohol vapour represents not less than 3 per cent and not more than 14 per cent by weight. One such explosion, Sir William thinks, had already happened, an aperture "in the deck near the hearth" having allowed alcohol vapour to escape from the hold below. Afraid of a really terrible explosion (there were 1,700 barrels in the cargo), Captain Briggs hurriedly got his family and crew into a boat; but by some accident they were drowned.

This theory resembles that put forward by J. H. Winchester, but is a good deal more scientific. The author of Sir William's principal source book, an American marine underwriter, Charles Edey Fay, offered facts but no theories.

Whatever happened on the *Mary Celeste* in 1872, she never had any luck afterwards. She went down in the world and ended up a wreck off the coast of Cuba in 1885. It was obvious from seawater-filled barrels aboard her which should have held molasses that something shady had been going on. Her captain and owner were subsequently arrested on a charge of wrecking her for the insurance. Previously she had been associated with other stories of murder and hauntings, none of them very well documented.

Like a true woman, the *Mary Celeste* kept her secret to the last.

7: PIRATES? SUBMARINE? OR BOTH?

When it comes to attaching nicknames to surnames, all Whites are "Chalky", all Clarks are "Nobby", and all Millers are "Dusty" — or, if they aren't, the Senior Service has changed. Lieutenant-Commander T. H. Miller was no exception to this tradition, and when he left the RNVR after the Second World War he carried his nickname more naturally than either of his Christian names. It was as "Dusty" Miller that he was known around the waterfronts and bars of the South Pacific in the years which followed.

He was one of those characters so beloved of thriller writers with a taste for sea settings: virile, tough, and with the blood of many seamen in his veins. Born in Cardiff just before the First World War of a long line of seafarers he had enlisted in the Merchant Service at the age of fourteen. The end of the war had found him in his late thirties in the prime of physical condition with a good rank and record to his credit. Women found him thrilling; men respected him; those who knew about seafaring acknowledged his ability.

War service had given Dusty Miller a taste for the Pacific and those free and easy islands which have attracted so many men of adventurous spirit. He worked in several vessels around the islands, always looking for something better to do. Occasionally he would strike off in small-time ventures of his own, some of them in the nature of gambles which might lead to bigger things, or, if they failed, would leave him that little bit less well placed than when he had begun. Unfortunately, whatever other attributes he possessed, Dusty Miller had no lucky streak. Each venture did, indeed, take him several steps back for each one forward. Then, in 1952, the fortunes of Dusty Miller suddenly showed promise of change.

In September of that year, a close friend, Dr. Ellen Katharine Luomala, an American lecturer in anthropology at the University of Hawaii, Honolulu, bought a fishing vessel bearing the romantic name of *Joyita*, Mexican for "Little Jewel", and chartered her to Miller. He began a series of expeditions to the fishing grounds between Fiji, the Christmas Islands and Honolulu, which he was convinced were going to restore his solvency once and for all. He little knew that on the contrary this "Little Jewel" was going to bear him to his death in circumstances which would give rise to one of the most baffling of all sea mysteries.

Joyita was just turned twenty-one when Dr. Luomala bought her. She had been built in Los Angeles in 1931 to the order of a motion-picture director, Roland West, who christened her after his wife, Jewel. As a movieland status symbol, *Joyita* had to be as luxurious as possible and West spared no expense. But she was no mere floating showplace. She was superbly built of two-inch cedar planking on oak frames and was fitted with twin diesel engines, enormous fuel and water tanks, all that was new in navigation aids, and an automatic pilot. She measured 69ft overall, with a 17ft beam, and drew 7ft 6in. Her gross tonnage was 70.

West used her for cruising and fishing — she was fitted with comfortable swivel fishing-chairs aft and had a deep-freeze compartment large enough to receive any fisherman's dream catch. But his enjoyment of her was short-lived. Thelma Todd, one of the screen's most popular blonde vamps of the day, who had been involved with *Joyita*'s owner for some time, died mysteriously on board and *Joyita* sold to another rich American who owned her until 1941 when she was commandeered by the United States Navy. She served throughout the war as a patrol vessel, her only dramatic experience being to run aground off the Hawaiian Islands, necessitating the re-planking of much of her hull. After the war she was sold off to a fishing firm who stripped her interior for conversion into refrigerated holds, building in more than 600 cubic feet of cork which not only insulated her but rendered her virtually unsinkable. They also put in new diesel engines.

This was her state when Dr. Luomala bought her and chartered her to Dusty Miller. He had a good craft, enough personal enthusiasm and experience to carry him through and a seemingly ready market in Hawaii for his frozen catch. But his expenses were high, higher than the return he found he could get from the fish he brought from the Canton Islands. Instead of making money, he lost it, three trips running. By the time his fourth trip in 1954 had ended Miller was desperate. He had hawked his catch around the merchants of Apia, the capital of Western Samoa, once German territory, but a New Zealand mandate since 1920. He found no buyer at a price he could afford to accept. He had taken it on to Pago Pago, capital of American-administered Samoa, still without result. Desperation increasing, he had returned to Apia again, where he had let the catch go for what it would fetch. Reduced to accepting menial jobs on shore in order to fight back his growing debts, he was now a sad shadow of the once spruce and confident naval gentleman. He applied to Dr. Luomala to ask what he should do about her boat, now lying idle in Apia harbour. She instructed him to sell it, settle his debts and come back to Honolulu. With yet another of his ventures in ruins, Miller started to look for a buyer.

Even now things did not go well for him. Although the twenties are prime years in a lady's life, they are not those of a ship which has lived hard and been through many hands. *Joyita* had been much converted and, of late, neglected through sheer lack of resources. Her engines in particular were far from good enough for work in the lonely vastness of the world's greatest ocean. No one would pay Miller's price.

For five months *Joyita* lay idle, deteriorating all the time. Then, at last, help came to Dusty Miller from a young New Zealand friend, R. D. Pearless, the recently appointed District Officer of the Tokelau Islands. Only twenty-nine, he was a conscientious and energetic official. Transport around the Pacific islands is not easily come by. There are few regular services, either by sea or air, except between the capitals of the main groups, and one can wait months for a passage or else go to the considerable expense of chartering a freelance skipper to make a special run. The Tokelaus, some 350 miles north-east of Samoa, are as inaccessible as any of the islands and in 1955 they were facing something of a crisis. Food and medical supplies were needed, copra, the islands' sole export, was piling up, waiting to be shipped. Pearless had the idea of serving the people he administered and at the same time doing a good turn to Miller. He asked the Western Samoan Government to charter *Joyita* for one or more trips to the Tokelaus and back.

The Government knew all about Dusty Miller and his troubles. They had been among those who had refused to buy *Joyita* from him, considering her not worth the asking price. They were reluctant even to charter her and were no doubt not a little relieved when Miller himself brought the negotiations to a decisive end by being unable to produce all the ship's papers without which no bargain could be officially made.

District Officer Pearless, described in one official document as "a very keen and enthusiastic officer", refused to let the matter rest. The crisis in the Tokelaus had worsened considerably during the past weeks. An airlift was out of the question and an earlier attempt by flying-boat had resulted in the aircraft's hull being ripped by coral as she taxied in the lagoon. No other sea vessel seemed to be available except *Joyita*, whose master, eating out his heart with despair, had sunk so low that he was painting the verandah furniture of the Returned Servicemen's Association club to eke out a bare living. Blocked officially, Pearless went to the general manager of an island trading concern and proposed that the firm charter the vessel to make at least one trip to the Tokelaus and back, carrying passengers and cargo each way. The company agreed, and, to the delight of Captain Miller, District Officer Pearless, a number of other administrative officials who had been wondering how they would ever get to the Tokelaus, and, not least, several natives of the Tokelaus stranded in Samoa, it was announced that *Joyita* would sail from Apia at about noon on Sunday, 2 October, 1955.

Having got his charter, Miller had to find a crew quickly. His own one-time faithfuls had long since dispersed to other jobs and he had only a matter of days in which to fill a dozen vital appointments ranging from mate and bosun to seamen, engineers, greasers and cook. Loyalty and affection persuaded some of his former hands to return. All were natives of the islands. As mate he was able to sign on a tough American, Chuck Simpson, known in the islands as "Captain Jah". This appointment was doubly fortunate: not only did Dusty Miller need a strong, experienced officer to share his responsibilities, but he also needed an American in his crew. Although he, the master, was a British subject, *Joyita* was owned by Dr. Luomala, an American, and was required by that country's regulations to have at least one of her nationals aboard as an officer. There was another American regulation, however, which Miller chose to ignore: *Joyita* was not licensed to carry passengers. The alternatives facing him were simple: carry passengers, or lose the last charter he might ever hope to obtain. Miller had faith in himself, he had faith in *Joyita*. He kept his mouth shut and as a consequence he, twenty-one other men, a woman and two children all perished.

Joyita's big tanks were filled with enough fuel to carry her far beyond the few hundred miles to the Tokelaus and back. She had plenty of water and provisions. The food and medical supplies for the islands, the chief reason for the trip being undertaken at all, were put aboard with piles of empty sacks to hold the copra on the return voyage. One of the seven European passengers, an employee of the chartering firm, carried with him £1,000 in cash with which to pay the islanders for their copra.

The other Europeans, besides Miller, his mate and Pearless, were two other employees of the company, a doctor from Apia Hospital and a dispenser. A European-sounding name in the crew list was that of Henry McCarthy, but he was, in fact, a native of Samoa. Only a few days before *Joyita* was due to sail, Dusty Miller signed him on as second engineer and must have been glad to do so. Long hours of sweating labour on *Joyita*'s twin 225hp diesels were necessary to get them into what appeared to be a fit state for the voyage. Even so, there was still some clutch trouble in the port engine which obstinately refused to be righted.

On the day of departure, a Sunday, as the passengers were settling down aboard *Joyita*, a worried superintendent of Apia Radio sent a message down to Dusty Miller. Ever since the sailing had been announced, the official, Mr. Bentham, had expected Miller to be in touch with him to arrange daily radio working schedules between them. It was not obligatory that he should, yet it surprised Mr. Bentham that he had not. So he sent to inform Miller that Radio Apia would be listening for him at 10 a.m. and 4 p.m. daily and suggested a test transmission of *Joyita*'s radio before she sailed. When this well-intentioned message was not acknowledged, Bentham took the trouble to go down to the wharf where he met Pearless and urged him to find out from Miller whether the proposed arrangement was agreeable. Once more, Bentham got no response.

Soon after noon, *Joyita*'s engines were started and she began to move towards the harbour mouth. She had not gone far when a Government official, watching her from his house overlooking the harbour, saw a puff of smoke appear from the vessel's port side and drift away. *Joyita*'s forward movement ceased. Slowly, she began to drift towards a reef, until after a few minutes an anchor was dropped. She lay there all that day and when darkness fell was still in the harbour. Some of the passengers came ashore with the news that the port engine was playing up and looked like taking some hours to fix. The Europeans amongst them made for their clubs where they were able to enjoy an evening's unexpected drinking. In the heat of *Joyita*'s engine-room, "Captain Jah" and the two native engineers wrestled with the stubborn piece of machinery. On deck or in his small chartroom, Dusty Miller waited tensely and must have cursed his unrelenting ill-fortune as he earnestly assured his charterer who had come hurrying aboard that there was no need to think of calling off the voyage. No doubt he was also afraid that if he did not leave soon word might reach the American authorities that he had passengers aboard and he would be forbidden to leave at all. But that, quite simply, would spell ruin.

At the radio station Mr. Bentham waited about until 7 p.m., hoping that some transmission might yet come from *Joyita*. None did and he went home. When he awoke next day and looked harbourwards he saw that *Joyita* had gone. Later that day he received a call from the charterer, passing on a message from Miller to say that *Joyita*'s call sign was WNIM and that he would contact Apia Radio at the times suggested. Accordingly, at 10 a.m. and 4 p.m. each day, Apia listened for WNIM and called her. There was no response. Those twenty-five people aboard *Joyita* were lost to the world.

On 6 October, after a report had come from Fakaofo in the Tokelaus that *Joyita* had not arrived there, the world began to search for them. That morning a Sunderland flying-boat of the Royal New Zealand Air Force thundered up in clouds of spray from Lauthala Bay, Fiji, and climbed to a height sufficient to enable her to sweep, visually and by radar, a range of ten miles to either side as she flew to Apia and thence to the Tokelaus. No trace of *Joyita* was seen. Every day for a week flying-boats continued to scan a vast area of the lonely Pacific in which *Joyita* must be if she were still afloat. Other shipping kept watch for her and Apia Radio listened and called in vain. *Joyita* was gone, not the first vessel to vanish into the Pacific's depths without trace or apparent cause. The search was called off. In the island clubs and bars it was agreed that Dusty Miller's ill luck, and his foolhardiness, some added this time, had finished him at last.

There was, however, at least one other theory: that Miller, having acquired the last substantial credit he was ever likely to get in Samoa, had never intended to sail to the Tokelaus at all. With far more fuel, water and provisions aboard than the short trip could possibly have justified, he had carried out a plan to sail *Joyita* to Honolulu, where he would hand her back to her owner, Dr. Luomala, who would presumably recompense him. How he would achieve this despite the protests of the other twenty-four persons on board was not precisely stated. It was enough that Dusty Miller was a resourceful and desperate man.

Joyita never did arrive at Honolulu or at any other port. Five weeks after she had sailed from Apia she was sighted, listing heavily and wallowing in an easterly swell, by the Gilbert and Ellice Islands' supply vessel *Tuvalu* which radioed to Fiji:

> Joyita *found waterlogged in position 14° 42' South 179° 45' East by dead reckoning. Boat sent across but nobody found on board but possibly in flooded compartments. Port side superstructure including funnel blown or washed away. Canvas awning rigged apparently subsequent to accident. No log book or message found.*

But when *Joyita* had been towed to a beach in Suva and the flooded compartments pumped out, no bodies were found. Word flashed round the world that there was another *Mary Celeste* story to add to the mysteries of the sea. *Joyita* was searched thoroughly. Not only had the passengers gone, with no message, however hurried, left behind, but quantities of the cargo and the whole of the £1,000 copra money were missing, too. Even more inexplicable, there was no damage to the hull. The water which had part-filled *Joyita*'s cork-lined hold might have got there from above, possibly from some great wave which had caught her beam-on, crashed down on her and flooded in. But, even assuming that a wave, or waves, might have carried away some of those on board, could this conceivably account for the disappearance of all twenty-five of them? *And* lifted a large part of the cargo out of the hold to accompany them?

A more likely explanation of *Joyita*'s predicament was offered by the finding of a break in a galvanized pipe, part of the cooling system of the port engine. Water could have flooded in through this and with the pumps failing the flooded engines would have stopped. There were no watertight bulkheads so the sea would have filled the other parts of the vessel. If Miller had tried to raise Apia Radio or some other station he would have failed because there was a break in the aerial lead which might have been found if he had not ignored Mr. Bentham's offer to test *Joyita*'s transmitter. *Joyita* had carried no lifeboat, only three floats. They were missing. The seas were scoured for them, but no trace was ever found.

Obviously, *Joyita* had become waterlogged, helpless; all aboard her had taken to the floats, only to be overwhelmed later by the sea and drowned. Yet there was a great deal that did not fit this simple explanation, and still does not.

For one thing, Dusty Miller knew his vessel to be unsinkable, as, indeed, she had proved. It is most unlikely that, even if all the others had chosen to transfer to the frail floats, he would have done so. He must have known that by far his best chance of surviving and being spotted by certain air search would be to stay with his vessel.

Again, what had happened to the items of cargo? *Had* they been washed away somehow? Or was there some more sinister explanation for their being missing?

Supposing, for instance…

Fiji rang with rumours about *Joyita*, and echoes of them resounded throughout the world. The newspaper *Fiji Times*, at the centre of a story of first-class interest, naturally played up the mystery angle vigorously:

> The locating of the *Joyita* deepens the mystery that has shrouded the circumstances of her disappearance.
> There has been a great deal of official secrecy about the discovery of the *Joyita*, What is it all about? Wherever our

reporters have gone in an attempt to present a true picture to the people of an event of world-shaking interest they have been frustrated by officialdom.

Overseas newspapers took their cue and began to circulate rumours already common currency around the islands. *Joyita* had been stopped by pirates, looted, and all aboard her killed or kidnapped. The pirates, it was suggested, were former Japanese soldiers, occupiers of Pacific islands who had never surrendered after the war. The most colourful rumour of all credited these desperadoes with possession of a submarine which they kept concealed in a perfectly camouflaged pen in the island bay which was their base. Other lone vessels had disappeared in the Pacific in recent years and might well have fallen prey to this same gang.

Another suggestion, again assuming the miscreants to be Japanese, was headlined by the *Fiji Times*, "ALL ABOARD *JOYITA* MURDERED?" The startling new theory, said to be inspired by official thinking, was that *Joyita* had accidentally run through the Japanese fishing fleet which operated unpopularly around the Fijis...

"...and that the *Joyita*'s people saw something the Japanese did not want them to see."

There was a young District Officer on board (Mr. Pearless) who possibly protested at something he had seen.

The suggestion was that resentful Japanese boarded the *Joyita*, murdered or took prisoner the passengers and crew, attempted to blow up the ship, and opened the seacock. The report explained:

> The *Fiji Times and Herald* informant stated that the *Koyo Maru*, mother ship of the Japanese fleet, was one of the most modern survey ships in the world and was fitted with the

most modern radar afloat. It is recalled that on her last visit to
Suva, when she called ostensibly to arrange salvage, shore
leave was not granted the crew who, on the visit before, had
swarmed all over Suva.

This report provoked an immediate reaction from the Fiji
Government. The Colonial Secretary broadcast from Suva,
denying emphatically that any such belief was being entertained
in official circles. All the same, island gossips and Pressmen
around the world continued to give currency to the more
colourful theories. There were whispers of gun- and drug-
running. The version of massacre by Japanese, whether pirates
or fishermen-spies, came sensationally to the surface again with
a report, admitted in official circles to be true, that several
knives of Japanese make had been found amongst the litter
aboard *Joyita* and were being tested for bloodstains. The story
died when the tests proved negative, and it was pointed out
that there was nothing remarkable about the presence of
Japanese-made knives aboard a vessel which had been chiefly
used for fishing.

It was not until the following February that fact had been
sufficiently disentangled from fancy for a Commission of
Inquiry to sit and judge the *Joyita* mystery impartially. Twenty-
eight witnesses testified to what they knew about the vessel's
seaworthiness, or lack of it, her engines, her radio, the purpose
of her trip, and, not least important, about the luckless Dusty
Miller's character and plans. The Commission unanimously
accepted the explanation that *Joyita* had flooded and become
immobilized. That was as far as its findings went. As to the
twenty-five missing souls:

Although your Commissioners find it possible to speak with a
reasonable degree of conviction as to the cause of casualty to

95

the ship, they are quite unable to do so with regard to the ship's personnel.

Pirates? Submarine? — or both? Enraged Japanese spies? All are the stuff of thriller-fiction, but behind the mystery of *Joyita* are facts. Nobody knows them. Robin Maugham, who became intrigued by the mystery, investigated it on the spot and ended up by buying *Joyita* himself and writing a book about it (*see Bibliography*) in which he put forward additional evidence and used it to reconstruct what, in his view, may well have happened on board. It makes plausible reading and may be the truth: but it is fairly certain that we shall never know.

8: THE HAUNTING OF U-BOAT 65

Ghosts are one thing. Accidents are another. When a ship has a reputation for both she is liable to be shunned by men who might otherwise have signed on with her. But in time of war a seaman has no choice. Whether he likes it or not he must leave his superstitions behind, even though he fears he may be sailing in a doomed vessel. Such was the case with the crew of the U-boat UB-65.

She was one of the light submarines launched by the Germans in 1916 to patrol the heavily protected Belgian coastline, thick with mines and nets. The earliest versions of these frail little craft had a surface speed of only 6–5 knots, and carried only two torpedoes. They plodded up and down Belgian waters, dodging British patrols, weaving in and out of sandbanks, edging up to terrorize fishing fleets or sink the occasional Allied ship. They pierced the Dover barrage and defied the famous Dover patrol. Little, but game, were the UBs.

UB-65 was new in 1916. Her surface speed was an improvement on that of her elder sisters — 13 knots. She carried a crew of thirty-four, including three officers. The trouble that was to make her the jinx of the German Navy began while she was still building. A steel girder was being slowly, steadily lowered into place. There was a jerk, a shout of warning, and the massive thing slid sideways and fell with a mighty crash. The noise of its fall and the splintering of wood were mingled with fearful screams. It had fallen on two workmen.

Slowly, with difficulty, their horrified mates raised the heavy mass as far as they could. But it was jammed, and the tackle had broken — they could not lift it clear of the two victims. One, it was obvious, was beyond help, a broken, bloody pulp. The other, trapped by the legs, screamed for an hour as they fought to free him. Soon after they got him out he died.

In the Dark Ages a blood sacrifice was made to bring good fortune to a new building. It seemed that UB-65 had taken her toll of blood, and would now be satisfied. But she had only begun.

Work was resumed, and for some weeks went on without mishap. Then came a second fatal mishap. The UB-65 was almost ready for launching when three workmen, putting the finishing touches to equipment in the engine-room, were heard coughing and calling for help. When help came, the engine-room door was found to be jammed. Inside was a haze of noxious fumes, and on the floor were three corpses. An inquiry produced no satisfactory reason for the escape of the fumes and the submarine was declared seaworthy.

"*Deutschland, Deutschland über alles!*" The Fatherland had a new weapon to hurl against the enemy. The UB-65 slid out for her trials. The day was calm, the omens propitious. She had scarcely got into the open sea before a sharp squall blew up. The sea rose, swamped her decks, and swept one of her ratings overboard. A boat was hastily lowered, but no trace of him was to be seen. Victim Number Six had died by drowning.

Then UB-65 was put through the diving trials in which a submarine must prove itself. A certain gloom prevailed amongst the crew. It was justified. Sure enough, when the U-boat was submerged a leak developed in one of her tanks with the result that submarine and crew were trapped underwater for twelve hours. Once again death-bringing fumes filled her, perhaps due to seawater in the batteries — it was never proved. When she finally surfaced and the officers and crew were released they were half-stupefied, sick, choking — but alive, *Gott sei dank*. For once the jinx had only been joking.

The next time was no joke. The submarine's private fiend had dealt out death by crushing, by asphyxiation and drowning. Now it experimented with explosives — and most successfully. The UB-65 made an uneventful maiden patrol, returned to base and started taking in torpedoes. Without warning, or reason, a warhead exploded. A fearful detonation, screams, chaos, followed, and five dead men lay huddled and twisted on the submarine's deck. Others were badly hurt. The fateful submarine, itself considerably damaged, went out of action for repairs during which any workmen in possession of good-luck charms undoubtedly wore them. A cemetery at Wilhelmshaven, the chief German naval station, received the bodies of the dead, including that of the second officer, a man of striking appearance.

Once more fighting fit, UB-65 was manned and prepared to sail. It was evening, and her captain and his officers were discussing plans in the wardroom while the crew settled in. Suddenly, the door burst open and a white-faced rating stood before them, panting and trembling. The captain's head jerked up, his beard bristling with affront.

"What's the meaning of this, Schmidt? Don't you know better than to enter the wardroom without knocking?"

"I beg pardon, Herr Oberleutnant, but the second officer... I — I've just seen him!" gasped out Schmidt.

The captain's lip curled sarcastically. "Not unlikely, Schmidt, as you're looking at him now!" The new second officer, who was indeed sitting at the captain's side, looked in surprise at the seaman.

"No, sir," stammered the man. "I mean the late second officer — the one who died in the explosion!"

The captain banged the table. "You're drunk, man — get out! You'll be in trouble for this!"

But the bluejacket stood his ground. He *had* seen the dead man, he repeated — strolling up the gangplank. And somebody else had seen him, a man called Petersen. They would both swear to it, and they were stone cold sober.

The captain sighed.

"All right. Bring Petersen here, and let him tell his own fairy-tale."

"He won't come, Herr Oberleutnant. He's up on deck, behind the conning tower. Shaking like a leaf, he is."

"Come along, gentlemen — we'd better investigate for ourselves," said the captain, and led the way on deck. There, indeed, was Petersen, huddled in a corner, in a worse state of fear than his shipmate. Patient questioning produced the information that he had seen the ghost of the dead officer come up the gangplank, stroll along to the bows, and stand there, arms folded, looking calmly out to sea. Petersen had rushed in panic to the corner where he was now crouching. When he dared to peer out again the phantom had gone.

The captain was a reasonable man. He knew the symptoms of drunkenness, and neither of these men had them. They had obviously seen something — but what? The captain had never believed in ghosts; he did not intend to start now. In his opinion, someone was either playing a grisly joke or deliberately trying to undermine the crew's morale. He investigated every possibility, questioned everyone who might have had access to UB-65, checked on the activities of other members of the crew. But no evidence of trickery came to light and he was obliged to let the matter rest. If a fake ghost had been produced with malicious intent, the faker must have been thoroughly satisfied, for the experience of the two sailors had infected the crew with panic. Petersen could not face the prospect of sailing on a death-boat. Two days before she was due to sail he vanished, risking the chance of a deserter's punishment.

Two years had passed since UB-65's keel had been laid. In the latter part of 1917 the U-boat menace had slowly been overcome by the Allies. Until the summer of that year the terror under the sea had been destroying British shipping at an alarming rate. In May, 1917, out of every four vessels that left British shores one had not returned. In April, U-boats had sunk 840,000 tons of British and Allied merchant shipping. But by the autumn the picture was changing. The Ministry of Shipping had boosted production; the convoy system was working. Germany would have to think hard and quickly if she were to win the war at sea and would need to throw every vessel she had into the fight. So UB-65, which in less needful times might have been written off, was kept in service.

On New Year's Day, 1918, she cruised from Heligoland to Zeebrugge where she spent ten days. To the immense relief of the crew, nothing untoward happened. They felt that their luck might have changed with the calendar. Then orders came to sail into the Channel, in search of merchant vessels and fishing fleets.

The evening of 21 January was wild as UB-65 ran on the surface. A gale was rising, the sea threatened to wash over the conning tower. It was a night to be down in the stuffy warmth of your cramped quarters if you were not absolutely obliged to be outside, like the starboard lookout, keeping his lonely watch. But suddenly, to his amazement, he saw that he was not alone. Below him, on the narrow, plunging deck, bathed in recurrent showers of spray, was the figure of an officer.

Cupping his hands, the lookout shouted a warning. "Don't stay there, sir — you'll be washed overboard!"

The officer looked up — with the face of the dead man who had appeared to Petersen and his mate. It was a frightened lookout who stammered out his tale to the captain as he came up through the hatch. Looking from the conning tower, the captain was just in time to see a figure. By the time he had blinked and looked again it had gone.

We are not told what eventually happened to the deserter Petersen, or to the other sailor who had first seen the apparition. But to the captain the sight he saw on 21 January was a death-warning. A few weeks later, while UB-65 was moored in a bombproof pen in a canal dock at Bruges, he went ashore to pass the evening at the local casino.

The air-raid sirens sounded as he walked through the streets: British planes were approaching. The captain's place was with his ship. He turned to go back — and a shell fragment severed his head from his body.

After this dreadful happening an official inquiry into the submarine's troubles was held. The investigating officer in charge of it did not transfer the crew wholesale to another vessel as they asked, but some neat paperwork resulted in most of them being drafted, one after another, to less alarming environments. The German Navy could not afford to have even one boat manned by demoralized men.

While the jinxed U-boat lay at Bruges it was someone's bright idea to have a pastor come aboard and hold a service of exorcism, bidding any devils who might be aboard to leave the ship, in the name of God. Nothing more tactless could have been planned. The new crew had heard unpleasant rumours from their predecessors and at this confirmation that there *were* devils sailing with them they became infected with fear. Ghost stories flew about until the captain issued an order that anyone who claimed to see even a vestige of a phantom would be heavily punished.

A first-hand account exists of the events of the next few months. A petty officer who served on UB-65 from beginning to end of the submarine's career wrote frankly of his experiences and beliefs.

"U.B. 65 was never a happy ship," he wrote, "though we were always fortunate in our officers. There was something in the atmosphere on board which made one uneasy. Perhaps, knowing her evil history, we imagined things, but I am convinced myself that she was haunted. One night at sea I saw an officer standing on deck. He was not one of us. I caught only a glimpse of him, but a shipmate who was nearer swore that he recognized our former second officer walk through the ship. He always went into the forward torpedo-room, but never came out again. Several of the bluejackets saw the ghost quite often, but others were unable to see it, even when it was pointed out to them standing only a few feet away.

"Our last captain but one would never admit the existence of anything supernatural, but once or twice, when coming on deck, I observed him to be very agitated, and was told by the men that the ghost had been walking on the foredeck. When the captain's attention was drawn to it he pretended to see nothing and scolded the watch for being a pack of nervous fools. But afterwards I heard from a mess steward at the officers' casino that our captain openly declared his ship to be haunted by devils."

During May, went on the storyteller, the U-boat was cruising up and down the Channel and off Spain. It was a terrible trip.

After two days at sea a torpedo gunner named Eberhard went screaming mad and had to be tied hand and foot and given morphia to quieten him. The treatment seemed to take effect and he was released and sent on deck for air in the company of another of the crew. No sooner did he reach the deck than he again went berserk. Pushing away the man at his side he leapt over the rail and went down like a stone. His body was never recovered.

Off Ushant, when high seas were raging, the chief engineer slipped and broke a leg. The submarine was hopefully chasing a British tramp steamer, firing with her deck gun, when waves towered over the gun-crew and washed one of them, Richard Meyer, overboard. He, too, was never seen again.

Now the submarine began to avoid encounters with British or Allied boats that would otherwise have seemed her natural prey — for each one might be the instrument of the final fate that her entire crew were sure was in store for her. "The men were so depressed that they went about like sleep-walkers, performing their duties automatically and starting at every unusual sound." They were not reassured to find themselves approaching the dreaded Straits of Dover, where three U-boats — UB-55, UB-33 and UC-79 — had just been blown up.

Their fears were justified. They were shot at on the surface, depth-charged when submerged and Coxswain Lohmann received injuries from which he died. A battered UB-65 limped away to Zeebrugge, almost sorry to have escaped. "Most of us felt that it was merely prolonging the agony."

At this point the storyteller, to his own immense relief, was attacked by such severe rheumatism that he was sent to hospital. He was visited there by another officer, Wernicke. The UB-65 was due to sail next day, and Wernicke felt that it would be the U-boat's last voyage — and his. He brought his messmate most of his personal belongings, to be sent on to his wife when the news everybody expected came.

It broke on 31 July. UB-65 was posted as missing. Her end was as mysterious as everything else that had happened to her.

On 10 July an American submarine off Cape Clear, on the west coast of Ireland, sighted a U-boat. Through the periscope her number could be made out — it was UB-65. Hasty orders were given for attack.

But just before the American torpedoes were fired, something happened that made it unnecessary. With a fearful detonation, UB-65 blew up.

The reason was never known. Possibly one of her own torpedoes exploded in its tube, or another U-boat attacked her by mistake and made off without being sighted by the American. But there were no remains on which to hold an inquest.

The mystery of UB-65, surely one of the strangest in naval history, was investigated thoroughly after the war by a psychologist, Professor Hecht, who published a pamphlet on the subject. In 1932 Hector C. Bywater, the English naval historian, followed this up with an investigation of his own, carefully checking all the evidence and testimonies. Neither Professor Hecht nor he was able to draw any firm conclusions. As a scientist, Dr. Hecht did not care for the supernatural explanation, but he could not suggest a watertight rational one. Today, so far away in time from the events, it would be even more difficult to do so. The ghost stories are convincing and well attested. But nothing is easier than to see a ghost if you expect to see one, and sailors, particularly the isolated, hemmed-in men on a submarine, are the most superstitious of folk. Given one convincing faked "appearance", the spectre seen walking up the gangplank, it was pretty certain that other apparent manifestations would follow, in the dark, in the mist, amidst flying spray.

Several who had sailed in UB-65 felt that there was malicious human agency behind the "accidents". Were they the work of a British secret agent? It is hard to see how some of them were contrived, and others, like the washing overboard of the gunner, and the beheading of the captain, were obvious coincidences. But the whole thing has a very strong smell of sabotage. Another possibility is that the "ghost" and various disasters were the work of some Till Eulenspiegel with a grudge, or a taste for killing. If the last accident of all was a planned one, the saboteur must have blown himself up with his victims. He might have saved himself the trouble, for within four months the war was over, and 138 U-boats were meekly brought as captives into Harwich.

9: THE HAND IN THE SAND

It was a boy on a beach — a New Zealand beach — who sparked off a seashore mystery which endured from 1885 until a few years ago. Three men were known to have had the answer to the puzzle: one of them a judge, one a barrister, and the third the protagonist himself. All took the secret with them to the grave, leaving the mystery seemingly insoluble. Then, after one of the present authors had written about the case in a New Zealand newspaper, he was sent the solution by a man whose mother knew the details of the act which had set the affair of the hand in the sand in motion. She, too, had since died, having confided her story to no one but her son.

Early one morning in October, 1885, a boy named Boot sauntered barefoot along Sumner Beach at Christchurch, in the South Island of New Zealand. The beach was almost deserted. The sea had been rough and cold-looking lately — the Antipodean summer had not yet begun — and there were no bathers about.

Boot vaulted over a breakwater, and almost landed on a pile of clothing. Puzzled, he gazed seaward again. He was sure he had seen no one swimming and several more minutes' watching confirmed this. He examined the clothing, and found a watch and chain wrapped in it. He went to the police.

Investigations soon showed that the property was that of Arthur Robert Ramage Howard, a fitter at the Addington railway workshops. His wife, when visited by the police, told them that he left home early that morning, saying he was going to Sumner Beach for a swim before work. Constables were sent to make inquiries of people living on the approaches to the beach and were rewarded with a good deal of information. A man fitting Howard's description had been encountered walking in the direction of the beach by several people that morning. He had greeted them and told them that he was on his way down for a swim. They had been surprised, with the sea so uninviting. But there was always someone willing to brave conditions which kept everyone else away. Now it seemed that the man's bravado had taken him to his death. Everyone's sympathy was with the widow and two children of so reckless a fool.

Inquiries which followed, however, suggested that the late Arthur Howard had not been so lacking in concern for his family's welfare. A year earlier he had insured his life for £1,000. A few months later he had taken out a further policy in the same sum with another company. More recently still he had signed up for another £400-worth with a third insurer. All this had made him liable to hand over half his weekly wage — he earned nine shillings a day — in insurance premiums, leaving his wife, in the event of his death, merely to prove that she was his widow in order to collect a total of £2,400. In all, he had provided magnificently for his dependants: now it only remained for Mrs. Howard to show that she was, indeed, his widow and not his wife.

After several days during which no body had been washed ashore she advertised in the Christchurch newspapers, offering a reward of £50 to anyone recovering the body "or the first portion received thereof recognizable". This brought a flurry of activity on Sumner Beach and at other parts of the coast where a corpse might conceivably come ashore, but many tides came and went without any of the eager searchers qualifying for the money. Interest died away. The insurance companies continued to refuse to pay Mrs. Howard her money until she could prove her husband's death and, at the insurers' request, the police kept an eye on all people boarding ships at New Zealand's ports.

Two months passed. No body was produced. The police scrutiny was relaxed and one of the insurance companies, anxious to clear up the matter, proposed to Mrs. Howard that she accept a smaller sum by way of a compromise settlement. While she was considering this a man named Elisha Godfrey walked into Christchurch police station carrying something wrapped in a copy of a local newspaper and asked to see the officer in charge. Inspector Pender came forward. Godfrey told him he had been walking on the beach at Taylor's Mistake that morning when he had come across the object which he now proceeded to disclose. It was a human hand, severed from the arm just above the wrist. It was brownish-black in colour and had clearly been dead for some time. One finger wore a gold ring, with the initials "A.H." scratched roughly on it.

The startled inspector ordered Godfrey to be detained until he got back and hurried round to Mrs. Howard's house. He told her: "Mrs. Howard, I have some news about your husband. Would you tell me what he wore when he disappeared, and anything in particular you could identify?" She described her husband's clothing again and added that she believed he had worn a gold ring on his left hand, a detail she had not mentioned before. When the inspector asked her why, she replied that she had only just recalled it. The shock of the sudden memory was evidently considerable: she swooned into the inspector's arms. He found that she had genuinely fainted.

When he had restored her, Inspector Pender took Mrs. Howard in a cab on a tour of the Christchurch jewellers, inviting her to show him a ring resembling the one her husband had worn. After a long search she picked one out.

Pender then allowed her to see the gruesome exhibit at the police station. With considerable emotion she told him it was her husband's hand and that the ring it wore was his.

Inspector Pender sent her home and sat down to review the other evidence he possessed. A jeweller had examined the ring and given his opinion that the initials in it had been scratched very recently and by an amateur. Doctors who had examined the hand had refused to accept that it had been bitten from the arm by a shark, as Elisha Godfrey had suggested when he brought it in, but declared that it had been *sawn off*. Furthermore, they said, it wasn't a man's hand at all: it was a woman's.

The inspector had Godfrey brought in and told him bluntly that his story of how he had found the hand would not do: he had better change it. Godfrey did. He confessed that he had been on Sumner Beach with his brother, fishing, when a stranger had approached. This had been a man wearing a wig, dark glasses and other items of obvious disguise. He had asked them to come and look at a human hand he had found behind some rocks. As they stood around the hand, which clutched a fragment of seaweed, the stranger suggested to the brothers that it must be the missing Arthur Howard's hand for which a £50 reward would be payable. He himself, as a "prominent person", was not anxious for publicity. If the brothers would care to take the hand to the police the money would be all theirs.

Elisha Godfrey had consented, but had pointed out that they had nothing to wrap the hand in. The stranger replied that he just happened to have a few sheets of newspaper about him, and whipped them out. He left the Godfreys to it. They wrapped the hand gingerly in newspaper, then, with extraordinary phlegm, they placed the bundle in the shade of a rock and went back to their fishing.

Seeing the case moving inexorably into the realms of the fantastic, Inspector Pender brought everyone back to reality by arresting Elisha Godfrey's brother and charging the pair with conspiring to defraud the insurance companies.

When they were brought to the magistrates' court the following day the crush of officials and spectators was so great that the accused almost had to stay outside while their case was heard. The celebrated hand — now pickled in a jar of spirit — was the real centre of attraction. It held up the proceedings while magistrate and lawyers argued whether it should be placed on the Bench, under the table, or out in the yard. The hearing was adjourned, pending further inquiries.

A few weeks later the sensational news rocked New Zealand that the "drowned" Arthur Howard had been arrested by a young constable in the Wellington area. He had been wearing a badly-fitting wig and had an easily identifiable scar on his neck. Just to make sure, the policeman had asked him to take his hands out of his pockets — not to see whether one of them was missing, but because Howard was known to be minus one thumb, which the suspect proved to be.

Howard and his wife were charged with conspiracy to defraud, so, not surprisingly, their trial began with the defence pointing out that, in law, a husband and wife cannot conspire, and therefore there could be no case to answer. But the Crown was ready for that one. Prosecuting counsel smoothly informed the court that the Howards had been married aboard a Scottish ship *en route* to New Zealand, without certificate or ring. Their union had no validity outside Scottish territorial waters: the charge could stand. After that the hearing itself was something of an anticlimax. The attempted deceit was so blatant that little defence could be offered. The jury found no criminal motives in the strange behaviour of the Godfreys and acquitted them. After discussion with the judge they also acquitted Mrs. Howard, for want of clear evidence against her. Arthur Robert Ramage Howard was found guilty. Sentencing him to two years' hard labour, the judge, Mr. Justice Johnston, remarked: "I assure you, and I say so sincerely, that I regret I cannot give you more as your fraud has been a most impudent and daring one."

So Arthur Howard went down; but all attempts to get him to say where he had obtained the hand met with silence. His movements were traced and many recent graves were opened in places where he had been. All the occupants were found to be intact. At length, a report reached the police from Masterton, in the North Island, which seemed sure to end the mystery. An undertaker stated that while he had been making the arrangements for the burial of a young woman who had just died an obviously disguised stranger had been seen hanging about the cemetery. After the burial, the sexton had partially filled in the grave and left it for a short time, returning later to find the job completed for him.

The body was exhumed. Both hands were intact.

Howard eventually told his counsel where he got the hand. Counsel told only one colleague. The three men died without allowing the mystery to be solved. Then, while living in New Zealand a few years ago, one of the present authors received the following letter:

> The hand was taken off a very respected clerk of the Public Works, Christchurch, who through excessive drinking was taken to Sunnyside Asylum, where he died just before the missing hand came to light.

My mother nearly upset their well-laid plan, but as it was two months before my brother was born my dad would not let her inform the police. Also the three sisters of the dead man were right against the public knowing their brother had died in Sunnyside, and that he was lying in his grave minus his hand.

The family recognized the hand. The two men who found the hand were, I believe, porter and cook at Sunnyside.

After Inspector Pender had lectured on his famous mystery, I wrote to him stating that if he would call and see my mother she would clear up the mystery for him.

After listening to her story, he said, "Well, well, well! — and to think that the hand came off a personal friend of mine!"

Just what part Howard himself played in obtaining the hand is, alas, unknown. But the identity of its former owner provides a perfect twist ending to the story of this bizarre crime, whose setting, if not on the sea, is beside it and which relied upon the sea for its effect.

10: THE SECRET OF THE
GROSVENOR

Every shipwreck is a disaster, somebody's tragedy; occasionally there is mystery, too. The saddest and most mysterious of all stories of lost ships is that of the East Indiaman *Grosvenor*, wrecked on the coast of Pondoland, a Kaffir territory south-west of Natal, on 4 August, 1782.

The *Grosvenor*'s tragedy has been the subject of books, essays, plays, detective exercises, stories and paintings. To this day, almost two centuries after it happened, it fascinates inquiring minds, for its riddles have never been solved. What happened to the bulk of the survivors from the wreck? Was the *Grosvenor* really a treasure-ship — and if so, what became of her precious cargo?

She was a handsome vessel, Thames-built. She had three decks, carried twenty-six guns or more, and contained ample cabin accommodation for passengers. Her master, John Coxon, whose firm, handsome face topped by a stiff white wig has survived in a miniature, first commanded her in 1778. He seems to have been a capable, much-respected captain, with a cool head and a reputation for enforcing discipline. He needed these qualities during the battle between the French and British fleets, in which the *Grosvenor* happened to become involved in April, 1782. But by June she had safely reached Ceylon, and left the port of Trincomalee, laden with passengers and merchandise, on 13 June. Captain Coxon cannot have been a superstitious man.

The names of the passengers have survived. There was Colonel Edward James of the Indian Army, his wife and their two servants, William Ellis and a maid, Sally. Also attached to the Army was Captain Walterhouse Adair. From the Navy — he had commanded HMS *Worcester* — was Captain George Talbot. There may well have been a little stiffness at meals between these gentlemen and two French officers, Lieutenant d'l'Isle and Colonel d'Espinette, prisoners of war being sent to England. Two merchants, a Mr. Taylor and a Mr. Williams, brothers-in-law; Charles Newman, a barrister of Bengal; Mr. William Hosea of the East India Company, and his young wife; and Mrs. Lydia Logie, only a few months married to the ship's Chief Mate, complete the list of adult passengers, except for servants. Six children were aboard. Mary Wilmot and Eleanor Dennis, who may have been the illegitimate daughters of rich Englishmen by Indian mothers, were probably on their way to England to be educated. Little Frances Hosea was a baby of twenty-two months. Also in her parents' charge was seven-year-old Thomas Chambers, a judge's son who was to go to school in England. Robert Saunders, son of a merchant, was also about seven, and so was William Law. The three small boys must have been good company for each other. It had been hard for their parents to part with them, but India was not a suitable place for the education of young gentlemen.

The weather was not too kind to the *Grosvenor* in the first weeks of her voyage and she was having trouble with her mainmast. A strong following wind had blown up on the flight of 3 August and there seemed no reason to anticipate danger. But then came violent squalls. Strange lights seen by the men on watch should have warned Captain Coxon that they were perilously near land, but he decided that they were at least three hundred miles from it. He was fatally out in his calculations. A terrible storm of rain, wind and lightning buffeted the vessel throughout the night and just before dawn she struck rocks.

Daybreak showed Captain Coxon a terrifying picture. The rocky reef on which the *Grosvenor* lay transfixed was off the coast of Africa, it seemed, for native huts and their inhabitants could be seen through telescopes. Boiling seas lay between the ship and the shore. As it was impossible to lower boats, two Italian seamen bravely offered to swim ashore with log-lines which they could then rig and bring passengers to safety by bo'sun's chair methods. One of them, Pandolpho, succeeded; his companion drowned. Their struggles were calmly watched by a number of natives, interested only in any valuable salvage that might drift ashore. A raft was launched with five of the crew on it and was instantly dashed to pieces, only one man surviving.

Hysteria broke out on board. The ship's drink stores were raided. Drunken sailors staggered about, looting what they could find, while women and children screamed and moaned. There seemed little hope for anybody. Then a miracle happened. A great wave lifted the starboard quarter of the hull and drove it almost on to the shore. All the passengers were got to land without serious injury and in all 123 people were saved. The natives made no attempt to help, collected any metal that was lying about — valuable souvenirs of an interesting morning — and strolled away, leaving the survivors to fend for themselves.

Temporary tents were rigged, as much food as possible was brought ashore, together with cooking utensils, carpenters' tools and anything that might be useful. But the natives again descended and robbed the sailors of every metal object they carried.

In the four days that followed, only the authority of Captain Coxon and his second mate, Mr. Shaw, preserved order in the frightened, demoralized little company. On Wednesday, 7 August, he called a general meeting. It was impossible for them to remain there any longer, he said. Shortage of food, and the menacing attitude of the natives, made it essential that they should try to reach the nearest Dutch settlement, which he thought to be about sixteen days' march away. So compelling was his speech that it met with no disagreements. He divided the company up into three divisions: one led by Mr. Shaw; one, which included women, children and other passengers, under Mr. Beale, the third mate; and one under the leadership of Captain Coxon himself, comprising the rest of the officers and crew. Mr. Logie, the chief mate, was so ill that he had to be carried in a hammock. Two men elected to stay behind and take their chances, but the rest set off as planned. Behind them, still beached and rocking in the waves, lay the split halves of the *Grosvenor*.

Constant plundering and attacks beset their journey. By Sunday, 11 August, their provisions were nearly all gone and morale was very low. The tougher members of the band now decided that it was time they forged ahead, leaving women, children and the feeble to save themselves as best they could, though hoping to bring help to them. A body of Lascars, the French prisoners, and about fifty of the crew put themselves under the leadership of Mr. Shaw and said their farewells to the rest of the party. With them went little William Law. He had become so fond of the ship's steward, Lillburne, that he cried bitterly at the thought of separation and Lillburne prevailed on the others to take him along.

There remained Captain Coxon, Mr. and Mrs. Logie, Mr. and Mrs. Hosea, Colonel and Mrs. James, other passengers, officers and crew — and all the children except William Law. Of this party, six Lascars reached friendly native territory, and two women — Betty, Mrs. Logie's maid, and Hoakim, maid to Mrs. Hosea. Of the rest of the forty-seven people nothing was ever seen again.

The terrible story of the journey made by Mr. Shaw's party does not belong to the realm of mystery and has no place here. It was set down by William Habberley, a young sailor who was one of the six survivors. He reached a friendly Dutch settlement on 14 January, 1783, after five months of indescribable sufferings. A kindly Providence and their own strong constitutions had saved him and five others from the dreadful deaths which had overtaken their companions. William Habberley dictated a full account of the nightmare trek to which we owe our knowledge. It is a simply told story of unimaginable courage, resource and endurance, almost too painful to read.

Of the fate of Captain Coxon's party Habberley knew nothing but what was told to his Dutch rescuers some months later. The two maids, Betty and Hoakim, had been found in different parts of the country. Betty said that the captain's party had begun to split up, that her master, Mr. Logie, was "almost dead when she left him", and that Colonel James was in nearly as bad a state. Mrs. James had begged her to stay and help, but she had deserted in the hope of catching up with the Lascars. She had joined some natives with whom she lived for a time — and one of them was wearing Captain Coxon's coat.

What happened to the rest? Throughout the years there have been persistent rumours that the women were captured by natives, and settled down with them. London newspapers published the theory as a fact, to the horror of relatives in England. A French traveller reported that the natives had killed all the survivors, except a few women. In 1789, seven years after the wreck, Colonel Gordon, commander of the forces at the Cape, told Bligh of the *Bounty* that he had heard there was a white woman with a child living with a native tribe. Gordon accordingly wrote letters of inquiry to be taken to the woman by the native who had given him the news. But he never heard anything more of her.

In 1790 a rescue expedition travelling in the territory of the Bomvana tribe heard that a number of descendants of Europeans who had been shipwrecked, were to be found on Bomvana territory — three of them women, living as wives to the chief. But these proved to be the descendants of castaways from a much earlier wreck than the *Grosvenor*.

A Danish traveller in Pondoland in 1927 alleged that he found there natives with fine features and a habitually sad expression, quite unlike the rest of their tribe. It is possible that these are the descendants of Captain Coxon's pathetic band. Of the three women, the young wife Lydia Logie was said to have been pregnant, and Mary Hosea was a pretty young woman with a baby. If they lived long enough to be captured, the local tribesmen may have taken them as wives, and that the two girls would have had no alternative but to accept this fate. Mrs. James, a woman in late middle age, had a poorer chance of survival, and may have refused to leave her dying husband. Her maid, Sally, seems to have been dead or to have deserted before the other maid, Betty, left the party. What happened to the two little girls, Mary Wilmot and Eleanor Dennis, is anybody's guess. But a rumour got about that they too "married" natives and were known to have died after a tribal uprising.

Over half a century afterwards, Charles Dickens wrote in *Household Words* an emotional account of the death of little

William Law during the journey made by the mate's party. And he referred to "the legends that were long afterwards received from time to time among the English officers at the Cape, of a white woman with an infant ... who was whisperingly associated with the remembrance of the missing ladies saved from the wrecked vessel, and who was often sought but never found".

Was she Mary Hosea, or Lydia Logie? It is too late to learn the answer now.

Attached to the *Grosvenor's* name is a mystery less tragic than the fate of Captain Coxon's party. It is this: was the *Grosvenor* a richly-laden treasure-ship? And did she carry in her hold the Peacock Throne of the Great Moguls?

The story has never died that she sailed from Trincomalee carrying chests full of gold bars and silver ingots up to a value of about three million pounds, more chests stuffed with diamonds, rubies, sapphires, emeralds and ivory, together with the valuable luggage of the wealthy passengers, and the load of silks and spices usually carried by a merchantman. It has always been supposed that these and other fabulous objects remained with her rotting timbers beneath the sea off the coast of Pondoland. But the facts do not seem to confirm this.

There were diamonds, certainly. A document remains to prove that at Madras she had taken on a considerable load of them — "twelve parcels" is the description — and that her cargo was reckoned at about £300,000. There is mention of miscellaneous goods, and of a "present" which Captain Coxon was taking home. There would also be money for the crew's wages, and for general expenses when the ship put into port.

After the wreck, gold coins were picked up from the sand round about by natives who valued them less than the odd bits of metal and the copper cooking implements they had wrenched from the castaways. Perhaps a whiff of these stimulated two Scotsmen's interest in the district, for in 1800 Alexander Lindsay and Captain Sydney Turner investigated the site and are said to have found two thousand gold coins.

In 1852 the Rev. Thomas Jenkins wrote a letter to a Captain Garden whose researches into the site of the wreck had resulted in the finding of what may have been part of *Grosvenor*'s ballast and some of her guns in the little "Bay of Muscles". Mr. Jenkins had found some more coins, gold and silver. In 1880 a Mr. Sidney Turner of Durban had the clever idea of dynamiting the rocks around the site. He discovered many coins, some of them minted in India, and all of the right date. It was this find and a newspaper reference to possible bullion treasure which seems to have led to the idea that the *Grosvenor* contained immense riches. But Turner's explorations revealed nothing substantial — only the coins, some bullets, and such pathetic relics as a button, cufflinks, part of a ring, and small commonplace objects that had been used aboard.

After more coins had appeared in 1896, public interest and greed was roused. In 1905 the Grosvenor Recovery Syndicate was registered in Johannesburg, with a reasonable capital and plenty of equipment. But the bones of the *Grosvenor* refused to be exhumed, and a diver went to join her in death. The syndicate disbanded and went home.

It was not until 1921 that a bigger and better syndicate was formed, the Grosvenor Bullion Syndicate, Ltd., "to endeavour to recover … all the gold, silver, tin, ivory, emeralds, rubies" that were still presumably waiting to enrich someone. Its prospectus gave mouth-watering details of the treasure, and all sorts of corroborative evidence, such as quotations from the *Grosvenor*'s log. Most of these, unfortunately for the syndicate's shareholders, were the work of a lively imagination. The brilliant research of Professor Percival R. Kirby of the University of Witwatersrand has uncovered the deceitful nature of this prospectus. The syndicate deservedly found nothing of interest or value, for all its elaborate tunnelling operations.

It was not long afterwards, in 1923, that the greatest *Grosvenor* legend was born. An anonymous writer in a South African newspaper wrote an article describing the work of the Bullion Syndicate, quoting the fictitious ship's log, and adding that, besides the bullion, there were indications that the *Grosvenor* carried the two priceless golden peacocks, looted from the Peacock Throne of the Grand Mogul. Made for Shah Jehan, builder of the Taj Mahal, it had stood proudly in the most famous building of the Imperial Palace at Delhi, the Diwan-i-Am, or Hall of Private Audience. The throne took its name, said one who saw it, from having the figures of two peacocks standing behind it, their tails spread, and both tails and bodies thickly encrusted with sapphires, rubies, emeralds, pearls and other jewels. Tavernier, the French jeweller, had seen it in 1665, and had described the throne as shaped like a bed, standing on four golden feet with bars above from which rose twelve columns to support the canopy, the bars being decorated with crosses of rubies and emeralds and the columns studded with splendid pearls. It was valued at £6,000,000.

In March, 1738, the Diwan-i-Am was raided by the hordes of Nadir Shah, the Persian invader, who stripped the palace of everything valuable, including the Peacock Throne, and took it back to Persia. In 1740 a similar throne was made from part of the original. According to the anonymous author, the peacocks were smuggled in chests back from Persia, and traced as far as Calcutta. He thoughtfully added that the tradition was somewhat nebulous.

But once started the rumour spread and later expeditions in search of the *Grosvenor* all appear to have had a vision of the golden peacocks in mind. For all the "it is said", "it may be possible", and other qualifications, the organizers wanted passionately to believe in a story which probably had no more foundation than the wildest tales of the Arabian Nights.

Or had it? What put the unknown writer on the track of the peacocks? Had he built the whole thing on the reference to some "present" which Captain Coxon was bringing home and could have been an oblique hint at something too rich to name? Was he only getting in a bit of propaganda for the Grosvenor Bullion Syndicate? Or was there, somewhere, a fragment of truth in the story?

Whether the diamonds carried by the *Grosvenor* still remain with her is also unknown. Probably not: Professor Kirby unfolds a most fascinating theory about them. But the stories fly about still and as recently as 1954 frogmen were diving in that much-explored stretch of water off the East African coast which by now may not even contain the wreck at all. Heavy seas and shifting sands have made her very position problematical and some of the discoveries of her cannon are distinctly suspect, for the Bay of Muscles was a noted spot for wrecks and the guns may well have belonged to other vessels. This, like everything else, about the *Grosvenor*, remains a mystery; and the sea is always reluctant to give up more than its dead.

11: THE WHITE NORTH HAS THEIR BONES

There is little mystery now about the end of the men who sailed with Sir John Franklin in the ships *Erebus* and *Terror*, northward-bound, in 1845. But in mid-Victorian times it was the most discussed of unsolved puzzles. One attempt after another was made to unravel it, until, at last, sad, conclusive news came back to England.

The story begins at the Battle of Trafalgar, for when the great *Bellerophon* sailed into action on 21 October, 1805, a young man called John Franklin was aboard her, serving in the dangerous post of signal midshipman. He was nineteen.

Young Franklin was lucky. Of forty-seven men on the quarterdeck only seven survived the French barrage and he was one of them. Calm and collected, he carried out his orders and kept the colours flying throughout the battle, unheeding the hail of shot that was killing his messmates like flies. The roar of the guns was frightening, certainly, but it did not stop Franklin doing his duty. Unwounded, he returned to England with his ship, was transferred to the *Bedford* and promoted to acting lieutenant.

Towards the end of the French wars, when America was involved and British troops were attacking New Orleans, Franklin was mentioned in dispatches as being the first man to board one of the American gun-boats. Next he was appointed first-lieutenant of the *Forth*, then was posted to the *Trent*, as second in command to Captain Buchan. With Buchan he first voyaged to the Arctic, where his future fate lay.

In 1819 Napoleon was safely incarcerated on St. Helena. Franklin must have been pleased that it was his old ship, affectionately nicknamed the *Billy Ruffian*, which intercepted the Emperor when, after Waterloo, he was preparing to make a bid for America and freedom. Now Franklin was free to follow in the footsteps of his hero, Nelson, who at the age of fourteen had edged himself into an Arctic expedition and killed a polar bear single-handed.

Exploring was in John Franklin's blood, or at least in his family. His uncle by marriage was Captain Matthew Flinders, who had won fame by his discoveries in the Antipodes. At the age of sixteen Franklin had served with Flinders in the *Investigator*, that aptly-named vessel which was sent to survey the sea-coast of Australia, and on this voyage he gained invaluable experience. He was a born seaman, but it was his urge to explore which took him in 1819 on his first amazing polar expedition into little-known waters, through unknown perils. All the man's simplicity and goodness are in his prayer before sailing, written in a letter to his sister.

> May the Almighty Power protect and guide us Who alone can order all things, and doth as seemeth best to His infinite wisdom. May we trust in Him and endeavour to do our utmost.

It was a voyage that has been described as "one of the most daring and hazardous exploits that has ever been accomplished in the interest of geographical research". Franklin and his companions were beset by unimaginable hardships. Terrible cold, famine, even murder reduced their number. But Franklin himself survived, and was back in England in October, 1822.

He was knighted, honoured, and appointed Governor of Tasmania, then called Van Diemen's Land, where from 1836 onwards he did his best to control the warring elements in the colony. But he was not happy in the post, nor outstandingly successful in it, and it was a relief to him when, in 1845, his seven years of office ended and he returned to England — just at the right moment. A great wave of interest and enthusiasm for polar discovery was sweeping the country. A new expedition was planned, using the ships *Erebus* and *Terror*. They had started off as bomb vessels, but had been adapted for polar use and had proved themselves in the south polar area under Sir James Ross. Ross was offered the command of the new venture, but declined. Franklin jumped at the chance of it and lost no time in applying to the Admiralty. They demurred because of his age — sixty. "No, no, my lord," he cried, "not sixty, but fifty-nine!" His lordship was won over. On 19 May, 1845, the greatest polar expedition ever organized up to that time left England. Franklin himself was in the *Erebus* with Commander James Fitzjames as his second-in-command and with them went Lieutenant Graham Gore and Mr. Charles Des Voeux. The *Terror* was commanded by Captain Crozier. Each ship held sixty-seven officers and men, and carried enough stores and provisions for three years. For the first time a polar expedition sailed under steam.

The object of the exercise was no less than to discover the North-West Passage. Franklin's orders from the Admiralty were to look for a passage to the Pacific, either to south or west of Lancaster Sound, north of Baffin Island. If he succeeded, the Atlantic and Pacific oceans would at last be linked. It was an ambitious project which appealed greatly to Franklin, and with his well-equipped vessels he saw no reason why it should not be successful.

On 4 July they reached Disco Bay in Greenland and wrote letters home, cheerful in tone. Twelve days later the whaling ship *Prince of Wales* met them in Melville Bay at the mouth of Lancaster Sound. The *Prince of Wales* sent a report back to England.

> 16 July, 1845. At 8 p.m. received on board ten of the chief officers of the expedition under the command of Captain Sir John Franklin, of the *Terror* and *Erebus*. Both ships' crews are all well and in remarkable spirits, expecting to finish the operation in good time. They are made fast to a large iceberg with a temporary observatory fixed upon it. They were in latitude 74° 48' N, longitude 66° 13' W.

Another whaler, the *Enterprise*, hailed Franklin, who told her master by megaphone that he had supplies enough to last for five years. He showed the captain a number of his men, busy on deck with the salting-down of seabirds for additional food.

And that was the last that was ever seen or heard of Franklin, his men, and the *Erebus* and *Terror*. "The knight-errant of the northern seas" had vanished without trace.

Nobody at home worried much for the first two years. In these days that would be an unthinkable time to be without news, but communications were poor in more frequented seaways than those of the Arctic and it was not till ten years later that the first Atlantic cable was laid. It was in the summer of 1848 that a council of naval officers was called by the Admiralty and the decision taken to send out a relief expedition. A veteran polar explorer, Dr. King, had already written gloomily to Earl Grey, the Colonial Secretary, suggesting that Franklin's ships had probably come to grief and that survivors had better be looked for along the course of Back's Fish River, in the south of King William Land. His opinion was not taken very seriously at the time.

But from 1848 several expeditions went out, always in vain. The *Investigator*, which had been the first ship to take Franklin exploring, started the search, accompanied by the *Enterprise*. Lady Franklin, that brave and hopeful wife, spent a large part of her private fortune in financing rescue operations. The Hudson's Bay Company came in, combing the extreme northern coastline of Canada. Between 1848 and 1859, thirty-two ships went out from England, three from America, and five from Hudson Bay. In 1850 and 1851 the rescue ships included the *Resolute*, the *Assistance*, the *Pioneer*, the *Lady Franklin*, the *Sophia*, and the *Felix*. They saw nothing of the missing vessels or men. But a curious sight was visible from the deck of the *Renovation*, a Canadian brig which happened to be off Newfoundland in April, 1851.

Ahead of her was the ghostly white form of an iceberg, not an unusual object in those parts. But deeply sunk among the white peaks and promontories of this iceberg were the remains of two wrecks caught like flies in aspic. The officer on watch was convinced that they were all that was left of *Erebus* and *Terror*. But there was no proof.

Lieutenant Osborn of the *Pioneer* reached Beechey Island where Franklin's ships had wintered, and anxious but still hopeful began the search. But all that was found was a cairn full of meat tins filled with gravel, some coal bags, rope, cinders, the pathetic vestiges of a small garden and the graves of three of the crew of the *Erebus* and *Terror*, their deaths recorded as having happened in 1845 and 1846. Two were seamen and one a marine.

In 1850 Captain Robert le Mesurier M'Clure, in the *Investigator*, made a great discovery. On the morning of 26 October, with six men and a sledge, he had left the ship and travelled through Barrow's Straits (now known as Melville

Straits). Standing on Banks Island, 600 feet above sea level, they looked northwards — and saw only sea. "The eyesight embraced a distance which precluded the possibility of any land lying in that direction between them and Melville Island. A *North-West Passage* was discovered." It was ironical that a ship searching for Franklin should accidentally have come upon the great object of his quest.

The following May M'Clure had another piece of luck of a rather different kind. He shot a large bear which proved to have in its stomach things indicating the proximity of civilized men. There were raisins, a few pieces of tobacco leaf, bits of pork fat cut into cubes and surgeon's sticking-plaster. M'Clure and his men rejoiced. Surely they were on the trail of Franklin at last!

But no more clues came to light until 1854, when a Dr. Rae, who had been searching for years on behalf of the Hudson's Bay Company, met a party of Esquimaux in Pelly Bay, King William Land. They told him that some years before, in the springtime, they had seen some forty white men struggling over the ice, dragging a boat and sledges. The men had managed to convey that their ships had been crushed in the ice and they were now trying to find food. They all looked thin and exhausted. The Esquimaux were killing seal at the time and the white men bought one from them. Later in the year the Esquimaux had found thirty corpses and some graves on the mainland and five bodies on a nearby island. Beside the bodies were relics which Dr. Rae was shown: a round silver plate engraved "Sir John Franklin, K.C.B.", some spoons with initials and crests which could be identified as those of officers. A more horrifying discovery was evidence that the unfortunate victims might have been reduced to cannibalism.

The British Government found this development sufficient grounds for calling off the search, particularly when John Anderson of the Hudson's Bay Company found more relics of the same kind. But Lady Franklin had not lost hope. She issued a gallant reply to the Government.

"What does all this prove? That the *Erebus* and the *Terror* had to be abandoned, perhaps, but no more. In fact, it does not even prove that. The unfortunate men to whom Dr. Rae refers may well have been a reconnaissance party sent out from the ships. After that they may have lost their way and been unable to return. Only 35 bodies were found, but the total party consisted of 129 officers and men. Are we to believe that there was not a single survivor left alive?"

She appealed to the Government for one last effort. They would not listen; private enterprise must come to the rescue. She bought a steam yacht, the *Fox*, and sent it out in July, 1857, under the command of the experienced and efficient Captain Francis L. M'Clintock. The Government, perhaps to appease its conscience for not wholly financing the expedition, supplied arms, shot, powder for ice-blasting, rockets, maroons and signal mortars. The Admiralty contributed 6,628 pounds of pemmican to the *Fox*'s stores and the Board of Trade gave meteorological and nautical instruments and journals. Ice-saws, ice-anchors and ice-claws, together with books and Arctic clothing, also came from the Admiralty. The whole expedition cost £6,000.

It seemed that with such equipment M'Clintock could not fail to strike the track of Franklin. But the *Fox* soon ran into trouble. She had left a warm English June behind her. Off Greenland she found premature winter conditions. Seventy miles west of Upernavik she reached the edge of the "middle ice" and found herself in a predicament which might have been fatal to a vessel without steam. M'Clintock, seeing no prospect of forging ahead in the direction they had been going, steered northwards towards Melville Bay. At Beechey Island he anchored and set up a marble memorial to the men they sought.

"To the memory of Franklin, Crozier, Fitzjames and all their valiant brother officers and men who suffered and perished in the cause of science and to the glory of their country, this tablet is erected near the spot where they spent their first Arctic winter."

Whatever M'Clintock expected to find, it was not living survivors.

They reached Melville Bay on 12 August, and again the ice closed in on them. For eight months the gallant little *Fox* struggled and drifted in the grip of her white enemy. M'Clintock's diligently kept journal is in itself a record of Victorian fortitude.

"My frequent visits to the crow's nest are not inspiriting. How absolutely distressing this imprisonment is to me no one without similar experience can form any idea. As yet the crew have but little suspicion how blighted our prospects are ... but I must not write on this subject. The men enjoy a game of rounders on the ice each evening."

He organized a "school" to keep the men's minds occupied, with lessons on everything from simple arithmetic to advanced navigation. On 5 November they had a celebration, with one of Lady Franklin's preserved plum-puddings and a firework party on the ice.

On 2 December one of the engineers, Scott, fell down a hatchway and was killed. His funeral took place by the light of the strange Mock Moons, those lunar phenomena which sometimes illuminate the Arctic night — "a complete halo

131

encircling the moon, through which passed a horizontal band of pale light that encompassed the Heavens; above the moon appeared the segments of two other halos, and there were also mock moons, to the number of six."

And so from day to day, from month to month, through another Arctic winter, that of 1857–58. Still the *Fox* remained locked in the ice. It was not until 27 March that gales released her, blowing her out to sea. To M'Clintock it was nothing short of a miraculous delivery. "It has pleased God," he wrote, "to accord to us a deliverance in which His merciful protection contrasts — how strongly! — with our own utter helplessness."

Now the *Fox* was free to pursue her quest. During the summer of 1858, M'Clintock explored all likely territory — Eclipse Sound, Pond's Bay, Regent's Inlet, Peel Strait, Bellot Strait — without finding any trace of the lost party. Another winter passed. On 1 March, 1859, the *Fox* was at "about the position of the Magnetic Pole". The crew halted to encamp and were pleased to meet with a small party of Esquimaux.

At first only bartering was discussed. Then something caught the eye of one of M'Clintock's men, glinting on the coat of one of the Esquimaux. It was a British naval button.

Discreet questions produced the information that the button had come from some white people who were starved upon an island "where there were salmon". Next day the entire village population arrived and M'Clintock got more news from them and more ominous relics. There were six silver spoons and forks, a silver medal bearing the name of Mr. McDonald, Franklin's assistant surgeon, part of a gold chain, more buttons, and knives, bows and arrows which the natives had made out of the wreck of the white men's ship.

During the next few months more and more clues to the fate of Franklin came to light. Two ships had been seen, long ago, by the inhabitants of King William Island. One of them had been seen to sink in deep water and nothing was obtained from her, but the other was forced on shore by the ice, at a place called Oot-loo-lik. This was the wreck which had provided the materials for the Esquimaux weapons. A young Esquimaux then revealed that a corpse had been found on board the ship, the body of a very large man, with long teeth. No, there had been no other corpses: all the other white people went away to the "large river" (Back's Fish River), taking a boat or boats with them. All that remained of these people was bones, M'Clintock was told by the reluctant natives — for Esquimaux dislike speaking of the dead.

He followed up the trail. On 25 May he made the first sad, conclusive discovery.

"I came upon a human skeleton, partly exposed, with here and there a few fragments of clothing appearing through the snow ... the dress appeared to be that of a steward or officer's servant ... we found a clothes-brush near and a horn pocket-comb."

An old woman had told them that the survivors "fell down and died as they walked along". This discovery proved her words.

Another clue came into M'Clintock's hands, a piece of flannel marked "F.D.V., 1845", which he sadly identified as part of the clothing of the mate, Des Voeux. Then, at Point Victory, about twelve miles from Cape Hershel, came written evidence. It was an Admiralty form, with a message written on it:

28 May, 1847. H.M. ships *Erebus* and *Terror* wintered in the ice in lat. 70° 05' N., long. 98° 23' W.

Having wintered, in 1846–7, at Beechy Island, in lat. 74° 43' 28" N., long. 91° 39' 15" W., after having ascended Wellington Channel to lat. 77° and returned by the west side of Cornwallis Island, Sir John Franklin commanding the expedition.

All well.

Party, consisting of two officers and six men, left the ships on Monday, 24 May, 1847.

The message was signed "Gm. Gore, Lieut." and "Chas. F. Des Voeux, Mate."

But the hope and cheerfulness of this was dispelled by smaller writing which filled in the margins of the paper.

25 April, 1848. H.M. ships *Terror* and *Erebus* were deserted on 22 April, five leagues NNW. of this, having been beset since 12 September, 1846. The officers and crews, consisting of 105 souls, under the command of Captain F. R. M. Crozier, landed here in lat. 69° 37' 42" N., long. 98° 41' W. Sir John Franklin died on 11 June, 1847, and the total loss by deaths in the expedition has been, to this date, nine officers and fifteen men.

The signatures now were "F. R. M. Crozier, Captain and Senior Officer" and "James Fitzjames, Captain H.M.S. *Erebus*".

A postscript said, "And start tomorrow, 26th, for Back's Fish River."

A brief, tragic epitaph, written by the living who were soon to join their dead comrades.

M'Clintock followed up the trail towards Back's Fish River. At the western extremity of King William Island he found a large, ruined boat. It was not empty. He and his companions gazed, "transfixed with awe", he tells us, at two human skeletons.

"One was that of a slight young person; the other of a large, strongly made middle-aged man..."

Animals had ravaged the bones, but plenty of identifiable objects were left in the boat. There were watches, guns, furs and some pathetic books, all of them Scriptural or devotional works, except *The Vicar of Wakefield*. One little volume, *Christian Melodies*, bore on the title-page an inscription to "G.G." — probably Graham Gore, the lieutenant who had written that cheerful message. These and many other small relics were carefully collected by M'Clintock's men.

So the fate of Franklin and his crews was solved. But of the cause of death of the two corpses in the boat a mystery remained. They had with them some tea, and nearly forty pounds of chocolate. Since M'Clintock's time in the present century several unopened tins of meat have been discovered at the spot and some opened which had been thrown away with their contents untouched, suggesting that the meat they had contained had been suspect. Perhaps poison from contaminated food had been the end of some of the survivors.

The *Erebus* and *Terror* were never found. All that remains of them is the wood and metal used by the Esquimaux to make weapons.

In spite of these all too convincing discoveries there were people in England who yet would not believe that Franklin and all his men were dead. Hall, the American explorer, had heard tales of mysterious white men living among the Esquimaux and himself took the hazardous northern route in the hope of finding them. But the Arctic is a cruel region; even legend cannot survive there long.

12: DERELICT

Of all the strange phenomena of the sea, the floating wreck, or derelict, is the most uncanny. No life aboard her, no life in her machinery, she is an unburied corpse that is quite dead but stubbornly refuses to lie down. To sailors each ship has her own personality and it is as though this persists after the vessel's "death". Sometimes the surviving spirit appears to be a malevolent one — a poltergeist of the sea. Here are two stories of dead ships which menaced the living.

In 1859, Captain Charles Hall of Rochester, New Hampshire, a blacksmith turned journalist, felt that he must make some attempt to solve the mystery of the vanished *Erebus* and *Terror* and rescue any of Franklin's party who might survive. Fifteen years had passed, but there was always hope in those days of poor communications. M'Clintock's discoveries in 1859 had proved Franklin's own death, but what of the others? It was only too likely that the white North had their bones, as Tennyson had written of their leader. But Hall was an optimist and anything was possible in the Arctic.

His offer to the American Geographical Society to equip an expedition was accepted, and with the proceeds of a public subscription he was able to fit out a whaler, the *George Henry*. Along with her in convoy he took a store-ship. This was the *Rescue*, a tough vessel which had already been out in 1850 on an unsuccessful search for Franklin. She had none too good a reputation. Sailors murmured of her as a bad-luck bringer. The mortality rate among her crews had been high and her sister ship, the *Advance*, had been smashed in Arctic ice-floes.

Hall's expedition had reached Frobisher Bay on Baffin Island in September, 1860, when the *Rescue* lived up to her reputation. While the two ships lay at anchor in the bay, a strong nor'-nor'-easter rose, bringing snow and gales which raged throughout the night of 27 September. The *Rescue* was visibly suffering. By mid-morning on the 28th she was in distress. The lookout on the *George Henry* reported to Captain Hall that the *Rescue* was dragging her anchors. Hall, who had previously been farseeing enough to transfer her crew to the *George Henry*, was saddened but not surprised to see his store-ship drifting helplessly shorewards.

For another twenty-four hours she continued to drift, her anchor-chains at full stretch. Then, while Hall and his crew watched, she gave a convulsive jump, heeled over, tossed wildly about, trembling like a frightened animal, then flopped, no longer a sturdy ship but a disintegrated object. Looking back to the scene in 1864, Hall remembered that as the *Rescue* lay "among the jagged crests of the rocks that were tearing her to pieces with the raging waves breaking over her deck, a snowstorm heaped its flakes around her as though swathing her in a gigantic winding-sheet".

The *Rescue* was dead; the *George Henry* sailed on. Hall had heard rumours of a party of white men living with the Esquimaux and was hoping to find them and also to do some whaling. In July, 1861, the *George Henry*, which had been laid up in winter quarters, returned to Frobisher Bay and cast anchor. During the night fog came up. Next morning Hall went on deck to have a look for the remains of the *Rescue*. There was nothing to be seen.

Baffled, he went ashore with a search party, but could find only small fragments of wood. The rest, it was decided, must have been washed away by the tide.

A few days later, on 27 July, the *George Henry* was near Whale Island, in the Hudson Strait, when Captain Hall was called on deck. About two miles distant, the lookout had sighted a battered hull floating on the waves. Something about it was familiar and became more so as the *George Henry* approached. The crew crowded up to see and a murmur spread among them: "The *Rescue*. It's her, all right. But we saw her smash up — broken to bits! She can't still be afloat."

Curiosity gave way to fear when it was noted that the *Rescue* seemed to be steering some sort of course rather than wallowing at the mercy of the waves. Perhaps there was someone aboard, ghosts or devils, for how could human hands steer her when the steering gear had gone? The ever-hopeful Hall wondered whether some survivors of the Franklin expedition might not have come across the wreck and fitted her out with help from the Esquimaux. How, without men aboard, could the *Rescue* have made her way round Cooper Island? The crew of the living ship watched keenly for some sign of life, some signal. But none came. Somewhat unhappily, they went back to their several jobs. They had never cared much for the *Rescue*, and considered her resurrection a very bad omen.

That night it seemed as though they were right. For the first time the *George Henry* was in trouble with the ice, great blocks threatening to splinter her sides. The crew hastily got to work to break it up — and as they did so, one of the men gave a cry of fear. He had raised his head from energetic pick-wielding to see, straight ahead, the dreaded form of the *Rescue*, surrounded by icebergs and moving steadily towards her old companion.

Something like panic set in. It seemed as though the *George Henry* could not avoid being rammed by the approaching hulk, still apparently under a sort of guidance. It would be a broadside collision when it came — most serious of all. Nearer and nearer she loomed, bringing death and destruction with her, for what hope would men have with ice and icy waters all about them and no one to help? Never had the *Rescue*'s name seemed more ironic. Some called on Captain Hall to abandon ship, but he steadily refused and was justified, for the hulk began to bear away astern of the *George Henry*, farther and farther away into the moonlit mist until she vanished altogether. The reprieved crew, half-paralysed with fear, gave humble thanks for their deliverance.

Next morning Hall lost no time in weighing anchor. It was imperative to get his ship away from the region where "the accursed thing", as he called it, was plying. She was nowhere in sight and a peaceful day followed for the threatened men. But during the evening meal there was a sudden clatter from the galley: the ship's cook had caught sight of the derelict lurking among the ice, as if watching the *George Henry* like a cat at a mouse-hole.

Cat and mouse was indeed the game the ships played for two more days, while the intrepid Hall studied the coastline in his quest for Franklin survivors. Not until 6 August did he and his dithering crew sail away, having seen, the night before, the *Rescue* departing seawards, as though she had done her worst with the *George Henry* and was summoned to mischief elsewhere.

Another dangerous derelict with icy connections was the *Frigorifique*. Her name referred not to the Frozen North, but to the fact that she was one of the first ships to be fitted up with refrigeration equipment. Throughout the history of shipping the greatest problem had always been to keep crews supplied with food during a long voyage, and even in Nelson's day the men were lucky to stay alive on rations described by John

Masefield as "nearly always bad, and sometimes villainous". The biscuit ration was liberal, but the biscuits themselves were made mainly of pea flour and bonemeal and were of an incredible hardness until long keeping softened them up — and bred weevils. The bread, so-called, was "as full of maggots as it could hold" and wise seamen left the eating of it until night when they could not see it so clearly. The meat preserved in salt, sometimes for years, was almost black and rock-hard — ideal material for the carving of souvenirs, but less suitable for consumption. Its origin was very dubious. There were tales of barking and neighing heard from slaughterhouses and of horseshoes in the meat-casts. The butter was edible on first putting to sea, but became putrid after a few weeks and the cheese was notable for a breed of red worms.

By 1814 the canning process ("can" was derived from "canister") had improved the meat situation, but it was very expensive and did not reach the lower deck until 1847. Throughout the middle years of the century the seamen's diet was becoming pleasanter and more varied. About 1850 the process of refrigerating food by pumping the heat out of an insulated chamber had been discovered and this was to revolutionize ships' food stores and the world's supplies in general. In 1880 the first cargo of beef came to England from Australia, and the trade soon spread to New Zealand, the Argentine and Europe.

The *Frigorifique*, once a British mailboat, was the first French ship to be fitted up with refrigerating equipment. In 1884 she had been plying successfully from country to country with frozen carcasses, and she was coming home to Rouen from Spain when she ran into fog. From the thick pea-souper around came the note of a siren — or was it? Nobody could be quite sure. The *Frigorifique*'s answering siren received no reply.

But then the other siren was heard again, this time very near, and another ship loomed up to starboard, silent and ominous, bearing down on the *Frigorifique*.

There was a rending crash as the collision came. The *Frigorifique*'s engines flooded, and she began to sink — she had been struck amidships. Her master gave the order to abandon ship and the vessel which had rammed her was quick to pick up the French sailors.

When they got aboard, they found her to be a British collier, the *Rumney*. The French guests were welcomed, given a tot of rum all round. They thanked their lucky stars that it was their ship, not themselves, on the way down to the bottom of the sea. The fog had swallowed her, and they were now moving away as fast as they could from the scene of the collision. Suddenly, out of the fog loomed a shape. It was a familiar one. The French sailors crossed themselves. *"Mais c'est impossible — la Frigorifique!"*

In these days somebody would have suggested that they were all suffering from collective hallucination. But the phrase was not then known and the thing which had appeared and was now moving away was thought to be a ghost-ship or a fog-wraith. In any case, it was now invisible again.

But not for long. Cries of alarm went up as the vision loomed up again like a materializing spirit, and before the master of the *Rumney* could give more than the briefest of orders the resurrected French ship rammed the vessel that had sunk her. It was as though an animal, driven away to lick its wounds after a fight, had returned to the attack and killed its enemy.

Now it was the *Rumney* that began to sink. Boats were lowered. Fortunately there were enough of them to hold the French seamen, as well as the *Rumney*'s crew. Soon the *Rumney* was empty and the boats rowed away. The fog was lifting now and they could see the *Frigorifique* still lurking, smoke coming from one funnel, and her screw turning.

One of the boats containing members of her crew reached her and climbed aboard. Investigation solved the mystery. She had not sunk. Water had stopped coming into her engine-room, her boilers were still at work, her wheel had been lashed so that she sailed in a circle that brought her twice across the *Rumney*'s path. The second collision had been her death-blow, and now she was sinking in earnest — happy, perhaps, to lie quiet in her ocean grave, having destroyed her slayer.

Less vindictive, but sufficient threat to other shipping, was the *Governor Parr* which was abandoned south of Newfoundland and went on to cruise about the Atlantic in 1923 and 1924, a menace to other craft. She mischievously resisted all efforts at capture. Government ships tried to take her in tow, but she broke loose and frisked away. They set her on fire and she blazed cheerfully for a short time, then extinguished herself and reverted to her old tricks. Everybody was relieved when the "phantom derelict" finally disappeared.

The *Fanny Wolston* holds the record for length of drift. After being abandoned in mid-Atlantic she continued to swim vaguely about for nearly four years. Like the *Governor Parr*, she was fired, but in vain. The last time she was seen was 1,408 days after her abandonment.

13: MERMAIDS AND MONSTERS

The mermaid has fascinated mankind from the beginning of time, or at least, from that time when they ceased to be entirely preoccupied with things of the land and began to turn their attention to the wide watery element that surrounded him. The inhabitants of the British Isles seem to have been particularly curious about the inhabitants of the sea and to have made up their minds very soon that under the waves were people something like themselves. After all, it made good sense. Fish could live in water; they were, so to speak, the animals of the sea. The presence of animals suggested the presence of superior beings who must, by reason of their superiority, be part-human. For the rest of their anatomy, a fish-tail was the most obvious and practical structure. And to these simple men who already believed in ghosts and fairies an element of magic was essential.

It was not long before sex, never far from the world of legend, crept into the landsman's picture of the sea-people. The female figure became dominant. A witch of the sea, beautiful, alluring, powerful, elusive, she lived in the mind of every sailor in those frail boats of early times. Woman-starved, he hoped, yet feared, to see her — for she was reputed to be able to lure sailors to their doom with her charms and her sweet singing, and to drag whole ships to the bottom of the sea with one wave of her hand.

The ancient Greeks had worshipped nereids — nymphs, the daughters of Neptune, who might protect or punish them — and the Romans were fascinated by the sirens, beautiful winged creatures who lived among the rocks and caves of the Italian coasts like great seabirds whose nests were made of the bones of drowned men.

But to the men of Britain it seems that the dangerous sea-lady very soon assumed the appearance of the typical girlfriend of any sailor, except for her scaly tail. The mermaid was plump, shapely, with long, fair, waving hair which she liked to comb as she sunned herself on a rock, admiring her face in a mirror at the same time. She became such a popular figure that when Christianity came to Britain she was not banished and carved images of her sometimes appeared as church decorations. Even the early Saints got involved with her. There is a legend that one of St. Columba's assistants in the Christian colony of Iona, off the coast of Scotland, held daily arguments with a mermaid who wanted a soul. She is said to have fallen in love with the holy man, though no account of their romance exists. St. Patrick is reputed to have dealt sharply with mermaids he found lounging about on the beaches of Ireland — though he managed to convert one of them to Christianity.

There are mermaid legends in plenty from those far-off times, but in 1197 comes the first "true account" of the capture of one. Unfortunately for the story's news value, the creature was male. The existence of mermen as well as mermaids had always been accepted, but their images had never been so popular. Now, at Orford in Suffolk, on the east coast of England, one was actually fished up by men out at sea with their nets. As the chronicler Holinshed put it (writing in 1577):

> A fish was taken by fishers in their nets as they were at sea, resembling in shape a wild or savage man whom they presented unto Sir Bartholomew de Glanville, Knight, that had then the keeping of the Cassel of Oreford in Suffolke. He was naked, and all his limbs and members resembling the

144

right proportion of a man … the crowne of his head was bald, his beard was long and rugged and his breast hairie. The knight caused him to be kept certaine daies and nights from the sea, meat set afore him he greedilie devoured and did eat fish both raw and sod. He would not or could not utter any speech, although to trie him they hung him up by the heeles and miserablie tormented him.

After some days of this cruel treatment, the poor merman was allowed to enter the sea again, with a row of strong nets set up to prevent him escaping. But, one is glad to know, he dived under the nets, emerged on the opposite side and "seemed as it were to mocke those on shore, for that he had deceived them".

He seems to have returned later, but only for a short time, "and was never after seene or heard of".

It is a circumstantial enough account. But Holinshed was writing four centuries after the event and the eyewitness, Ralph of Coggeshall, may have been letting his imagination run away with him. His own version (written up by monks) says that the merman was taken to church but took no part in the ceremonies. If he was some kind of seal, which seems possible, it is not altogether surprising.

In 1403 a Dutch mermaid appeared through a broken dyke near Edam and was rescued from the mud by some women on their way to milk cows in the water-meadows. At first they were afraid of her, but overcoming their fear they took her to the house of one of them where "she suffered herself to be clothed and fed with bread, milk and other meats, and learned to spinne and perform other pettie offices of women". Often the wretched captive tried to steal down to the sea again, but was always brought back and lived in Harlem for fifteen years, never once speaking. Because she had learnt to kneel before the Crucifix she was granted Christian burial. No account of her appearance survives except that when captured she was covered with sea-moss which the women picked off her.

Columbus is reported to have seen three mermaids jumping about in the sea in 1493, but thought them "not so faire as they are painted". Throughout the sixteenth century, the great age of voyaging and discovery, countless tales were brought back from sea of mermaids and their doings, none of them particularly well authenticated. But in 1608, Henry Hudson, sailing in search of a passage to the East Indies, recorded in his log that two of his crew, Thomas Hilles and Robert Raynar, were lucky enough to see a mermaid closely resembling the familiar romantic descriptions.

"Her back and breasts were like a woman's … her skin very white; and long haire hanging down behinde, of colour blacke; in her going downe they saw her tayle, which was like the tayle of a porpoise, and speckled like a macrell".

Again in 1608, apparently a vintage year for mermaids, another charming creature appeared off Newfoundland, a beautiful, well-proportioned maiden with blue hair and white shoulders who "looked cheerfully" upon the ship's crew that had sighted her. But, most unchivalrously, they struck her on the head and drove her away.

A few years later a green-haired charmer was seen in West Indian waters and beguiled a susceptible captain into the beginnings of love — until he saw her tail, which put him off completely.

In 1717 a book was published in French which contained what purported to be the authentic picture of a mermaid — green-haired, swarthy of complexion, with webbed fingers and pink hairs on her tail. The painter swore to her reality, but nobody seemed able to give any details about her.

An unpleasant eighteenth-century story of mermaids and mermen being eaten by hungry sailors records that they tasted rather like veal and, when captured, cried and grieved — not, one feels, without cause. It seems that by now the early superstitions about mermaids no longer protected them from being callously hunted like the seals they resembled. They were clubbed, speared, mutilated, and otherwise maltreated. But they continued to survive, even into the matter-of-fact nineteenth century.

In 1809 the north of Scotland rang with controversy over a mermaid sighted by a highly respectable schoolmaster of Thurso, William Munro, whose account actually appeared in *The Times*. It had all happened, he said, about 1797, when strolling on the shore he had found himself confronted by "a figure resembling an unclothed human female, sitting upon a rock extending into the sea, and apparently in the action of combing its hair, which flowed around its shoulders, and was of a light brown colour ... the forehead round, the face plump, the cheeks ruddy, the eyes blue, the mouth and lips of a natural form... It remained on the rock three or four minutes after I observed it, and was exercised during that period in combing its hair, which was long and thick, and of which it appeared proud, and then dropped into the sea".

Neighbours of Mr. Munro's, to whom he told the tale, surprisingly replied that they had seen similar appearances. All reliable, God-fearing folk, they were prepared solemnly to stand by their stories. So were those who saw the mermaid of Campbeltown, Argyllshire, in 1811. Campbeltown's staple industry is whisky distilling, but nowhere in the impressive testimonies of the witnesses is there any suggestion that they had been over-indulging in the local product. Their mermaid was hairy and rather plain, more resembling a boy than a woman.

But the strangest and most touching of Scottish mermaid stories comes from the Hebridean island of Benbecula and belongs to the year 1830. William IV had just come to the throne. Victoria was a young girl. Charles Dickens was a reporter in the Law Courts. The Liverpool and Manchester Railway had been opened. London was illuminated by gas-lamps. It was an age of scientific and social progress; the world of legend was reserved For Amusement Only. And yet to a number of Hebridean peasants gathering seaweed there appeared a mermaid.

She was a child, not a woman. Those who saw her said she seemed to be aged about three or four, but with the full bosom of a grown girl. Her hair was dark, long and shining, her skin white. From the waist down she was like a salmon. She was playing in the sea, swimming and leaping as a land-child might do. The spectators watched, enthralled, some, no doubt, crossing themselves. Then the inevitable happened — a boy picked up some stones and threw them at her. One struck her between the shoulders, and she disappeared. A few days later they saw her again: but now she lay limp on the shore, killed by the cruel stone.

The most touching, and convincing, part of the story is its ending. Duncan Shaw, land-agent for the local laird, ordered a coffin and shroud to be made for the small corpse and she was buried not in the churchyard but by the sea which was her element. And there, beneath the sands of Benbecula, still lies the little mermaid of whom Hans Andersen might well have heard.

Up to modern times there have been reports of mermaids, although credulity is less than it was in those days when showmen could exhibit a "mermaid" in a fairground booth, as they did in the days of Shakespeare, who himself frequented the Mermaid Tavern, famous rendezvous of wits and poets. The present authors saw two of these strange exhibits at the British Museum's exhibition of fakes in 1961. They were small, shrivelled creatures, cunningly compounded of the top halves of monkeys and the tails of fishes and were as unlike the glamorous siren of legend as could be.

There was no mystery about them: and yet the mystery remains. Why, if the mermaid was solely a piece of wishful thinking on the part of superstitious and sex-starved sailors — or the survival of a pagan belief in sea-gods — do so many varied, and, on the whole, unattractive descriptions of her survive? The most popular scientific explanation is that she is based on the Dugong or Manatee, a cetacean of singular ugliness which, when suckling its young in an upright position, might look very roughly like a woman. But the viewer's eyesight and the light would have to be equally bad. Nor does the Dugong live off the Scottish coast. Did some other creature, semi-human in form, blue- or green-haired as in the description of the most modern sightings, exist in the sea? And does it exist there still, or has modern shipping driven it out of existence? The poet Gerard Manley Hopkins summed up the situation with melancholy neatness.

White loom'd my rock, the water gurgling o'er,
Whence oft I watch but see those Mermaids now no more.

Even deeper-rooted in mythology than the mermaid is that other phenomenon of the marine world, the sea serpent. He was Midgard of the ancient Norwegian sagas, the great snake whose tail encircled the known universe. He appears among the constellations as Cetus, the sea monster sent to devour the

149

chained Andromeda. There is no end to the legends about him, crediting him with gigantic size and terrible savagery. Old drawings show him coiling around a whale in strangling folds, swooping on a ship and seizing it in his huge jaws.

He is sometimes described as having fiery eyes and a habit of snapping sailors up from the deck.

All these stories we may take as seriously as we take the things encountered by Odysseus on his wanderings: one-eyed man-eating giants, nymphs turning men into pigs, and similar marvels. But the sea serpent legend, far from dying out with the spread of knowledge and communications, has grown stronger and is remarkably well documented. Reading the great file of accounts of "sightings" during the last century in particular, one is forced to believe that something very large, very strange and unknown to science is responsible for these stories.

Accounts begin to be circumstantial in the eighteenth century. Pontoppidan, Bishop of Bergen in Norway, writing his *Natural History of Norway* in 1755, said that he had never believed in the sea serpent "till that suspicion was removed by full and sufficient evidence from creditable and experienced fishermen and sailors in Norway, of which there are hundreds, who can testify that they have annually seen them." Another churchman, Bishop Egede, made a missionary voyage to Greenland in 1734 and records in his Journal: "On 6 July, 1734, when off the south coast of Greenland, a sea-monster appeared to us whose head, when raised, was on a level with our main-top. Its snout was long and sharp and it blew water almost like a whale; it had large broad paws; its body was covered with scales: its skin was rough and uneven; in other respects it was as a serpent; and when it dived, its tail, which was raised in the air, appeared to be a whole ship's length from its body."

Lawrence de Ferry, a captain in the Norwegian navy, actually wounded such a monster, and brought two of his men into court to testify to the fact. It seemed to have a grey head, a black mouth, and a long white mane, and there was about a fathom distance between each fold or coil of its body. But Pontoppidan thought that the typical sea-snake of Norway was dark brown and spotted like tortoiseshell, with large blue eyes like a couple of pewter plates.

In the next century more sightings occurred, usually by highly respectable people such as Captain Schielderup, Postmaster of Otersoen, a former captain, who had never believed in the stories until in 1849 he actually saw one of the creatures for himself, two hundred yards away from his boat. It seemed to be about 600 feet long, was greyish, and made a "a loud crackling noise" when it moved. Its head was like a snake's, and it smelt unpleasant (Shakespeare's "ancient and fish-like smell", apparently). Other people in the neighbourhood saw the same or similar monsters — called by them kraken — and the Bishop of the Nordlands, at Alstahoug, saw two swimming together.

Though popularly known as "the Norwegian sea serpent", the thing was seen many times off the coast of Scotland during the early years of the nineteenth century, particularly off Inverness-shire. At this point a forecast of the most famous of all monsters, "Nessie", creeps into the stories. The *Inverness Courier*, in 1872, remarks that "the huge serpent invariably appears in still, warm weather ... and is scarcely ever seen in the open sea. In the present case, the limit in which the animal has been seen on our coast is Loch Duich to the north and the Sound of Mull to the south ... and it is in that part it should be most looked for. If it chances to turn up once more, some full and accurate account of the phenomenon would certainly be most desirable".

Not far eastwards from Loch Duich and in a line with the Sound of Mull is Loch Ness and the "sighting" of the 1872 monster, by the Reverend John McRae and the Reverend David Twopeny, is quite astonishingly in agreement with the various descriptions of "Nessie". A series of "black lumps" undulated across the water. There is a small flat head, a sort of fin, an equable and smooth motion, "like that of a log towed rapidly". They are almost the identical phrases used by modern viewers lucky enough to be by Loch Ness at the right moment.

But some varieties of the sea serpent did frequent the open sea. One of the best-authenticated accounts was made by Captain Peter M'Quhae, of HMS *Daedalus*, on 6 August, 1848. She was homeward bound from India, about 300 miles westward from the southern corner of Africa. It was a dull day and *Daedalus* was beating up into a strong nor'-wester. The captain, his sailing master, and Lieutenant Edgar Drummond were on deck. Stationed forward were midshipman Sartoris and the bo'sun's mate. At the wheel was an able seaman, with the quartermaster nearby. All these witnesses saw, and swore to, the appearance of an enormous serpent with its small, snaky head about four feet above the surface, a dark brown body with yellowish-white round the throat, and a mane-like growth on its back. Swimming at twelve to fifteen knots, it went briskly past the ship without a sideways glance — no doubt to the intense relief of the watchers.

The captain's report was published in the *Illustrated London News* with a sketch of what had been seen. Professor Richard Owen, the eminent naturalist, did his best to demolish Captain M'Quhae. No remains of any such monster had ever been found, so how could it exist? But in 1883 some remains were found. While cruising in a saltwater inlet of New Florida, the President of the United States Humane Society found his anchor tangled up in something large and unpleasant. It was the decaying corpse of a monstrous serpent-like creature, forty-two feet long and six feet round. The carcass was hauled ashore, and plans made to give the skeleton to a museum. But before anything could be done the sea had taken it back.

Not long after the encounter between *Daedalus* and the sea serpent, a Lieutenant-Colonel Thomas Steele of the Coldstream Guards wrote to the *Zoologist* to back up Captain M'Quhae. He too, and everybody on board the *Barham*, bound for India, had seen an even more startling apparition — the head and neck of an enormous snake, spouting water. On its back was a crest like a cock's comb, and its colour was green, with light spots. One of the ship's officers corroborated this in a long statement and mentioned that the creature was surrounded by hundreds of birds.

Throughout the last quarter of the century sea serpents seem to have been as common as herring. The Royal Yacht *Osborne* saw one in June, 1877. It had a smooth skin and the head and mouth of an alligator. So slowly did it move that Lieutenant Hynes made a pencil sketch of it, which is very like the drawing made of one seen from the American ship *Sacramento*, a month later, by the man at the wheel, John Hart.

In 1879 the *City of Baltimore* encountered one in the Gulf of Aden. A Major Senior, of the Bengal Staff Corps, spotted it level with the ship's stern and excitedly shouted: "Sea serpent! Sea serpent! Call the captain!" This one had a head "not unlike pictures of the dragon, with a bulldog appearance of the forehead and eyebrow". From the *Nestor*, between Malacca and Penang, came a description of something with a dragon-like, black, white-striped tail and a body fifty feet broad; and the master of the barque *Pauline* recorded in his log a dramatic encounter between a monster sea serpent and a large sperm whale. The whale lost. His account was corroborated at the police court at Chittagong by his officers and crew in a sworn statement made before a magistrate. The postscript to it tells of yet another sighting of a similar monster which was seen to look threateningly towards the vessel.

The century turned. In 1903 the steamship *Tresco*, bound from Philadelphia to Santiago de Cuba, saw what was at first thought to be a derelict. The second officer, Joseph Grey, gave orders for the ship to change course and inspect it. A derelict was always a menace to other shipping. But the thing which had looked like the hull of a vessel proved to be a menace of another kind: "A mighty and horrible head came out of the water, surmounting a tall, powerful neck that had the thickness and strength of a cathedral pillar." The men on watch panicked and fled below. Grey and the man at the wheel, a Portuguese, stood their ground, but Grey thought it wiser to steer from the wheelhouse in case "this fellow" decided to charge the ship.

Nearer it came and Grey studied at close quarters the awful head, about five feet long. Two immense molars curved down and backwards from its mouth, which was red. Its eyes were also reddish and were remarkable for having no pupils. They watched the ship with a baleful, unwinking glare. The creature's dull scales were the colour of antique bronze. Suddenly, to Grey's horror, the fins on the back rose into a great webbed crest which began to glow as if with anger. It approached the ship and for a time swam alongside it, Grey and the Portuguese anticipating every moment that it would attack. Then slowly it began to turn away, with remarkable grace for anything so huge, and sank down into the water. The statement reads like a vision seen in delirium tremens. But it bears the affidavit of Grey and of four other men, one of them the master.

In 1925 an unidentifiable monster was found dead on the beach at Margate, on the south coast of Natal. It was fifteen feet long, six feet broad, and two feet thick, covered with longish white hair. Decomposition prevented any more details being noted.

Still reports come in of the Loch Ness monster and its relations, and still modern science fails to capture, photograph or identify them satisfactorily. Certain factors are common to the creatures seen and described throughout the ages: a snake's head, or an alligator head resembling that of a dragon, a long neck, and a barrel-like body, a fin, or fins, which look like a horse's mane. The appearances have most often been seen in the summer months, June, July or August. In no authenticated case has a monster attacked a ship, and Grey of the *Tresco* may well have wrongly interpreted the "baleful glare" of the creature's eyes. Reptilian faces are not noted for their range of expression and if the monster had had savage intentions there is no reason why it should not have carried them out. The general conclusion, therefore, is that the unknown creatures are harmless, elusive, and fall, broadly speaking, into two types, dragon or snake.

A number of other explanations have been put forward. The sea serpent could be a school of porpoises, swimming in line, or two basking sharks, which doing the same would produce the effect of a body sixty feet or more long. Sea-lions, seals, giant squids (which sometimes grow to a length of fifty feet) are also popular theories. One interpretation of the monster-whale conflict seen by the *Pauline* is that the whale was the attacker, not the attacked, and was in fact eating a giant squid whose tentacles looked like the coils of a snake. Some have thought the sea serpent to be no more than an overgrown conger eel.

The serpent's habit of diving and disappearing under the water implies that it is a non-air-breathing creature — or, more accurately, one which can exist for a brief period on the surface but normally lives below it. This seems to knock out the most interesting and attractive theory, that it is an Enaliosaur, a survival of those prehistoric monsters such as the Plesiosaur, whose gigantic bones are more fascinating than the most elaborate production of the taxidermist's art. The small head, long neck, thick body and immense tail of the snake-type monster all resemble this, just as the dragon-type is singularly like the Dinosaur. It may be that when land life became impossible for them, some of these took to the water and adapted themselves to a new element. The Coelacanth has survived the passage of millions of years: why not the great lizards?

That all the witnesses of sea-serpent manifestations throughout history were lying is unlikely — particularly in the case of nineteenth-century testimonies made when a Bible oath was taken very seriously. That all the witnesses were drunk on duty, or all needed spectacles, is impossible. Sailors and fishermen are used enough to the sight of seals, basking sharks, schools of porpoises and squids, and there is no reason to suppose they would be deceived by such creatures swimming in line or take them for anything else. The sea serpent can fairly be said to belong to the region of fact, not that of myth. But like the mermaid its debatable character and the legends that have grown up about it have added much to the romance of the element in which it flourishes. Sailors' yarns would not be the same without it: it is, in a sense, the great nautical household pet. And poets, too, have dwelt lingeringly, lovingly, on its coils from the earliest ballad-days to those of James Elroy Flecker and his "The Dragon-green, the luminous, the dark, the serpent-haunted sea".

14: THE TRIAL OF THOMAS DOUGHTY

A recurrent cause of trouble at sea until recent times has been a lack of contact between officers and seamen. Sharp class divisions aboard prepared the way for trouble of all kinds, especially mutiny. Sir Francis Drake recognized this four centuries ago and spoke forcefully of it to his assembled crews as they waited to sail from Port St. Julian, Santa Cruz, towards the perilous Straits of Magellan, in August, 1578.

"By the life of God!" swore the fiery Queen's Admiral. "It doth even take my wits from me to think on it! Here is such controversy between the sailors and the gentlemen, and such stomaching between the gentlemen and sailors, that it doth even make me mad to hear it. But, my masters, I must have it left. For I must have the gentlemen to haul and draw with the mariner and the mariner with the gentlemen. What! Let us show ourselves all to be of a company, and let us not give occasion to the enemy to rejoice at our decay and overthrow."

He had some provocation for his speech. One of the gentleman officers who had sailed with him from England had been guilty of plotting the decay and overthrow of Drake, his ships, and the entire hazardous royally-ordered expedition. The story of this "gentleman" and his relations with Drake is one of the strangest psychological puzzles in the history of seafaring.

Drake, for all his strong language and firm discipline — he was notoriously strict with his crews — was an enlightened, civilized man for that Elizabethan Age when brutality was still a part of daily life, in curious contrast with the splendour of literature and music then coming to full flower. Drake did not inspire the protective love felt by Nelson's tars towards their Admiral; he was not that kind of man. But, like Captain Corcoran, he was "a really popular commander", honest, forthright, sincerely religious. Most remarkable of all, he was humane. One of his most outstanding virtues was his kindly treatment of prisoners, a thing so rare as to be almost unknown in those times, especially when given to Spaniards, bitter enemies of England and themselves notorious for cruelty. We have his own word for it, modestly and factually expressed in a letter to Walsingham:

> The Portingals I have always commanded to be used well, and set them ashore without the wanting of any of their apparel, and have made them to know that it was unto me a great grief that I was driven to hurt of theirs to the value of one real of plate, but that I found them employed for the Spaniard's services…

He inspired poetic eulogies as no other great sailor but Nelson has done.

You, whose exploits the world itself admired,
Admire the strange exploits of peerless DRAKE;
And you whom neither lands nor seas have tired,
Have tired your tongues when they rehearsal make
What hard adventures he did undertake;
Then if that such Atlantes are too weak,
What marvell if their weight or shoulders break?

He that hath been where none but he hath been,
Leaving the world behind him as he went;
He that hath seen that none but he hath seen,
Searching if any other world unkent
Lay yet within the Ocean's bosom pent:

Even he was DRAKE: O could I say "he is",
No music would revive the soul like this.[3]

But for all Drake's virtues, it would have been odd if there had not been some ruthlessness and superstition in his temperament. The sixteenth century was full of both. Even so, nothing can adequately explain Drake's part in the extraordinary affair of the trial and death of Thomas Doughty.

It was the year 1577. Four years previously Drake had returned to England with two ships laden with Spanish gold, collected during his exploits in the Spanish Main. In the words of a contemporary, "he got some store of money by playing the seaman and the pirate".

It had been an extraordinarily successful enterprise, dealing a sharp blow at England's enemy, Spain, and contributing handsomely to the coffers of Queen Elizabeth. The Queen, who was extremely fond of money, might have been expected to reward Drake fittingly.

But unfortunately for him he had arrived back just at the moment when England and Spain had patched up an uncomfortable truce. Their basic enmity had not changed; it had merely been put temporarily on one side for economic reasons. Drake, therefore, appeared in the light of a pirate rather than a hero. He was only in his early thirties, a comparatively unknown sea captain. The expedient thing to do was to keep him out of sight until the political situation worsened and he could again be sent out to harass Spain. Elizabeth had no scruples about using her fighting men as pawns, moving them as the game demanded.

Drake, then, staged a diplomatic disappearance, doubtless on the Queen's orders, for two years. In 1575 he emerged; the

---

[3] *On Sir Francis Drake* — Charles Fitz-Geffery.

Queen had need of him. He was taken back into favour, accepted at Court, his past triumphs were praised. In 1577 a high honour came to him. An expedition was planned by some of the Queen's right-hand men — Walsingham, the Earl of Leicester, Sir Christopher Hatton, the Earl of Lincoln, Lord High Admiral, and Sir John Hawkins, Drake's kinsman, Treasurer of the Navy. The expedition was to be one of exploration. Beyond the Straits of Magellan lay an uncharted country; they called it Terra Australis Incognita. Drake, with his flair for such ventures, was to establish relations between the ruler or rulers of this country, and provide England with new trade interests. This would cut out any possibility of Spain doing the same thing.

For this reason the expedition's purpose was to remain secret. Elizabeth wished to appear still on friendly terms with King Philip and she therefore preferred to remain officially ignorant of the enterprise. Walsingham, that wily man, was asked to approach Drake and ask for suggestions, on paper, as to the most favourable areas for undermining the trade of Spain. Drake, however, refused to put anything in writing and the Queen finally sent for him herself.

To her he suggested that instead of making for the unknown land at once, he should, after leaving the Straits of Magellan, make another raid on Spanish waters and their richly-loaded ships, thereby ensuring the financial success of the venture, even if the unknown land proved disappointing or altogether inaccessible. Elizabeth agreed with the proviso that Burghley, her Lord Treasurer, should know nothing about it. If anyone leaked the news to him their heads would roll: and when Elizabeth said this, she meant it literally.

The expedition was fitted out, its ostensible purpose being a voyage to Alexandria in connection with a trading scheme.

Drake's fleet consisted of five ships and four pinnaces, with crews totalling about 166. Drake's own vessel was the *Pelican*, one day to be renowned as *The Golden Hind*. With him went two of his relations, his brother Thomas Drake and his nephew John. And a man called Thomas Doughty.

It is not known for certain where Drake and Doughty met, but they probably came across each other when Drake was doing some fighting in Ireland during his period of diplomatic obscurity. Captain Thomas Doughty was what would nowadays be described as a smooth type: well-born, educated, easy-mannered. He had been friend and something like aide-de-camp to Walter, Earl of Essex, commander of the English forces in Ireland. The association had come to an abrupt end when Doughty was found to have been making mischief between Essex in Ireland and Leicester at Court. The flare-up that ensued between the two earls revealed Doughty's part in the business and he was dismissed from Essex's service. Writing him off as a double-dealer, Essex told Leicester how thoroughly taken in he had been by the man's charm and apparent sincerity. "I was rather induced to give him credit because he had before that time spoken as much as any other of his devotion to me and my cause."

Doughty then transferred to the service of Sir Christopher Hatton, and presumably became increasingly friendly with Drake as he was invited to accompany him on the expedition. Drake may even have trusted him with the real purpose behind the ostensible one. If he did not, Doughty was wily enough to have found it out for himself. It may have been, in fact, the reason why he sailed with Drake at all. From the moment the fleet left Falmouth on 13 December, 1577, Doughty seems to have set out deliberately to undermine the morale of the men and to prevent Drake from carrying out his instructions.

Why should he have done this? He acted on too large a scale to be prompted purely by malice. If he was in the pay of someone, that someone can only have been Lord Treasurer Burghley, whose policy was "peace at any price". Burghley knew that if Drake succeeded in capturing more treasure-ships King Philip would inevitably renew the war. It would be the end of the uneasy armistice, of England's trade hopes, and possibly of England as a free Protestant country. Like Walsingham, Burghley had his spies. If Doughty was on Burghley's payroll, his job was to sabotage the expedition by undercover means.

Trouble first arose when Drake told his crews their real destination, though not the object of the enterprise. They were dismayed. The dangerous Magellan Straits were most unpopular with sailors, particularly sailors who had expected to voyage to the Mediterranean or the West Indies. They grumbled and fretted and Doughty made good capital out of their apprehensions.

But apart from bad weather at the beginning of the voyage, all went well for some time. Two Portuguese ships were captured and Doughty was put in command of one of them which Drake had re-named the *Mary*. Also aboard her went Drake's trumpeter, Brewer, and his young brother Thomas. It was at the Island of La Brava that Brewer brought news to Drake. Doughty had been caught stealing from the cargo of the captured Portuguese. A violent scene followed. Drake swore and raged at Doughty. Doughty smoothly defended himself. Yes, he had a few things belonging to the Portuguese crews, he admitted, but they had all been given to him as presents. This story was not hard to disprove and Drake's temper grew even fiercer. Then Doughty committed one of the silly mistakes that make him such a puzzle: he accused Thomas Drake of having stolen the goods.

It would have been natural for Drake to have written off Doughty completely at this point. But, although he deprived him of the command of the *Mary*, which he gave to Thomas, he immediately reinstated Doughty in a position of authority on the *Pelican*, himself remaining in the *Mary*.

The voyage was long, and the boredom of the men on the tedious stretch between the coast of Guinea and the coast of Brazil must have been intense. In such circumstances men will do strange things to pass the time, such as playing silly and painful practical jokes on each other. But it is impossible to understand why Doughty risked playing one that might have been deliberately calculated to infuriate Drake.

Brewer, the trumpeter, had rowed over to the *Pelican* from the *Mary* with a polite message to Doughty and an inquiry about the general state of the ship and the temper of her men. His greeting was rough. A party led by Doughty debagged him and gave him a sound thwacking. This playful trick, known as a "cobbey", might have been taken in good part, if hardly welcomed, by an ordinary seaman. Brewer, Drake's personal messenger, was seriously affronted and hurt, not only in his feelings. He reported back to the *Pelican* exactly what had happened, naming Doughty as the ringleader.

Drake reacted as might have been expected. Orders went to the *Mary* that Doughty was to report to him instantly. This time the messenger was not debagged, and Doughty duly rowed over to the flagship. What was his expression as he looked up from the boat at Drake above him on the *Pelican*'s deck? Was it fear, truculence, amusement? Drake's short beard bristled with temper and his aspect was what his contemporaries would have called "cholerick". "Stay there,

Thomas Doughty," he shouted, "for I must send you to another place!"

Doughty was transferred to the *Swan*, the fleet's store-ship. John Chester, her captain, was to hold him there until further orders.

It was curious, not at all typical, behaviour on the part of Drake. A flaming row with Doughty, followed by an admonition not to play pranks again, would have been more in character. To put Doughty at once into cold storage suggests that Drake was by now certain that the man was a dangerous element aboard either the *Pelican* or the *Mary*. If the "cobbey" incident was regarded as part of Doughty's effort to incite unrest or even mutiny, Drake must have thought it a very odd one, drawing direct punishment on Doughty himself as it did.

Now the story becomes downright fantastic. It is said that when the fleet at length came in sight of the coast of Brazil and was in turn sighted by the natives, the Brazilians lit fires to propitiate the many devils who ruled that part of the world and danced round them chanting incantations to raise storms and wreck the approaching ships. The sight must have been a daunting one to the Englishmen who had not seen land for many weeks. They were even more daunted to find that the natives' charms appeared to work. Terrible gales and mists beset them and drove them off their course. Miraculously, the little ships weathered all. They were incredibly small by modern standards — the *Pelican* only just over 100 tons, the *Benedict* of only 15 tons. Gamely they ploughed along the line of the eastern coast of South America towards the Straits so dreaded by navigators.

On 29 May they sailed into the port of St. Julian, north of the Straits of Magellan. Here they were to spend two months, laying in provisions and servicing the fleet. Magellan had halted

165

in this same place in 1520 before attacking the dangerous passage now called after him, and mutiny had broken out. The men who had led it had been hanged. Drake's crews, when they came ashore, found gruesome evidence of this — a rotting mast which had once been an improvised gallows. Was it morbid curiosity that made them dig round the foot of it? They found the bones they were looking for, and the *Pelican's* carpenter whittled out lumps of gallows-wood and carved it into cups from which the less squeamish of his companions drank their supper-ale. Death and decomposition are constantly recurring themes in the literature of the Elizabethans: on one side of the medal the glittering Virgin Queen and her gallant ships, on the other a grinning wormy skull. Not many years after this voyage, Shakespeare was to put into the mouth of the young, tender Juliet a speech in which the ghastly terrors of burial alive in the Capulet vault were lingered over, almost enjoyed.

This was the spirit in which the disgruntled crews of Drake's fleet dug up the skeletons of those who had once suffered for mutiny. What the reactions of Doughty were to this episode is not recorded, or to the encounter with a band of Patagonian natives armed with bows and arrows, who killed two of Drake's men, one of them his gunner. Drake snatched the gun from the dead man's hand, rammed in a fresh charge and fired at the killer, "and, striking him in the paunch with hail shot, sent his guts abroad with great torment, as it seemed by his cry, which was so hideous and terrible a roar, as if ten bulls had joined together in roaring".

Drake's blood was up and now he abandoned his temporizing policy with regard to Doughty. Perhaps the grim atmosphere of Port St. Julian had something to do with this. But he seems to have been partly motivated by fear — not of mutiny, but of the supernatural. For Doughty had done another silly, inexplicable thing. He had allowed his brother John to go about saying that both the Doughtys were wizards, able to raise the devil "and make him to meet any man in the likeness of a bear, a lion, or a man in harness".

It is useless to conjecture how any sane man can have made such a boast in that superstition-ridden age, knowing what retribution might fall on him, Witches, male or female, were hunted, tortured and burnt if enough evidence could be gathered against them: and here was Doughty boasting of being a practitioner of the Black Art. Did he believe he had magical powers and suppose that they would render him a desirable leader in the eyes of the seamen, in the event of mutiny? Did he entertain some muddled hope of terrifying Drake who, like most of his contemporaries, would face any mortal enemy, but run from a ghost or a devil?

Whatever he meant by it, the effect on Drake was disastrous to Doughty's interests. Drake began a sharp investigation into Doughty's words and actions. Questioned, his men made it clear that Doughty had been a subversive influence throughout the voyage. Drake put him on trial.

It was an impromptu affair, but perfectly valid. Drake appointed himself both judge and prosecuting counsel. A jury of forty was drawn from the officers and men, their foreman being John Wynter, commander of the *Elizabeth* and Drake's Vice-Admiral. The charge, in Drake's own words, was:

"Thomas Doughty, you have here sought by divers means, inasmuch as you may, to discredit me to the great hindrance and overthrow of this voyage, besides other great matters where I have to charge you withal."

Doughty had no objection to standing trial, but threw doubts on the validity of this one. He hoped that Drake's commission was good, he said. He already knew that it was: the crew of the *Pelican* could testify that he had said publicly that Drake's commission from the Queen put him in a position to order an execution, if necessary. Perhaps he had forgotten having said this. The trial proceeded.

Evidence was given that Doughty had been overheard by one Edward Bright plotting — in, of all places, Drake's own garden — and that he had actually been heard to say that Burghley "had a plot of the voyage". "No, that he hath not!" interrupted Drake. And now came the most extraordinary moment of this strange case. For Doughty, instead of denying this, agreed with Bright's evidence. Yes, Burghley had known all about the real object of the voyage, he admitted.

"How?" asked Drake.

"He had it from me," coolly answered Doughty: and, in answering, put a rope round his own neck.

If this was meant to light the fire of Drake's ready temper it succeeded. He burst out furiously:

"Lo, my masters, what this fellow hath done! God will have all his treachery known. For Her Majesty gave me special commandment that of all men my Lord Treasurer should not know it. But see how his own mouth hath betrayed him!"

It does not seem to have occurred to Drake to ask *why* Doughty's own mouth had betrayed him. He accepted the confession and pressed for a verdict. "Guilty of treachery," declared the jury, and voted unanimously for Doughty's execution. It was fixed for two days hence. The strange prisoner left the stand, apparently without any great emotion.

With equal casualness, it seems, he suggested that a pleasant alternative to the gallows might be that he should be put ashore, preferably in Peru. Drake rejected this and the other suggestion made by John Wynter, who seems to have been a friend of Doughty's, that he himself should be appointed Doughty's jailer throughout the voyage and back to England, where a more formal trial could be held. The hanging must take place as appointed. No mention had been made during the trial of the "other great matters" with which Drake had promised to charge Doughty. Presumably these included the witchcraft indictment. Doughty's confession had made this charge superfluous and an inquiry into exactly how the two Doughtys did their devil-raising would have prolonged the proceedings undesirably. It is a pity that no more is heard of this curious factor in the case.

The final hours of Doughty's life make almost unbelievable reading. By now it was to be expected that all pretence of friendship was over between accuser and accused. Yet, when Doughty took Holy Communion for the last time, Drake took it beside him and, kneeling before the fleet's chaplain, heard the condemned man boldly affirm his complete innocence of everything with which he had been charged. The chaplain, Fletcher, fully believed this to be true.

This denial makes Doughty even more of a riddle. Having once confessed his guilt, there was no point in making a lying retraction of it, particularly at such a solemn moment. The strongly religious Drake, hearing such a lie, might well have recoiled from the man kneeling at his side in horror and disgust. He did nothing of the kind. From the bread and wine of the Sacrament, judge and condemned man proceeded to Drake's quarters, where they "dined at the same table together as cheerfully in sobriety as ever in their lives they had done aforetime, each cheering up the other and taking their leave by drinking to each other as if some journey only had been at hand".

If only some other account remained of this fantastic scene! There was cheerful, commonplace conversation, there were light toasts — but what else? Was no mention made of the events that had gone before — of the strange confession at the Communion table? Apparently not. It is hard to envisage Elizabethan seamen sticking to the Victorian rule of etiquette that forbade unpleasant subjects to be discussed at table, but so they did.

Any solemn converse between them was reserved, probably by previous agreement, for a later hour. Doughty, a guard on either side, was about to be led away to the block that awaited him. He had been granted the privilege of a gentleman — beheading, not hanging. He asked for, and was allowed, a short private interview with Drake. What was said in it nobody heard, nobody will ever know. Then, calmly, cheerfully, with that odd lightness of spirit which seems to have characterized the man, Doughty went with his guards to the place appointed, and Drake watched as his friend's head leapt from the body at one stroke of a sword.

And Drake observed, "Lo! this is the end of traitors."

Did he sincerely believe that Doughty was a traitor? If so, what had he made of the denial to the chaplain? If he did not believe that Doughty was a traitor, why did he let the execution proceed? But if he *did* believe it, how does one explain the friendly, even cordial, terms on which the two men remained up to the last moment of Doughty's life?

Throughout the voyage, too, his behaviour was strange. Drake was no fool, and even before they reached Port St. Julian there had been plenty of pointers to Doughty's treachery. Yet Drake appears to have been most reluctant to take any action against him and, when forced to take action, was very moderate about it. Was there a strong personal friendship between them — and Elizabethan men were much given to warm friendships which were not in any sense sexual — and did this tie of soul make it impossible for Drake to treat his friend harshly until the situation got out of hand?

None of Drake's behaviour in this matter makes sense. Doughty's belongs even more to the world of fantasy. To condemn himself out of his own mouth, deliberately having provoked his commander's wrath with petty thefts, horseplay and silly stories about wizardry — never did a secret agent behave more irresponsibly. The final denial of his guilt is as impossible to understand as the rest of his conduct.

We have just used the phrase "the world of fantasy". This may well be the clue to the riddle that was Doughty. For it is just possible that he was never an agent of Burghley's at all. The evidence at the trial was not conclusively damning, though Doughty was condemned on the strength of it. Some witnesses may have been lying because they disliked the prisoner. Others, his known friends, obviously were telling what they thought to be the truth. Doughty lived long before the age of analysts, their couches and their case-books, but he fits rather neatly into a certain category of psychiatric patient. A man of charm and talent, with no particular outlet for it, restless, unreliable, rather too intellectual for the sailor's life and too adventurous for that of the scholar, having a side to his nature which enjoyed mischief-making (we know this from the Essex-Leicester quarrel): he may very well have made the whole Burghley story up. That he caused trouble in the fleet and made subversive remarks and statements cannot be denied. But it all ties in with the character of a man who desires, at all costs, to make an impression on other people, to cause a sensation.

He must have known that he was digging his own grave. But though the expression "death-wish" did not exist in 1578, the thing itself certainly existed, and occurs frequently in the literature of the time. "I will encounter darkness as a bride, and hug it in mine arms," says Claudio in *Measure for Measure*, a man, like Doughty, condemned to execution. The lemming-like impulse to rush on to his doom may have been present in Doughty, combined with that amazing fortitude so often met with in Elizabethan fighting men and in the age's martyrs, to whom pain and death were as nothing.

It is the only explanation that fits the behaviour of Doughty. That of Drake is inexplicable. Soon after the execution he sailed on his perilous way towards new discoveries and triumphs.

> *So, in the May-tide of his summer age,*
> *Valour enmoved the mind of vent'rous DRAKE,*
> *To lay his life with winds and waves in gage,*
> *And bold and hard adventures t' undertake,*
> *Leaving his country for his country's sake:*
> *Loathing the life that cowardice doth stain,*
> *Preferring death, if death might honour gain.*

Did he think, on that long voyage, of the friend he had left at Port St. Julian? And had that friend confessed to him, at the last, that he too preferred death, if death might honour gain? Answer comes there none.

15: THE HORSE THAT "SWAM" TO
THE NATIONAL

It seemed like a fishing story to end them all.

One day in 1904 a party of fishermen set off from a point on England's Irish Sea coast near Liverpool. It was a rough day, and their hopes of a good catch were not high. Least of all, they never expected to return home with a racehorse.

Their fishing trip took them to a tiny, uninhabited island, off which they proceeded to cast their nets. As they bobbed and rolled in the troughs of the sea, they were suddenly astonished to hear what was unmistakably the whinnying of a horse.

Knowing perfectly well that no life of any kind existed on the island, the wary fishermen put ashore — and found that their imagination had not been playing tricks. There stood a horse.

In the name of humanity there was only one thing to do. After a great deal of difficulty in the conditions prevailing, they succeeded at length in coaxing the animal into their boat, and put back to the mainland. Their astonishment at finding the animal at all was nothing to that of onlookers who saw a fishing expedition return with most of their small boat taken up by what was clearly a massive specimen of horseflesh. A local newspaper reporter quickly heard about the excitement and sent off details to the National Press, blowing up the affair into an immediate sensation with mysterious implications. The horse, sound in wind and limb, was no beauty — he was, in truth, large and ugly — but it needed only a glance to appreciate that he was far removed from your common run of horses. Who, then, was he? And how came he on an uninhabited island several miles out in the sea?

The mystery was not long-lived, though the wonder of it remains. The horse was claimed by a Mr. Spencer Gollan, who identified himself as the owner of one of New Zealand's leading studs and his animal as Moifaa, nine-year-old offspring of the mare Denbigh and sire Natator, which, appropriately enough, is Latin for "swimmer".

Moifaa had been on his way to England for training. In the Irish Sea the ship carrying him and his owner towards Liverpool had been suddenly battered so mercilessly by wind and sea that the master had decided to lower the boats and had ordered passengers and crew into them. He was barely in time. Waves crashed over the stricken vessel, beam-on to the sea, and she seemed to have only minutes left to live. Then someone remembered Moifaa, tethered in his stall. Braving the sea, a man fought his way below and released the animal, giving him the slender chance of surviving.

Moifaa took his chance. The power and courage which that unlovely exterior concealed enabled him to get clear of the foundering ship and to swim and swim, until at last he staggered ashore on that uninhabited island.

That, really, is all there is to the short-lived mystery of a seahorse who stood seventeen hands high; but to leave Moifaa's story at that point would be to leave a good yarn unspun.

As the sensation surrounding him faded away he was taken to his training establishment, apparently none the worse for his experience. Soon he ran in three steeplechases, and failed in them all. The experts sneered. A horse as ungainly as that would never clear the high English fences.

Moifaa sneered back. In fact, he was always sneering, his lip perpetually curled in a grimace which matched his graceless appearance. "A starved elephant, the ugliest devil you ever saw," said Lord Marcus Beresford, the English owner, after seeing him. Moifaa's retort was to do a practice run on the Grand National course at Aintree and whistle effortlessly over every fence. "Moifaa is a great machine at high pressure over fences," conceded Beresford.

The bookies gave Moifaa 25–1 for the National, with King Edward VII's Ambush II favourite at 7–2. The King himself watched and shared the general amazement as, with his jockey lacking strength to subdue the gigantic amalgam of surging shoulders and whirling legs, Moifaa flung himself immediately into the lead. The bookies smiled. Even if he cleared his fences at this reckless pace he would drop from exhaustion before the finish.

Moifaa did not drop. He was never passed during the entire race, finishing eight lengths ahead of the second runner, Kirkland, and the Gunner a neck behind for third.

King Edward bought him on the spot, and, after another year, Moifaa seethed impatiently at the start of the Aintree course. Again he charged into the lead and looked like repeating his sensational win. But he was ten years old, and heavy, and his wind was not what it had been. By the second circuit he was flagging. Becher's Brook loomed ahead. Full of courage still, he made a great lunge, hit, and sprawled to the turf. His runner up of the previous year, Kirkland, went on to win.

Still sneering, Moifaa was pensioned off: but he hadn't done badly for a horse obliged to swim to fame.

Curiously enough, there is another recorded instance of a fishing boat returning to harbour with a horse aboard. It dates from the 1850s.

A fishing boat from the Biminis, a group of islands in the Florida Strait of Miami, crossed to another island, Great Isaac, for a day's trawling. Towards evening, as they were about to pack up for the day, the fishermen distinctly heard the whinnying of a horse from the nearby shore. Astonished, they went to investigate and found a pure white stallion, reeling about on the beach, apparently terrified. As they approached it collapsed, kicked briefly, and lay still. They found it dead, with a broken neck.

Along the beach, previously hidden from them, they saw the remains of a four-masted ship. Bodies were floating in the sea nearby. The fishermen dragged a few ashore, but all were dead — except one. Clutched in the already stiffened arms of a young woman was a baby. Almost impossibly, it was still breathing.

The fishermen hurried back to their boat with the child, having thrown up a rough enclosure of stones round the young woman's body, intending to return next day and bury her. When they did there was no trace of her. The night's high tide had carried her away.

It was just at this time that the Victoria lighthouse, which had proved one of the attractions of the Great Exhibition in London in 1851, where it had stood in a make-believe sea of grass in Hyde Park, was shipped in the barques *Hero* and *Stanley* to Great Isaac, where men set to work to erect it for the benefit of shipping using the Florida Straits. On several occasions the workmen reported seeing the figure of a young woman wandering on Great Isaac's shore as if looking for something. She continued to be seen throughout the last century and was encountered as recently as 1913 by one of the lighthouse men who had the unnerving experience of meeting her on the spiral staircase of the lighthouse late one evening. His successor saw her, too, and determined to get rid of her for ever. He held a service of exorcism. The distraught young mother has never been seen since.

There is at least one more sea mystery involving animals on an island. In 1911 the steamship *Tottenham* — one of the vessels which had searched for the *Waratah* three years before — herself came to grief off the island of Juan da Nova, in the Mozambique Channel, halfway between Mozambique and Madagascar, when she struck a reef in the dark. Her crew managed to struggle ashore to find themselves awaited by a reception committee — of dogs.

Crowds of dogs, of every breed and colour, stood in complete silence, watching the survivors land. It was an eerie experience for the men, who would have minded less if the dogs had performed as expected and set up a chorus of barking. Instead, they just stood there as though they had forgotten how to bark, as lonely men sometimes forget how to speak. Their tails, instead of wagging, hung limply, wolf-fashion, between their legs.

One of the seamen, hoping to get some reaction from this weird congregation, fired a shot in the air. The dogs ran away in a body. They were heard whining in the night, but they were never seen again.

What was their strange story? Nobody knows. At least we know, from another incident, what that most penetrating of all minds would have inferred from it:

Inspector Gregory: "Is there any other point to which you would wish to draw my attention?"

Sherlock Holmes: "To the curious incident of the dog in the night-time."

Inspector Gregory: "The dog did nothing in the night-time."

Sherlock Holmes: "That was the curious incident..."

16: TREASURE AT TOBERMORY

"God blew with His winds and they were scattered."

It was September, 1588. The formidable combination of God, Francis Drake and Lord Howard of Effingham had effectively disposed of the Armada, that fleet which was the hope and pride of Spain, sent to conquer England for Philip II, capture the arrogant Queen Elizabeth, bring the country under Catholic rule and end English sea power which was damaging so seriously the trade of Spain in the Americas and Indies.

The story of the Armada's defeat is an amazing one. The odds were heavy against England, yet she won through, as she had done before and was often to do again. The Invincible Armada was vanquished. When the Duke of Medina Sidonia, its commander, got back to Spain in late September he had to report to his king the loss of 72 ships and 10,185 men. Over twenty of those that did not return found themselves in trouble round the wild and rocky coasts of Ireland and Scotland. Reports of their movements went to London for the information of Walsingham, head of Elizabeth's secret service.

Mr. Ashby, Walsingham's correspondent at the English Embassy in Scotland, wrote to him on 6 November that "a great shippe of Spain that has been for some six weeks on the West Coast is now off Mula (Mull) in Maclean's country, is unable to sail, is supplied by the Irish people with victuals, but they are not able to possess her, for she is well furnished with shot and men. If there bee any English shippes of war in Ireland, they might have a great prey of this shippe, for she is thought to be *verie riche.*"

Previously he had reported that this ship, which he described as being of 1,400 tons, having 800 soldiers on board with their commander, was lying at an island called Isla (Islay) in the west part of Scotland, there driven by weather. Guided by a fisherman, she had arrived in Tobermory Bay in the Hebridean island of Mull and there dropped anchor. She had been lucky to find friendly natives in both her havens. Many Spaniards who came ashore from their ships or swam there from wrecks were cruelly murdered and robbed by those to whom they appealed for help, or, in Ireland, killed by forces of the English government who were afraid of their inciting the Catholic Irish to rebellion. Some were luckier, and lived to hand down a legacy of dark eyes and curved Spanish noses.

When the tired galleon limped into the bay, Tobermory seemed at first a heaven-sent refuge. The town of Tobermory ("Well of Mary") did not exist officially until 1788, but two centuries before it was a fishing community living around the shores of a natural harbour.

What was the name of this galleon, which was so "verie riche"? Various names have been suggested. She could have been the *San Juan di Bautista*, or the *San Juan di Sicilia*, or the *San Francisco*. All ships of Spain bore resounding and holy names, invoking the formidable saints of a Catholic heaven, whereas the ships of England were more apt to be called the *Lion*, the *Swan*, the *Rose* — suggestive of pubs rather than of principalities and powers. The *San Francisco*'s full name was the *Galeon del Gran Duque di Florencia di Nombre San Francisco*. She had been loaned to Spain by the city of Florence, her commander was Captain Don Antonio Pereira, and around her had grown the legend that she was the principal treasure-ship of the Spanish fleet, with the Paymaster General and the pay-chest for the entire Armada aboard.

179

Let us examine the evidence for this report. It is, alas, very scanty. The Paymaster and his treasure (said to be over three million pounds in gold doubloons) were reputed to be aboard the *San Salvador*, which was damaged in action and had to be abandoned, her treasure then being distributed among other ships. But which ships? Presumably the *Duque di Florencia* was one of them. But nobody knows for certain. The seventh Earl of Argyll (the noble family whose name has for centuries been associated with the Tobermory mystery) is said to have heard the story from a descendant of Captain Pereira whom he met in Spain.

Was it, in fact, the *Florencia* which sailed into Tobermory Bay? Walsingham's agent irritatingly forbore to mention the galleon's name — an omission which would not have recommended him to MI5. Local tradition talks of the *Florence*, the *Florida*, the *Admiral of Florence* — but perhaps these names date from the information given by the seventh Earl. The present authors are told by Rear-Admiral Patrick McLaughlin, who was in charge of the most recent attempt to locate the galleon, that the Duke of Argyll had spoken with a direct descendant of Don Pedro de Valdes, who with his ship *El Capitana* was taken prisoner by Drake in the *Revenge*. This lady told the Duke that it has always been a tradition in the family that the Tobermory ship *was* the *Florencia*, carrying a great deal of treasure. She added that when the wreck was eventually located the emblem of a five-petalled flower would be found carved on the door of the after-cabin.

So far the evidence, though nebulous, points to the galleon being the *Florencia* rather than any other. Against this there is a story that the *Florencia* was never anywhere near Tobermory, but was captured off the west coast of England and brought as a prize into Weymouth Bay.

The mystery of the Tobermory ship sinking in the bay, from mishap or hostile intent, is almost as great as that of her name. This is what is popularly supposed to have happened.

After the galleon had anchored, the captain went ashore and approached the local chieftain, Lachlan Mor McLean of Duart, for victuals and water. To the Spaniards' relief, McLean, a far-seeing man, agreed courteously — but only on condition that the captain loaned him one hundred fighting men. It appeared that he was engaged on an intensive campaign to put down the Macdonalds, an enemy clan. The captain held no brief for the Macdonalds; he duly supplied McLean with soldiers and McLean promptly raided the islands of Rum, Eigg and Muck, committing fearful slaughter.

Then, says legend, Spaniard and Scot quarrelled, perhaps over the price of victuals, perhaps over the return of the Spanish troops. Whatever the reason, the chieftain sent a young relative, Donald Glas McLean, on board the galleon. The captain held him as hostage, so Donald, evidently a youth of fiery temper, having heard that the ship was preparing to sail, managed to set light to the powder-magazine and blew the galleon and himself out of existence. Nobody called Donald Glas McLean has been traced as living in the area at that time, so perhaps legend got the name wrong. But a much more likely story is that the ship was blown up by one of Walsingham's agents, a man called John Smollett, ancestor of the author, Tobias Smollett, who was under orders to prevent the ship leaving Tobermory.

The contemporary version of this story runs thus:

This day (18 November) word is come that the great ship that lay in the West Iles is blown in the air by the devise of John Smollett; most part of the men are slaine. The maner is this: McLean entertaining great friendship with them, desireth the borrowing of 2 cannon and 100 halberdiers ... and delivered a foster-son of his as pledge for safe delivery of them again. John Smollett, a man that has great trust among the Spaniards, entered the ship and cast in the powder a piece of lint, and so departed. After a short time the lint took fire and burnt ship and men.

On 13 November Ashby wrote to Walsingham that the galleon had been "burnt ... by treacherie and almost all the men within consumed by fire. It is thought to be one of the principall shippes, and someone of great accompt within; for he was alwais, as they say, served in sylver."

Here the Campbells, Earls of Argyll, come into the picture. As a reward for his father's information about the galleon being a treasure-ship, the eighth Earl had received a Deed of Gift from Charles I, allowing him salvage rights in the wreck. This seriously annoyed the McLeans and they may well have attempted a little piratical salvage of their own.

But the Earl was never able to exercise his rights, for he was executed for treason in 1661. Poor "Gellespie Grumach", or "the glaed-eyed marquis", so called from his squint, had changed sides once too often. Charles II regarded the Campbells "with one auspicious and one dropping eye", like Hamlet's stepfather. The late Earl had certainly set the crown on Charles's head during his exile, but some of his other activities, such as serving as Member for Aberdeenshire in the Commonwealth parliament, rather weakened the king's confidence in the Campbell loyalty to the Throne. When Archibald Campbell, the ninth Earl, wanted to exercise the salvage rights granted to his grandfather, Charles opposed him on the grounds that they only applied to the reign of Charles I and were now extinct. An attempt at salvage had been made in 1661, in the late Earl's lifetime, by means of a diving-bell newly invented by the Swedes. The ninth Earl contested the King's decision in the courts of session in Edinburgh and won back his family's right in the wreck. The claim stands to this day.

The diving-bell went down again, manned by two Swedish divers. A cannon was retrieved, but the divers and the bell were lost, somewhere around 1677.

In 1683 a diver named Archibald Miller went down and his report can be seen in the Bodleian library at Oxford. He described the ship as the *Florence*, of Spain, and reported her position, not more than nine fathoms deep at low water, twelve at high water, her stern pointing shorewards. He retrieved some guns and a silver bell, but though he hooked an object which he thought was a crown he was unable to get it out. He found no deck, except on the poop.

The ninth Earl of Argyll followed his father to the scaffold, also on a charge of treason, in 1685. His son joined William of Orange at an auspicious moment, retrieved the title and estates, and in 1701 was created first Duke of Argyll. His younger son, who became the third Duke, decided in 1740 to have another shot at the treasure. Like his ancestors, he was a soldier and a politician, very often in disfavour with the Crown but wise enough to keep his head on his shoulders. In 1711 he had been Ambassador and Commander-in-Chief in Spain, but was probably too busy to pick up any first-hand clues about the treasure. Under his directions an improvised diving-bell was sent down. A number of gold and silver coins were retrieved — and a greater prize, a bronze cannon wrought at Fontainebleau by the great Benvenuto Cellini. It can be seen today at the present Duke's castle of Inveraray. But it bore, alas, no ship's name.

Nothing remarkable seems to have happened at Tobermory for a century and a half. One diver sent down during the nineteenth century reported that the wreck had disappeared under a mass of silt and sand. No doubt he made his explorations wearing the "close" diving suit and helmet, fitted with air inlet and regulating outlet valves, which had been invented in 1830 by the enterprising Augustus Siebe.

A Glasgow treasure syndicate was formed in 1903 after the chance discovery of a gold coin and an ancient, sea-encrusted anchor. With the Duke's permission and the promise of an equal share-out, one Captain Burns used all the resources of contemporary diving equipment to explore the bottom of the bay. He found more cannon, weapons and some coins, but not the wreck itself. Suction-pumps and steam shovels were no more effective than cruder methods had been.

Then somebody had the bright idea of employing a dowser. The sensitive, quivering hazel twig used by these gifted people can locate either hidden water or hidden metal. This particular twig correctly indicated the presence of metal which turned out to be silver, but not much of it.

A new syndicate was formed, under the leadership of an American, Colonel Kenneth Foss. It was his theory that the diver, Archibald Miller, had been misleading everybody about the wreck's position so that he could quietly cash in on it for himself. Whether this was the case or not, Foss was right in his calculations, for he found the wreck under thirty feet of silt, eighty-four yards distant from Tobermory Pier and forty-eight feet under water at low tide. He located the captain's cabin in the stern (the hold was never penetrated), and his divers brought up two small cannon, pieces of gold and pewter plate, some crystal, and fragments of arms and armour.

When war came in 1914, Foss's operations were stopped. He returned after the Armistice and found coins dated 1588. But his luck turned. He got in the way of a high-pressure hose, whose powerful jet broke his ribs and inflicted other serious injuries. He never recovered, and there were whispers in the legend-ridden Hebrides of a curse on the hidden treasure.

There were less romantic whispers that unpublicized nibbles at it had been taken by nameless persons who had suddenly begun to flourish without visible cause. It is difficult to see how this could have happened without the knowledge of interested spectators on shore.

Two more syndicates made attempts, the Anglo-Dutch Diving and Salvage Company, and an English one. But war again stopped play.

The years crept on to 1949, when Ian Douglas Campbell, the eleventh Duke of Argyll, resumed the search his ancestors had begun. The Royal Navy collaborated with him and a contract was drawn up with the Admiralty which lent two small craft and a fishery protection vessel, the Duke financing the costly enterprise.

On 8 May, 1950, naval divers came upon the wreck of an oak vessel, sixty feet below the surface of the bay, buried twenty-four feet in silt. It was in pieces, and the marks of fire were visible. Working in spite of the strong tides and currents that trouble the Isle of Mull, they reported that "on two occasions the probes struck substantial metal within the body of the ship, and it appears possible that these contacts were part of the ship's armament". Two small gold medallions of sixteenth-century Italian design were brought to light.

In 1955 the expert team under the command of Rear-Admiral Patrick McLaughlin, by then retired from the Navy, was joined by a man who was in the next year to be himself the subject of a mystery which is dealt with elsewhere in this book. He was Commander Lionel K. Crabb, the famous frogman, a wartime diving hero. The problems of the team, operating from the salvage ship *Reclaim*, and later the *Ardchattan*, were twofold. They had to identify the sunken vessel, then get it up from the silt.

First that frustrating layer had to be penetrated. A long metal pipe was lowered from compressors in the ship to suck up the silt at the rate of thirty-five tons an hour. Altogether it was reckoned that there were about 12,000 tons to be removed. As it was brought up, the silt was sieved into a hopper-ship. The first loads produced a rusty sword blade — perhaps a herald of greater things. But results were disappointing. More weapons, and fragments of them, some pottery, coins — these were all the team's reward. They retrieved no chests of gold and silver, no jewelled crown as described by Archibald Miller (rumoured, most improbably, to have been a gift from Pope Sixtus V for King Philip to wear when he added the English crown to his own); and, sad to relate, they got no glimpse of that most attractive lady who features in one of the legends, the statue of a golden Virgin, with eyes of sapphire. Nothing substantial was found to add to the collection in Inveraray Castle.

The enormous cost of the enterprise meant that it had to be abandoned when there was no prospect of quick returns. Even when the expenses were shared between the Duke and interested financiers, they were prohibitive. "Operation Galleon" was called off. Once again the lovely Bay of Tobermory was left undisturbed and whatever lay at the bottom sank once more into the silt of that glacial channel.

And there the mystery rests, eternally tantalizing. The Duke of Argyll firmly believed, as did most people who knew the facts, that a great Spanish ship lay there with rich treasure aboard. On the other hand, the naval historian, Sir Julian Corbett, pointed out that there were two captains called Pereira commanding Armada vessels, which may have led to confusion in the stories about the *Florencia*; and also that a ship of the *Florencia*'s size would not have been able to carry the weight of troops, crew, armour and over 750 tons of coins alleged to have been aboard her. Andrew Lang, the Scottish writer and historian, worked out to his own satisfaction that the vessel was the *San Juan Bautista* of Sicily, another ship on loan to King Philip.

Soon perhaps, if the funds can be raised, another attempt will be made to plumb the cold blue waters where lie the bones of — what?

17: NOAH'S ARK, AND THE INVASION THAT NEVER WAS

There was a time when all the world was sea. That the Flood really happened is certain: that Noah built an Ark is not.

Attempts to pinpoint the spot where the Ark made her safe landfall continue to this day and every decade or so sees a new theory propounded. The most enthusiastic searchers believe that they will in time find the remains of the Ark herself, and since Mount Ararat lies in a wild region of Turkey there remains considerable scope for their optimism.

In 1883, however, the search seemed to be over. The world's Press buzzed with a firm report that Noah's Ark had been found. Said the *San Francisco Examiner*, its excitement outstripping its grammar: "The evidence upon which the statement that Noah's Ark has been discovered is so well sustained that it seems difficult to successfully question it... The story is a remarkable one, which we would be inclined to disbelieve were it not authoritatively confirmed... If it be not the veritable Noah's Ark, it is difficult to tell what else it is."

The Times of London, of all newspapers not the one given to printing uncorroborated news, carried the report of the finding of the Ark. So did nearly every other newspaper in Great Britain, together with many on the Continent, in the United States and in other parts of the world. The story began with a series of devastating avalanches which had recently occurred in the Mount Ararat region of Armenia. Hundreds had been killed and several villages completely obliterated. The Turkish government had despatched a rescue and investigation commission to look into the disaster. According to a local newspaper, the *Levant Herald*, the commission had penetrated a deep valley below Mount Ararat and had come to the foot of a glacier, where, embedded in the ice of a glacier, they had found to their astonishment an enormous wooden structure, towering forty to fifty feet above the ice. The depth to which it was embedded could not be measured.

Villagers in that remote part declared that they had known of its existence for several years. Whenever they had gone near it strange voices had reached their ears and once a wrathful-looking face had glared out at them. Thereafter they had left the mysterious wooden thing alone.

The commissioners, one of whom was reported to be a Captain Gascoyne, "a well-known scientific investigator formerly attached to the British Embassy in Constantinople", were made of sterner stuff. They approached the strange object, found a break in its wooden outer covering, and climbed in.

The interior proved to be virtually a solid block of ice, but enough space remained to enable them to crawl from the room, or compartment, in which they found themselves into another and then another. To their increasing amazement, it occurred to them that they were in some form of ship: the notion that it might be the one and only Noah's Ark followed in a flash. Feverishly, they fell to examining the wood of which the ship was made. It was of a kind not grown anywhere in the neighbourhood. In fact, someone recognized it came from as far away as the low, steamy valleys of the Euphrates, where it was known to the natives as "zim". It was nothing less than the gopher wood of the Scriptures.

Many of the newspaper reports went on to quote the commissioners' own description of their sensational find:

It was in a good state of preservation, being painted or stained on the outside with a dark brown pigment, and constructed of great strength. It was a good deal broken at the angles, from being subjected to somewhat rough usage by the moraines during the slow descent of the glacier from the lofty peaks towering away beyond the head of the valley to a height of over 17,000 feet, a process which, considering the nature of the country and the slow pace at which these snow rivers travel, especially in the higher altitudes, must have required thousands of years.

The conclusion to be drawn from this was inescapable. Deposited on the peak of Mount Ararat, 17,230 feet high, by the Flood, the Ark must have continued to lie where it had stranded long after the waters had receded, and Noah, his family and their beasts and birds had wandered off to get on with the restoration of human and animal life on earth. In course of time snow had enveloped the Ark, carrying it eventually into the stream of the glacier which, over the ages, had borne it down to the mountain foot where it now lay.

The report finally stated that the commissioners had just returned to Constantinople, where they had made known their discovery directly to the Sultan of Turkey. The German Ambassador to Turkey had since intervened to insist upon immediate measures being taken to preserve the Ark, as it had come to his ears that an enterprising American traveller was already starting to negotiate for its purchase and shipment to the United States for exhibition.

The story caused world-wide interest and speculation, but not everyone took it seriously. Some newspapers waxed positively flippant about it, such as the American one which stated that a reporter, instructed to follow up the details, had found in an insurance company's archives a policy, dated 2,300

B.C., on "An Ark, constructed by Noah, the property of Noah and Sons. Tonnage, 42,413,950; length, 525ft.; width, 87ft. 6in.; Gopher wood. Destination ——. Transport of passengers and animals. Classed A1."

Many people were not amused by such humour, and debated earnestly the details and implications of the discovery. But it was the jokers who proved to be right, as a long report in another newspaper, the *New Zealand Herald*, revealed nearly eight months after the initial news item.

The pricker of the bubble was G. M. Reed, the writer of a weekly column of whimsical humour in the newspaper under the pen-name "Pollex". He owned up that on 27 March a genuine Reuter cable had reached the office, reporting briefly the avalanches in Armenia. The mention of Mount Ararat had caught his humorist's attention at the very moment when he had been wondering what he might put in his column to mark the approaching All Fools' Day. He had, accordingly, dashed off the story which had, to his surprise, been seized upon by the world Press as a serious news item. Perhaps his attributing the details to the *Levant Herald* had given them sufficient credence; though if any editor had cared to check up he would have found that the *Levant Herald* had been defunct for more than two years and that its editor was languishing in a Turkish prison, paying the penalty for publishing ill-judged criticism of members of the government. If Reed's story had appeared on 1 April it might have stood a better chance of being rumbled. But All Fools' Day that year fell on a Sunday, a day on which the newspaper was not published.

Having confessed, and, in passing, expressed astonishment at the way the small joke had snowballed, the columnist took farewell of his invention:

Dear Gascoyne, farewell! Well-known scientist, former member of the British Embassy, now Gascoyne Pasha of the Turkish Service, you have served me well.

Spirit of fierce aspect looking out of the upstairs window, adieu. Cease to frighten the unhappy villagers of Bayazid, and take now repose amid your icy chambers.

And thou, O Barnum, "enterprising American traveller", who triedst to buy my Ark from the Pasha of Van, retire; and the curtain descends on the drama of All Fools' Day, 1883.

The newspaper sensation created by the Noah's Ark story calls to mind another which had burst upon a staggered New Zealand public ten years earlier. Its chief ingredient was a mysterious event at sea.

It was on the morning of 17 February, 1873, that many Auckland residents received the worst shock of their lives as they unfolded the *Daily Southern Cross* to read the multiple headline: WAR WITH RUSSIA — A CALAMITY FOR AUCKLAND — HOSTILE VISIT OF A RUSSIAN IRON-CLAD.

The threat of war between Russia and Britain and her Empire had been on people's minds for some time. One can, indeed, still see on the outskirts of New Zealand's capital city, Wellington, a battlemented fort with gun emplacements and loopholes for small-arms fire, built at that time for defence against the Russians. Nevertheless, it was with stunned horror that people read of an event:

...productive of great disaster to New Zealand, and destructive of the ancient prestige of England and her boasted supremacy as Sovereign of the Seas.

That event was the sudden appearance of the hostile ironclad man-o'-war, the *Kaskowiski*, which took possession of the British warship lying in the waters of the Waitemata

(Auckland's harbour), seized our principal citizens as hostages, demanded a heavy ransom for the city, and emptied the coffers of the banks of all the gold and specie they contained.

At this moment we are under the domination of Russia, our own guns in our man-of-war being pointed against the city, ready to be opened on us at any moment that the barbarous caprice of her captors may select.

As Aucklanders read these words, pandemonium broke out in many parts of the city. Women fainted, men hurried to buckle on whatever weapons they could find or else locked and barricaded their doors. Shops closed and put up their shutters and one shopkeeper stationed himself in front of his premises with a shotgun. Wealthy householders hastily dug in their gardens and buried their jewels. One old lady, whose livelihood depended on taking in laundry, frantically worked to bury her most precious possession — her washtub.

Excitement was greatest on the waterfront. Boatmen pulled up their boats and refused to accept fares. Crowds gathered densely, straining their eyes to see what was going on aboard the British warship, HMS *Blanch*, at anchor in the roadstead. It was the *Blanch*'s invariable custom to break out her ensign precisely at eight o'clock in the morning. This morning one man stared anxiously out across the water, his watch in his hand. The hour hand reached eight. No ensign appeared. At two minutes past, with not a sign of activity on the *Blanch*, the man hurried away into town, shouting to everyone he met that the story was indeed true. His story of the non-appearance of the ensign was quickly embroidered, and worried folk who came galloping in on horseback from country districts were met with the news that the British warship was now flying the Russian colours.

As the crowds waited and watched for the next dreadful move, they discussed with awe the newspaper's detailed account of what had occurred.

On the evening of 15 February, it stated, the steamer *Wonga Wonga* had left for Australia with a large number of passengers. Off Kawau Island, approaching Auckland, her watch had seen a large vessel, hull down. Darkness had fallen soon after, but in the early evening a shell had suddenly screamed across the *Wonga Wonga*'s bows. She stopped at once and before long a boat appeared out of the darkness. It was full of sailors. Recognizing them as Russians, a British naval officer travelling in the steamer got some other men to help him heave a small brass cannon off its mounting and send it crashing down into the boat below, smashing it and sinking it together with its crew. All lights on the *Wonga Wonga* were extinguished and she fled back towards Auckland. As the moon rose at midnight a mighty warship could be seen pursuing her. The *Wonga Wonga* ran into the shelter of a bay and persuaded the fast cutter *Volunteer* to race on to Auckland with a warning message. The cutter had arrived in Auckland too late. The Russians were already in control.

The Russian warship *Kaskowiski* had slid into the waters of the Waitemata still under cover of darkness and had at once despatched her submarine pinnace, equipped with the deadly water-gas apparatus, to deal with the *Blanch*, while other detachments were sent ashore to seize vital points. They were followed ashore by a main force of eighty Russian sailors, armed with rocket tubes, who proceeded to rifle the banks systematically, while a smaller body of sailors and marines, equipped with cutlasses and repeating needle-carbines, escorted their commander, Vice-Admiral Herodskoff, to take over the Provincial Government Chamber, to which he summoned the

Mayor, members of the Assembly and all the bankers. They were placed in the centre of the floor, surrounded by armed men.

Speaking in good English, the Admiral demanded a ransom of one and a half million roubles (£250,000 sterling) for the city. He set a time limit of three hours, after which Auckland would be burned to the ground if the money were not raised. The bankers and officials conferred. Little more than half the sum demanded could be raised they told the Admiral. With a curt gesture he ordered the guards to take the hostages aboard the warship, and set off immediately in pursuit of the *Wonga Wonga*, to prevent her carrying the news to Australia. Sufficient men were left aboard the overpowered *Blanch* to ensure dominance over the city until the man-o'-war's return.

From some source the newspaper had managed to get hold of precise details of the mighty *Kaskowiski* and her formidable armament. Her complement was 953 officers and men. She mounted twelve 30-ton guns and machinery for manufacturing the deadly water-gas, invented by the late General Todtleben, which could be used either to suffocate or scorch its victims. Little wonder, then, that Auckland lived through those early-morning hours of 17 February, 1873, in abject panic.

But had the man with the watch, who had so anxiously waited in the waterfront crowd, lingered for a minute or two more — or, better still, had his watch not been several minutes fast — he would have seen, precisely at eight o'clock, the customary running-up of HMS *Blanch*'s ensign and would have heard the rest of the crowd assuring one another, though perhaps a little uncertainly, that all was well after all. For, like the Noah's Ark affair, it had all been a joke.

Many years later, in 1938, Orson Welles would panic a gullible American public with his radio adaptation of H. G.

Wells's novel of an invasion from outer space, *The War of the Worlds*, an achievement which certainly went beyond the bounds of Welles's expectations and moved his near-namesake to a vigorous protest about the liberties that had been taken with his book. In a smaller way, this is what a New Zealand journalist, D. M. Luckie, had succeeded in doing to a gullible Auckland public. He, too, had underestimated the credulity of newspaper readers. A small asterisk in the headlines had drawn attention to a footnote in minute type which, together with the absurdity of a warship — even a Russian one — bearing a name so like "cask o whisky" — might have been expected to give the game away. Unfortunately, many people, confronted with such headlines, had panicked and read no further. Many of those who had seen the joke wrote to congratulate Luckie on a journalistic triumph.

At least he could remind himself that his story had not been intended as a cheap stunt. His object in fabricating it had been to draw attention to the parlous position the isolated, scarcely defended New Zealand would be in if war with Russia should break out in reality. Her first intimation of events might, indeed, have been the seizure of a port by an ironclad — or even a wind-borne whiff for the populace of General Todtleben's water-gas.

18: "CAST UP BY THE SEA"

The discovery of wireless telegraphy changed the nature of life at sea. Previously, a ship in trouble had had no way of asking for help beyond the flying of distress signals; and these were useless when there was no other vessel near enough to see them. A shipwrecked crew in a lifeboat could do little beyond hoisting somebody's shirt or lighting a fire to attract attention. Only one other method remained: a plea for help, giving the ship's position, might be sealed in a bottle and thrown into the waves to take its chance. With extreme good luck, it could reach friendly hands in time to save the lives of those aboard.

But more likely, the bottle would never be seen; or faked messages, the work of cruel hoaxers, might even mislead the authorities and bring untold suspense and disappointment to relatives at home. Mystery has always surrounded such messages, only a few of which have proved to be genuine, as in the case of the SS *President*, a fine steamship which left New York harbour on 11 March, 1841, bound for Liverpool.

Captain Roberts had a good reputation. Nobody worried much about the *President*'s chances of reaching port, even when unusually stiff gales blew up just after her departure, and when, by 1 April, there had been no news, *The Times* calmly announced that the ship had been delayed by storms. A week later her passenger list was published. It included the name of Tyrone Power. A century later that name was to be famous in the film world, but in 1841 the holder was a popular Irish stage actor, leading comedian at Drury Lane Theatre. London audiences had last seen him at the Haymarket in 1840, since when he had been playing in America. He was forty-four, lively and popular. At home his wife waited.

On 13 April, news came to Birmingham, carried by a special train from Liverpool, that the *President* had docked at Merseyside, but had been damaged by storms. The rumour was quite untrue. The joker had started on his career. Next came a message to Lloyds of London, supposedly from Captain Roberts's wife. It said that she had heard that the *President* was at Madeira, undergoing repairs. Again, it was a fiction, followed by a faked letter to the family of a passenger.

Mrs. Tyrone Power was the worst hit. The postman brought her three letters in succession, all saying that her husband was safe. Two of them may have been sincere efforts at comfort from somebody who had heard a mistaken report. The third was signed with her husband's name, and was quite obviously forged. Yet another letter came to raise her hopes, this time from the *President*'s former master, reassuring her that the steamship was too good a vessel to have come to any harm. She was probably in Bermuda, he thought. In fact, the brother-in-law of Captain Roberts was told soon after, again by letter, that the *President* was about to sail out of Bermuda. The letter writer stated that the news had come to him by way of a ship which had been in Bermuda at the same time, and had just arrived at Waterford, in the south of Ireland. Inquiries in Waterford proved this to be no more true than the other messages.

Then came more news. This time the traditional bottle was picked up, with a note inside signed by the *President*'s most famous passenger. "The *President* is sinking. God help us all," it said.

Nothing more was ever seen of the splendid *President*. It may be that Charles Dickens, when he travelled to America in the following year, sailed over her bones. Nor was the perverse torturer of Mrs. Power and other relatives of those aboard ever traced. Did he write the final message? Or was it, indeed, the actor's very last contact with his public?

There was no long voyage ahead for another ship, the *Vienne*, when on 10 December, 1903, she left Rochefort harbour, her holds loaded with armaments. She was only bound for Toulon, via Cape Ortegal, Cape St. Vincent, Gibraltar and Cape Gata. She had, in fact, to skirt the coast of south-west France and circle Spain and Portugal. In bad weather the journey had been known to take as much as thirty days, but this trip was scheduled for ten. The crew of fifty should be in Toulon on 20 December, in good time for Christmas. As they sailed out of harbour the sea began to roughen, and the captain gloomily noted that they might easily lose a couple of days. But that was nothing, after all: although a ship plying coastal routes was not compelled to carry the customary three months' supply of food, including iron rations, the *Vienne* was well provisioned. There was nothing to worry about.

By 27 December, a week after her scheduled date of arrival, the *Vienne* had still not arrived in Toulon. The owners were getting worried and a Press conference was called to allay the rumours that there had been a cargo explosion — the ship was carrying, among other explosives, thirty-eight cases of shells — and that she had gone down with all hands. Bodies were reported to be floating in coastal waters. All quite untrue, said a spokesman. A cruiser, the *Galilee*, had certainly been sent out, but only to contact the missing ship and ascertain the cause of delay. There was no reason to think that the *Vienne* had come to any harm other than a bit of trouble with December storms. Under canvas she could not make more than two knots. And she would never be far from port along those coasts.

The *Galilee*, scouting along the *Vienne*'s route, was not expecting to find anything tragic. Commander Jaures surmised that at the worst the *Vienne* had been driven off course. Off Gibraltar his lookout sighted a cargo-boat ahead. Her name was made out to be the *Romsdal*, a Norwegian. Perhaps she might have seen something of the *Vienne*: Jaures decided to confer with her captain. But there were difficulties. The cargo-boat was going along the coast of Algeria, the *Galilee* along that of Spain. Jaures decided to change course for Algeria, and catch up with the *Romsdal*, which was well ahead though moving slowly. But engine trouble developed and forced him to put into Carthagena, while the *Romsdal* sailed on to Oran. Jaures reflected that it was a pity, but after all the captain of the *Romsdal* had probably seen nothing of the *Vienne*. Those were days before wireless telegraphy annihilated space.

Fate had played a cruel trick. On 29 December, Captain Oddo Madson of the *Romsdal* had been notified by his officer of the watch that a ship had been sighted some three miles away. The seas were high and visibility poor, but the Norwegian could make out the tricolour flying at the stranger's stern. She was a French naval vessel, a three-master, moving very slowly and apparently in some trouble. But after all, Madson agreed with the officer, Gibraltar was only about 120 miles away. The Frenchman could put in there easily enough. All the same, something prompted him to make contact with her, for he had heard of the *Vienne*'s disappearance and wondered if by any chance this could be she. He hesitated whether to change course and find out. But the *Romsdal* was not having a smooth passage: she, too, had some engine trouble and was only just keeping on course. If she found herself steamless she would be unlikely to make the port of Oran on the scheduled date. No, Madson decided, it would be unwise to change course. If this were the *Vienne* and she really were in difficulties she could always signal for help, which she had not done. The *Romsdal* proceeded.

At Toulon the authorities were getting seriously worried. A number of reports and messages had come in, but none of them had been at all helpful. A spiritualist medium had reported a vision of the *Vienne* "in a great black space where all was calm", but said that help was needed urgently, for those aboard were already in touch with the next world. From Bayonne came more concrete news — a derelict lifeboat from the *Vienne* had been found. It proved to be from an Austrian vessel, also confusingly called *Vienne*. By this time Commander Jaures was giving up hope, feeling deeply frustrated by his single-handed job. With one ship he was now expected to comb the Atlantic for the *Vienne*, for she could not have been blown in any other direction. He set course for Tangier, but the onset of a storm decided him to alter his plan and make for Gibraltar instead. The alteration in timing which resulted meant that the *Galilee* had left Gibraltar hours before a message arrived from Toulon telling the captain to set a course for Cape St. Vincent. If he had received that message and done so, he might have encountered the *Vienne*. Instead, he was sailing ever farther away from her. He had reached Casablanca by the time he heard of the report from the *Romsdal*. Now he turned, and went back to Cape St. Vincent, but too late.

While the *Galilee* searched, the *Guichen*, a naval vessel fitted with primitive wireless equipment, was also on the trail; and so were others — the destroyer *Taillebourg*, the cargo-boat *Emilie*, the sloop *Alcyon*. They found nothing, only false clues. But at Rochefort the authorities were examining something that had turned up in a fisherman's net. It was a bottle, loosely corked so that the sea had filtered in and blurred the message on the paper inside. Only one letter of one word could be clearly read — the letter V. On the heels of this not very satisfactory discovery came another report, also from a fisherman. He had seen a ship's mainyard bobbing about in the waves off Fouras. And at the mouth of the Gironde the master of a ketch had seen a mast and rigging floating.

Early in February, 1904, came something more definite and more alarming. On the beach of the Ile d'Oleron, off Rochefort, another bottle was washed up. This time the message was legible. It said that the *Vienne* was 150 miles west of the Rochebonne Hulk and added cryptically "Hurricane".

Evidence piled up. At the end of February, on the beach of Bourg de Batz, on the Croisic peninsula, a lifebelt and other wreckage floated ashore. They were followed up by something more identifiable — a case which had contained explosives. Three days later the sea gave up its final relic of the dead ship — a chronometer with the mark "Leroy 322", which, it was discovered, had been a gift to the *Vienne* by the Port of Cherbourg in the previous year.

It was conclusive of the *Vienne*'s fate, but it did not solve her mystery. A naval chronometer is too heavy to float. How had it arrived on shore? And why was wreckage from the *Vienne* found so near Rochefort, when the message in the bottle had indicated otherwise, and when she had been seen near Gibraltar?

The mystery rests there. No answers to these questions were ever given, and nothing more of the fated *Vienne* was ever seen.

A year before the *Vienne* disappeared a steamer from Glasgow preceded her into oblivion. She was the *Huronian*, bound for Newfoundland, and she, too, was the subject of conflicting reports. First came the news that she had been wrecked not far from Sable Island, off Nova Scotia. Investigation showed that what had been mistaken for her was an ancient wreck. Then someone thought they saw her making for St. John, New Brunswick. She never arrived there. In April, 1902, *Huronian* was given up for lost.

In June came dramatic, hopeful news. Off Owl's Head, Nova Scotia — still in the same region as the last report — a bottle was found floating with a message inside. It purported to have been written by a survivor of the *Huronian*, who, with thirteen shipmates, had got off in an open boat. A search was made, but no trace of the boat or its occupants was found.

Far away, at Castlerock, off the coast of Ireland, another message in a bottle came to shore. This one had the ring of authenticity, for it was signed by one of the *Huronian*'s crew, Charles McFall, a greaser, and it contained a sad, brief goodbye to his mother and sister. As he wrote, it said, the ship had heeled over and was sinking fast. McFall's pathetic note was all that was ever heard of the *Huronian*.

Two macabre messages of a different kind proved all too genuine. The first involved two wrecks — one a complete mystery. The *Essex*, a whaler, had gone down, and her crew managed to land on Ducie Island, in the same Pacific group as Pitcairn Island, on which the *Bounty*'s mutineers had settled. Ducie is a small uninhabited atoll. But when the *Essex* men landed there they found signs of life: carved on a tree was the name "Elizabeth". They searched the island and found, in a cave, eight human skeletons. Which bony hand had made the inscription, and whether it was the name of a ship or a woman, will never be known. It is a curious coincidence that Henderson Island, west of Ducie, is also called Elizabeth Island.

An Australian beach saw an even stranger sight. Two boys, wandering on the shore at Fremantle, found a great bird in distress. It was an albatross and was almost choked to death by something round its long neck — a tin can, crushed and twisted into a ring. On this cruel collar a message had been written in French. Thirteen sailors, it said, had been cast away on the Crozet Islands. Help, for the love of God! they begged.

The date on the message was only twelve days old, but red tape held up rescue operations and it was weeks before an expedition was sent to the Crozet Islands. They found the site where the thirteen men had camped — and another message, also on a can, saying that food supplies had come to an end and the sailors had launched their boat and sailed away in search of help.

No trace of them was ever found. Perhaps the curse that beset Coleridge's Ancient Mariner had followed them. For the albatross had died soon after the boys picked it up.

19: THE MYSTERY OF THE
MADAGASCAR

Far across the sea, my lassie,
I'm bound away, my lassie,
Far across the sea, my lassie,
I'm bound away.

This and other anchor shanties like it were heard drifting shorewards as the "Blackwallers" sailed down London River in the early 1850s, bound for Australia and her goldfields. These fine ships were so called because they were built in the East India Company's shipyard at Blackwall, on the Thames. They carried not only precious cargoes but rich passengers, for their cabins were comfortable by the standards of those days. They took the minimum time for the long voyage, and, judging by their portraits, were as beautiful as they were efficient.

Among the most popular of the Blackwallers was the *Madagascar*. She was a frigate-built, square-rigged vessel of more than 1,000 tons, capable of carrying something like 600 passengers. Her master and officers were respected; she had no history of ill-luck, that bane of the sailor. As she lay at her moorings in Hobson's Bay, Melbourne, on a pleasant autumn day in 1853, there was no reason to suppose she would not reach England safely. She carried more gold than usual and her full complement of passengers.

But after she sailed from Melbourne an ominous silence fell. News came home that she had left port, that was all. Since then no human being had set eyes on her. Several ships went down between her sailing-date and Christmas, and were mournfully logged as wrecks: the *Annie Jane* of Liverpool, the brig *Harwood,* the *Dalhousie,* the screw-steamer *Marshall,* the emigrant ship *Tayleur.* The following year, 1854, brought a catalogue of horrors — a troopship sunk with 350 rank and file of the Madras Light Infantry, the steamship *Prince* lost "with 144 lives, and a cargo worth £500,000, indispensable to the army in the Crimea". But the *Madagascar's* fate remained unknown. Like Mary of Dee Sands in a popular poem of the times, "never home came she".

For thirty years, despite reports from other ships that the weather had been fine and fair without squalls or sudden storms, it was assumed that some unknown calamity had overtaken the *Madagascar* and she had been lost with all aboard her. Then came quite another explanation. Unfortunately, no date, name or exact locality has been given to it. But it seems that an old woman in Brazil, finding herself about to die, had decided to tell the true story of the fate of the *Madagascar* in which she had been a passenger.

They had sailed from Melbourne in fair weather and with minds as untroubled as the seas — except for one thing: there had been a lot of publicity about the ship's large cargo of gold, and this had worried some of the women on board. The behaviour of the crew had not been reassuring. As a rule, lady passengers had no fears aboard such a ship. The sometimes unprintable words of a shanty would be changed or moderated if it was likely to reach feminine ears, and discipline was strict. But the crew on this voyage looked a dangerous, surly lot.

Three weeks after leaving Melbourne, the *Madagascar* rounded the Horn as scheduled. Then the trouble started. At eight bells in the dog-watch, a confusion of voices brought passengers scurrying out of their cabins. There were shouts, followed by shots and a tramp of hurrying footsteps. The women screamed as they saw a horde of menacing faces crowding in on them.

It was mutiny.

On deck lay the master and the first mate, shot to death. They had been taken by surprise, without a chance of saving themselves. The other officers were still fighting a losing battle with the mutineers, while the passengers huddled together like terrified animals.

"Get back to your cabins!" was the mutineers' order. Some of the male passengers offered resistance and were shot or clubbed. The rest were herded into the cabins and the doors locked. There they stayed for two hours, listening to the dreadful sounds of cries, shots, curses and drunken laughter from above. There seemed little hope that any of the officers could survive what had evidently been a long-planned mutiny.

At last the din of fighting ceased. Then there were other sounds — the chests of gold being hauled up and then loaded into boats. The cooped-up passengers began to feel something like hope.

"If they get away with the gold they won't concern themselves with us," one of them suggested. "In weather like this we could keep the ship afloat."

A naval officer among the passengers volunteered to take over. It seemed that everything was not lost.

But new sounds put an end to their cheerful speculations: the sound of the hatches being battened down, and a more sinister one which the naval officer alone recognized.

"They're going to scuttle the ship," he told his fellow prisoners. At first his words did not penetrate their numbed minds. Then they understood.

"They'll sink us! They're leaving us to drown!"

A terrible confusion of screams and cries broke out. The prisoners banged on the cabin doors and hatch covers and begged the mutineers to let them out, promising co-operation, anything, so long as they were not left to a miserable death.

The answer was mocking laughter and shots through the cabin doors. Then one of the crew had a good idea.

"Some o' them gals is worth savin'. Let's take 'em with us — eh, lads?"

There was a shout of approval. The cabin doors were unlocked and any women who were reasonably young and good-looking were dragged out and driven on deck. Husbands or parents who fought for them were ruthlessly shot down and the doors locked again.

Now water could be heard rushing into the ship through large holes bored with augers in her bottom. At the same time the crew went over the side.

Among the young women seized and flung into a boat was the storyteller of Brazil. She was comparatively lucky. Her captor was a shade less evil than his companions. He had enough compassion not to make the terrified girl watch the sinking of the ship, as the other men made their captives. But though she sat huddled with eyes shut and her hands over her ears, the awful cries from the trapped, drowning passengers reached her and were to haunt her for the rest of her life. When she dared to look up, the tall masts were submerged and all that remained visible of the lovely Blackwaller were floating bodies — those of her murdered officers.

The mutineers sailed away with their women and their loot. But there was not so much loot as they had hoped. They were a drunken stupid lot, capable of mass murder, but without proper co-ordination or leadership afterwards — or even much skill in handling boats. As they landed in Brazil, two of the boats overturned and the precious gold in them went to the bottom of the Atlantic. The share-out of the rest led to the inevitable quarrels and to the death of some of the mutineers. But the man who had captured the storyteller escaped with her from the general confusion, a portion of the gold in his pocket. From her account of his subsequent conduct it seems that he was weak-willed rather than downright bad. He had joined the mutiny largely because he feared for his skin if he refused, and now he wanted nothing better than to lead an honest life: which, in fact, he proceeded to do. He married his prisoner, who by now liked and respected him although she had, in any case, little choice in the matter, being a penniless, friendless girl in a strange country. They were reasonably happy together and agreed to tell no one of what had happened on the *Madagascar*. But in her dying confession the woman felt she should disclose the truth at last.

It is a sound, likely story and there is backing for it in an account written for the *Melbourne Argus* by a port detective who saw the *Madagascar* in harbour before she sailed. He was unpleasantly struck by the scenes taking place aboard.

> Drunkenness, fighting, swearing, and men, women and children in a state of semi-nudity, howling like wild animals. The crew were composed of men of the most motley kind that ever signed articles. Some of the passengers were a rough lot. A pang of horror shot through me as the thought rose to my brain — should evil overtake the *Madagascar*, what would become of the young women and girls, and the better class of passengers?

The old woman in Brazil said nothing to indicate that there were other bad characters on board, as well as the crew. Perhaps she had forgotten. Or perhaps the detective, having already heard the mutiny story, was dressing up with the picturesque detail some fight he had happened to see.

Other theories for the ship's disappearance have been put forward. The *Sydney Daily Telegraph* of 10 April, 1917, said: "The mystery surrounding the loss of the old Blackwall liner *Madagascar* in 1853 has been revived in New Zealand. Those who have heard the old story of the mysterious treasure-laden ship believed to have been wrecked near Doughty Point on the west coast of Stewart Island are in doubt as to any definite details, but they are all fairly unanimous that a large vessel named *Madagascar* met her doom in that locality in the '50's. There still lives at the Bluff an old Maori who states that he saw a vessel wrecked in a storm near Doughty Bay about that period, and he maintains that she was the *Madagascar* and that not a soul escaped."

A few years later a letter appeared in the *Liverpool Weekly Courier*.

"I have a correspondent in Portland, Oregon, a retired sailor, who wrote to me (August, 1917) saying that he was on the *Hawea* with an excursion, at Christmas, 1876, to certain sounds on the New Zealand coast. At one of them, at dead low water of a big spring tide, could be seen (in fact, he saw it himself) the well-preserved wreck of a ship built of good hard wood. The natives in that quarter believe that she was the *Madagascar*, but they have never been able to make sure of the fact. With various variations they had the story of the gold and the cut-throats. Their legend was that some of the crew had smuggled ex-convicts on board. At any rate there is nothing particularly out of the common in people being murdered for the lure of gold; indeed, much less valuable cargo has been looted, under the same circumstances, by undesirables on many ships.

"It is quite possible, and always feasible, for the *Madagascar* to have had highly experienced and thoroughly desperate criminals on board, bent on murder and stealing the gold — but then gold can buy them nothing at sea. I should fancy they would have had a better preference for the ship's liquor. Once this was broached, and, say, an officer or two out of the way, it would be the easiest thing in the world to lose the *Madagascar*."

It seems curious that if a mutiny really did take place no other echo of it has ever been heard beyond the old woman's story. English-speaking men turning up with gold in their pockets on the coast of Brazil would probably have created a certain stir, especially if they were accompanied by unwilling women: and it would not be unreasonable to expect some other deathbed confession to have come to light. "Let none admire that riches grow in Hell," said Milton, "that soil doth best deserve the precious bane." The stolen gold of the *Madagascar*, if stolen it was, no doubt carried its own Hell with it.

But perhaps she sank off Doughty Point after all, and there never was a mutiny.

20: ACCIDENT OR SABOTAGE?

Many sea tragedies have been brought about by fire, explosion, or both. Ships have always been vulnerable to these destructive forces, both by nature of the cargoes they have to convey in confined spaces and because their own need for self-sufficiency means carrying large quantities of fuel and other inflammables, including, in the case of warships, explosives. Elaborate precautions against fire have for centuries been part of ships' working regulations, but, inevitably, there have been many mishaps and errors resulting in swift disaster.

Usually the cause of a fire or explosion can be found, even after a ship has gone to the bottom. In a few cases, though, doubt and even mystery remain. This is especially so in wartime.

It was, for instance, the blowing up of the American cruiser *Maine* in Havana harbour in 1898 which precipitated the Spanish–American War. Perhaps she went up, as many have claimed, because of accidental or spontaneous ignition of her explosives. Many another warship had done, and has done since. But there are plenty who believe that the ship was sunk by Cuban saboteurs wishing to discredit their Spanish oppressors by making the Americans think they had done it. If this was the object, it succeeded, but no one has ever really known.

During the First World War, Great Britain suffered no fewer than five serious losses through warship explosions, four of them occurring when the ships were lying peacefully in protected anchorages. It has never been stated categorically what caused any of these explosions, at least two of which may well have been due to sabotage.

HMS *Bulwark* was one of several battleships laid down in 1899, displacing 15,000 tons and armed with four 12-inch and twelve 6-inch guns. When the war broke out she was, therefore, no longer a ship of the first rank, now occupied by the Dreadnoughts and super-Dreadnoughts, but still worthy of her place in the Fifth Battle Squadron, based at Sheerness, in Kent, maintaining an anti-invasion patrol of the English Channel. Her complement was nearly 800 officers and men, commanded by Captain Guy Sclater.

On 26 November, 1914, she lay with her sister ships in one of the reaches of the River Medway, some four miles from Sheerness itself. It was a little before eight o'clock in the morning. The officers were finishing breakfast. An ammunition party had almost completed re-stowing shells. Midshipmen and some ratings were taking a breather after their daily physical jerks, and the Royal Marines' band was making the air pleasant with light music, prior to the formal ceremony of hoisting the colours.

Suddenly, without even fractional warning, the battleship exploded with a noise loud enough to startle people at Southend and Westcliff, some twenty miles away. They saw a dense cloud of greenish smoke arise from the Sheerness direction and hang in the air for ten minutes. In Sheerness itself windows were shattered and plaster shaken from ceilings. Then an appalling rain began to fall on the district for miles around. It consisted of great twisted chunks of armour-plating, pieces of wood, charred papers, shattered objects of furniture, photographs, clothing, and, most horribly, mutilated portions of human bodies.

When the smoke cleared away, HMS *Bulwark* had disappeared. Boats racing urgently towards the spot where she had lain had to plough their way through water strewn with debris of all kinds. Few bodies were picked up, most of them unidentifiable. When the whole search for survivors was over, fourteen had been found, most of them seriously injured. Two soon died.

The first thought of shocked officers in other ships and ashore was that the *Bulwark* had been torpedoed. The new anti-U-boat boom extending from Sheerness to the Isle of Grain across the Medway was hastily closed and defence vessels vigorously swept the whole of the enclosed area. Although there was one report of the sighting of a periscope, nothing was found. Nor has the cause of the *Bulwark*'s destruction ever been determined beyond doubt. A Court of Inquiry, held in the lost vessel's sister ship, HMS *London*, only two days after the disaster, was unable to ascertain any concrete reason why the explosion had occurred — not surprisingly, since the few available witnesses were shocked and injured ratings who had been at breakfast one moment and in the sea the next, with only a vague recollection of an immense force which had blown them high into the air. The court found that: "It is clear from the evidence which has been produced that the explosion which caused the loss of the ship was due to the accidental ignition of ammunition on board. There is no evidence to support a suggestion that the explosion was due either to treachery on board ship or to an act of the enemy."

There was no evidence either that it had been due to the accidental ignition of ammunition. Whichever view is preferred, it can only be on the basis of a guess: the mystery remains.

Eighteen months later, all but one day, and within sight of Kethole Reach where the ironclad had blown up, an auxiliary minelayer, *Princess Irene*, 5,934 tons, lay off Port Victoria, the old port of the Isle of Grain. Shipwrights were at work aboard the fine, modern ship, completed only the year before to the order of the Canadian Pacific Railway and immediately bought in by the Admiralty for conversion to a minelayer. Some 400 officers and men were aboard, as well as about 80 civilian workmen. At 11.15 a.m. a colossal explosion and an enormous cloud of smoke were heard and seen by people ashore and on ships lying nearby. When the smoke cleared, *Princess Irene* was nowhere to be seen.

Again, debris fell miles away, houses were damaged, windows blown in. At Upchurch, five miles distant, the church tower partially collapsed. Papers and two of the ship's towels were picked up as far as twelve miles away. Many people were injured by falling metal. Of nearly 500 men who had been aboard the ship only one survived, badly injured. The cause of her destruction could never be ascertained, but she had been heavily loaded with mines, ready for her next mission, and the possibility of mishandling is perhaps the most likely.

Just over a month later there occurred the most mysterious of all these unexplained wartime losses. The scene this time was far north, in Cromarty Firth, a twenty-mile inlet on the east coast of the Scottish county of Ross-shire. Close to the austere main base of the Grand Fleet at Scapa Flow was a station well provided with repair facilities and amenities for rest and relaxation to suit all ranks, and the many warships based on Scapa took welcome turns to go there and combine business with pleasure.

One of the warships lucky enough to be in Cromarty Firth for Christmas, 1915, was the cruiser HMS *Natal*, 13,550 tons, commanded by Captain Eric Back, whose wife and children, like the families of other senior officers who could afford and arrange it, had taken up residence in the district with the chance of reasonably frequent reunions.

When Captain Back decided to hold a film show in his ship's wardroom on the afternoon of 30 December, to which a number of visitors from shore would be invited, he naturally asked his own family along. So did two other officers. Another civilian family was also asked to attend, and three nursing sisters from the hospital ship *Drina* lying nearby. When the time came, Mrs. Back arrived without her two children so that the civilians totalled just under one dozen.

The little party began immediately after luncheon, for darkness falls early in those parts in December and the guests were expecting to leave for the shore again by about 3.30. If they had left by 3 p.m., or even 3.15, they might have survived the day: for at 3.20 HMS *Natal* blew up.

She did not go with one great bang, but with a series, the first of them so muffled that it was not heard aboard nearby vessels. Flames and smoke leapt from aft, setting the wooden decking alight. There were over 600 persons aboard (103 lucky officers and ratings were on shore leave at the time) and most of them were killed instantly, but some were trapped below to burn to death, or suffocate, or drown. Survivors who could manage to do so tried briefly to fight the raging fires and carry out rescues, but both tasks were hopeless. The cruiser had begun to list almost immediately, and as fresh explosions tore at her innards she heeled over more and more acutely. Within five minutes, which seemed a lifetime to those who lived through it, *Natal* was upside down in the chilly waters of Cromarty Firth, her keel showing above the surface like the back of a basking whale.

Within moments, boats from a dozen other ships of the Fourth Battle Squadron were speeding to the scene to join others from the shore in a frantic race to pick up survivors. But many men died in the water and many more did not live long after being hauled into the boats. None of the civilians was seen. Captain Back, too, was amongst those who died below decks.

Within hours of the disaster the Commander-in-Chief of the Grand Fleet, Admiral Jellicoe, was on board the hospital ship *Drina*, anxiously questioning survivors for himself. None of them, however, was able to dispel or confirm his fears that a U-boat had penetrated the anchorage defences or tell him exactly how the explosion had been caused. All that could be remembered were sudden great surges of heat and flame which had bowled men over or flung them great distances to crash dazedly against metal walls, followed by the ripple of explosions.

The usual inquiry into the loss of the ship was held, but its findings were not made public. Attempts to discuss it in Parliament were firmly rejected. On New Year's Day, Jellicoe was present aboard the cruiser HMS *Shannon* for a solemn service near to the upturned hull of *Natal*.

Before writing this chapter, we asked a former naval officer who had been serving at the time of the *Natal* disaster what he believed had caused it. He replied at once that the wardroom film show had been to blame. The film — highly inflammable stuff in those days — had caught fire in the projector. The projectionist had dragged it free and flung the flaming reel from him, igniting curtains and setting the whole wardroom ablaze. In moments the fire had spread to a nearby magazine.

This is, indeed, one of the most often repeated myths of the First World War; surprisingly so, for it has been perpetuated by many naval men who must surely know that no warship has a magazine adjacent to its wardroom and that flames would have a long way to travel and many thick steel bulkheads to pass before they could reach any place where explosives were stored. No fire alarm was given aboard *Natal*. No one ran out of the wardroom. No woman or child was heard to scream with fear. It is virtually certain that explosion preceded fire, not vice versa. What is less certain is what caused the explosion — accident or sabotage? It is known that during the First World War a number of ingenious weapons of sabotage were devised, amongst them faked lumps of coal containing explosives, drums of "oil" and "paint" actually filled with highly inflammable liquids and fitted with time-clock devices and tiny cigar-sized metal tubes containing separate compartments filled with acid, which when they had eaten through a lead partition and mingled, produced a jet of flame of incendiary-bomb intensity. Many such devices were detected aboard merchantmen, and no doubt a number of mysterious conflagrations and explosions in vessels at sea and in port were caused by ones which searchers had failed to spot. Whether any such infernal machine caused the destruction of the *Bulwark* and *Natal* can only be guessed at: but it could have happened.

It could also have happened in both the last cases which make up these five mysterious explosions in the First World War. One of them concerned the monitor *Glatton*, lying towards the end of the war in the security of Dover harbour, well protected by defences and surrounded by other shipping. On 16 September, 1918, as evening approached, a tremendous explosion shook Dover and *Glatton* was seen to be burning fiercely, though not heeling over. As small boats swarmed to pick up survivors, it became obvious that a colossal danger threatened not only the rest of the shipping in the harbour, but the entire town of Dover itself. *Glatton* and other monitors had been preparing to bombard the Belgian coast and were heavily loaded with shells for the purpose. Nearby lay a merchantman full of ammunition for the forces in France. As the flames swept the *Glatton* it was plain that at any moment all these ships could go up in a devastating series of explosions. Ordering troops down to the seafront to herd the crowds of sightseers into the safety of back streets, the Commander-in-Chief, Admiral Keyes, gave instructions for *Glatton* to be destroyed on the spot. She was torpedoed by a destroyer and went down before her main magazines could explode. What caused her to explode and burn in the first place was never determined.

The most tragic of the five disasters, in terms of sheer numbers of those killed and maimed, had happened over a year before this. HMS *Vanguard*, 19,250 tons, was a Dreadnought of the Fourth Battle Squadron of the Grand Fleet, now commanded by Admiral Beatty, since Jellicoe's departure to the Admiralty to become First Sea Lord. On the night of 9 July, 1917, watchkeepers on other ships in Scapa Flow saw a great tongue of flame leap up from *Vanguard*'s upper deck. Moments later, a thunderclap of an explosion awoke the sleeping fleet. It was followed instantly by another. A dense cloud of fiery smoke welled up, obscuring *Vanguard* from all eyes. When the smoke drifted away the Dreadnought had disappeared.

Debris, much of it red hot, rained down on other ships and their crews had to take prompt action to prevent further fires. Fires were caused also on shore. A large part of one of *Vanguard*'s armour-plated gun turrets landed on another battleship. It weighed tons, yet it had been tossed through the air as lightly as if it had been a discarded tin can. All night fires were fought and the dark anchorage searched for survivors. This was a hopeless quest. The Dreadnought had blown up with such violence that only three of the 800 men who had been aboard her were found alive, and one of them, the only surviving officer, died shortly afterwards.

Again, it has never been discovered what destroyed the *Vanguard*, still lying at the bottom of Scapa Flow, entombing the hundreds who went down with her. Wartime censorship and caution prevented the matter being discussed in the Press or debated at any length in Parliament, though not before one Member had asked whether any connection had been established between the losses of *Vanguard*, *Bulwark* and the *Princess Irene*, and whether any arrests had been made. He received no answer.

Thus three of our five cases were linked briefly at the time in some people's minds, and before long a fourth link was added to the chain when it was discovered that both *Vanguard* and *Natal* had had civilian ordnance fitters working aboard them shortly before the explosions had occurred, and that one of these men had been on both jobs, returning to the shore with what might seem to be a suspiciously narrow margin of time to spare before the disasters. These men — in particular, this one man — were interrogated several times, but nothing incriminating emerged. Unfortunately, the destruction of a ship and all aboard her by a great internal explosion is so complete that only external evidence of sabotage can be obtained. In the five cases we have mentioned, no such evidence, as opposed to ingenious and even plausible theory, has emerged: and so five mysteries remain.

21: "THOSE COWARDLY CAPTAINS"

Sir —

I had little hopes, on Monday last, but to have supped in your cabin: but it pleased God to order it otherwise; I am thankful for it. As for those cowardly captains who deserted you, hang them up; for, by God, they deserve it.

Yours,
Ducasse.

The mystery of six days in August, 1702, is not what — but why? That Admiral John Benbow's last action lives in naval history as one of the most disgraceful debacles of all time is beyond doubt. Reasons were assigned at the time and men punished with the utmost rigour of the law. By all accounts they deserved what they got; yet no account tells us precisely why "those cowardly captains" deliberately followed a course of action which they must have known could only have the direst consequences. Cowardice is not explanation enough.

In 1701, England faced one of her many conflicts with France, this time allied with Spain, over her interests in the West Indies. The Spanish had been first in the West Indies, explored by Columbus in several expeditions, and had established settlements on many of the islands, whose people they had promptly proceeded to enslave and oppress. The English had followed, early in the seventeenth century, staking claims first on the tiny island of St. Christopher (later called St. Kitts), then quickly expanding to more and bigger islands, basing their occupation on that sound agricultural planning which has remained the West Indies' principal benefit to this day.

The British had shortly been followed by the French, and by the end of the century all three countries had substantial interests in the sunny isles. But with the succession to the Spanish throne in dispute, and Louis XIV of France with his boundless territorial ambitions backing one of the candidates, a Franco-Spanish squeeze upon England's West Indian settlements seemed highly likely.

Accordingly, in September, 1701, John Benbow, Vice-Admiral of the Blue, serving in the Grand Fleet under Sir George Rooke, was invited to command a squadron sailing for the West Indies to safeguard British lives and property. King William III was reluctant to let him go: he liked men of Benbow's kind about him and often consulted and confided in him. Other candidates were suggested. They hastened to ask to be excused: at that time the West Indies was a station looked upon — and rightly — more as a fever-trap than a paradise.

"Well then," sighed the king, consoling himself with a jest, "I find we must spare our beaux and send honest Benbow."

The pun, if it was ever made, was an apt one: there was every difference in the world between "honest Benbow" and his courtier-colleagues. Benbow was a "tarpaulin", and proud of it — a self-made man who had raised himself from nothing to high rank in a service in which wealth and favour so often counted for more than ability and courage. A courtier or gentleman with enough money and the right connections could get himself an officer's appointment in a favoured ship, no matter how little he knew about working her or handling men, a disgraceful state of affairs which was to persist, in decreasing degree, until the post-Trafalgar years. For an ordinary seaman to achieve the right to walk the quarterdeck, though not unknown, was exceedingly rare. Even down to our own time argument has continued as to whether gentlemen or ex-rankers make the best officers: there is, of course, no answer. Everything depends on the man.

Bill Benbow, the tanner, at Shrewsbury did dwell,
He taught his son Johnny and thrashed him as well;
He 'prenticed him early a butcher to be,
But John loved adventure and ran off to sea.

Benbow was of the type which constituted the cream of naval seamen: as tough as they came, "with every hair a rope-yarn, every tooth a marlin-spike, every finger a fish-hook, and his blood right good Stockhollum tar". He had been born in 1653, son of a Shropshire tanner, and had served since a boy in the Merchant Marine, from where the Navy found those experienced, no-nonsense officers who could hand, reef, steer and, if need be, do any other task aboard those complicated marvels of ingenuity and beauty, the great wooden ships. He had entered the Navy, aged twenty-five, as a Master's Mate in the *Rupert* under Captain Philip Herbert, later Earl of Torrington. Pepys had written of Herbert, "Of all the worst men living he is the only man I do not know to have any one virtue to compound for all his vices." And he must have been just the commander to appreciate Benbow's rough-and-ready nature, for he himself was even rougher and readier with a number of extra, singularly nasty traits thrown in. A weakness shared by many "tarpaulins" was that of overdoing their natural coarseness and boasting of it as a virtue, a habit which tended to disgust more moderate professional officers every bit as much as it offended — as it was intended to — foppish amateurs. Benbow was guilty of this weakness, and his manner combined with the favour shown to him by someone of

Herbert's stamp must have told against him in many decent men's minds. Amongst those he most despised, it must have kindled actual hatred.

> *So John was a sailor and lived merrily,*
> *A-hunting the Frenchman all over the sea,*
> *He caught twelve black pirates a-raiding the main,*
> *And had their heads pickled and sold them to Spain.*

Herbert gave him a command, and he distinguished himself in a minor way in a couple of Mediterranean engagements against Algerian pirates. But his ship was then paid off and he found himself back in the Merchant Service, this time as master and part owner of a frigate in the Levant trade. It was during this time that there is said to have occurred one of the most famous incidents associated with his name. His ship, the *Benbow*, was attacked and boarded by a Sallee rover. The native pirates swarmed everywhere, fighting with their usual ferocity, but Benbow's men stood firm and drove them off. Thirteen native corpses lay in their blood on his deck. He ordered their heads to be sliced off and tossed into a tub of pork-pickle and the bodies thrown over the side. This was no mere gesture of contempt. Pirates' heads were worth money, if produced to the Spanish authorities, and Benbow was making for Cadiz.

As they entered the port he ordered his servant to decant the pickled heads into a sack, throw it over his shoulder and follow his master ashore. As the two men stepped on land, revenue officers came up, asking to know what was in the sack. Benbow, not a man to tolerate petty officialdom, refused to tell them. Still polite, they insisted upon knowing. Provisions, he grudgingly admitted. Might they take a look, just to make sure? This was too much for the fiery Englishman who bellowed that he was hanged if he was going to have his word questioned in a port where he was so well known. Very well, replied the customs officers, who evidently knew their man: he could complain to the magistrates who happened just then to be in session in a building nearby. If they would take his word, then there would be nothing more to say.

Benbow must have known what was coming and we can imagine his wink to his man Caesar as they were shown into the courtroom. The matter was explained to the magistrates who in their turn courteously asked for the sack to be opened. Benbow still pretended reluctance and indignation, until, having been assured that there was no question of victimisation, and that even the highest Spanish nobleman would have to submit to customs examination, he allowed himself to be persuaded. Turning with a sigh to his servant, he ordered his "salt provisions" to be turned out on to the table, adding that if the magistrates wanted them they could keep them.

When the Spaniards had got over their astonishment and horror at the sight of thirteen pickled human heads, they abandoned the dignity of the court and crowded round Benbow, congratulating him on being a jolly fellow and hero enough to have overcome so many Moorish marauders. The story, which even if not true is not uncharacteristic of Benbow, goes on to say that the magistrates reported the affair to the King of Spain, who invited Benbow to court to tell him about the adventure in his own words. (It is not recorded whether he was required to take the heads along.) The king wrote to James II of England, singing Benbow's praises and recommending him as a fitting leader of men, and thus it was that Benbow was invited to rejoin the Royal Navy with every implied prospect of rapid promotion.

So more and more famous John Benbow he grew;

225

They made him a captain, and admiral too;
In battle and tempest for years he was tossed,
Yet never a battle he fought but he lost.

Whatever the truth of this, he certainly got on quickly —
from Third Lieutenant to Captain in four months. A few
months later he was Master of Chatham Dockyard; a little later
Master of Deptford Dockyard; and, within a few more weeks,
Master of the Fleet at the Battle of Beachy Head, in 1690,
when his admiral was his old soul-mate, Philip Herbert, now
Earl of Torrington.

The battle was not the Royal Navy's brightest encounter, the
superior French force driving the Anglo-Dutch warships all the
way back to the Thames, where they hastily took refuge and
pulled up the buoys after them to prevent being followed and
burned where they lay. Torrington was peremptorily dismissed
from the Service and imprisoned in the Tower of London, but
was soon court-martialled and acquitted, partly, without doubt,
because of Benbow's evidence on his behalf. The trial had a
partial echo a few years later, though. Torrington's defence was
that he had chosen to run from the French rather than fight
them because "most men were in fear that the French would
invade; but I was always of another opinion, for I always said
that, whilst we had a fleet in being, they would not dare to
make an attempt." Something of this philosophy, though less
artfully expressed, can be detected in the defence offered by
Benbow's "cowardly captains" after the disgrace of August,
1702.

Benbow emerged from the Beachy Head disgrace without a
stain on his record. By now he was becoming a popular figure,
termed "the famous Captain Benbow" in print, and generally
admired as the very model of an outspoken sea dog. That his
name and fame, such as it was, have endured at all is perhaps

due more to the colour of his personality and the quality of his courage than to his actual deeds. He won no outstanding battles. He went on to play his part at the Battle of Barfleur and in sorties against French ports before being sent to the West Indies as Rear-Admiral in command of a squadron charged with defending British interests and hounding down such piratical embarrassments as Captain Kidd. He acquired more enemies on his own side during this time by throwing his weight about unnecessarily, insulting officials, pressing crew members — regulations did not permit this in colonial ports — and seeming to care more for the welfare and health of his sailors who were dying like flies than for the feelings of officials and his own senior officers.

There was no little relief felt when he was ordered home in 1700 and no less dismay when he returned to the West Indies the following year. He soon began pressing men into his ships despite the commands, protests and pleas of the islands' administrators. "Necessity has no law," he replied gruffly when taxed about it by the Secretary to the Admiralty.

The war over the Spanish succession at last broke out in May, 1702, and it was not long before news reached Benbow that a small French naval force was approaching the West Indies under the command of an enterprising admiral named Ducasse, a man of courage, eager to rid the Caribbean of all interests other than French. On this occasion, however, Ducasse was not looking for a fight. He was escorting three transports carrying troops to garrison Cartagena, the French-owned Colombian port and city which was to be used as a war base, and was only thinking about getting them there safely when on 19 August he ran into Benbow. Ducasse was not far from his destination, and Benbow wasted no time. It was one o'clock in the afternoon, with plenty of daylight left. Within a few minutes his flagship, the *Breda*, 70 guns, was flying the signal to attack. And now began six days of frustration and humiliation for Benbow, and of disgrace for England.

His captains were cravens and would not obey;
He swore, and they swore, and Du Casse got away,
A cannon-ball knocked off his leg with a bump —
John merely said "——" and fought on with the stump.

In order to form line of battle as laid down in the fighting instructions which commanders were strictly bound to obey, Benbow had to wait for his other ships to come up from several miles astern. To his surprise (or perhaps he was not altogether surprised: it is part of the mystery) several of his captains showed no haste to comply. It took all of three hours for the line to form and bear down on Ducasse's reluctant little fleet. Then, after the exchange of a few broadsides, the Admiral found himself and one other ship, the *Ruby* of 48 guns, left alone in the combat. The rest had either turned away or simply kept their distance, making no effort to close with the enemy.

It was the same next day, *Breda* and *Ruby* doing all the chasing and firing, the others standing several miles off, ignoring every order to come into line and fight. By the following day *Ruby* was showing the effects of the close-quarters action and, her rigging in tatters, had to be towed out of range of the French guns by *Breda*'s boats. She was too badly damaged to rejoin the action and was ordered back to Jamaica. Yet still the other English ships, fresh and unharmed, looked on and did nothing.

On the fourth day Benbow received the welcome support of one of the waverers, *Falmouth*, 48 guns, whose captain sent his lieutenant to the flagship to ask whether he might leave his station in the line and assist, a doubly significant question as would later transpire. Benbow accepted, and what had been the *Breda*'s and the *Ruby*'s fight now became the *Breda*'s and the *Falmouth*'s, the remaining ships confining themselves to quick tip-and-run sorties, coming close enough to fire an occasional token broadside, then retiring again to a safe distance for the rest of the day.

After five days of this remarkable exhibition which astonished the French and disgusted Ducasse — as he later made plain in a letter to Benbow quoted at the beginning of this chapter — Benbow scored what seemed to be a tangible success, taking the *Anne*, a former English ship, and so battering the rearmost ship in the French line during the night that it seemed certain she would become an English prize by daylight. But before then Benbow had suffered the wound which the song records.

The leg was shattered, not severed, but the pain he suffered was none the less for that. Yet, refusing to be kept below, he ordered his cot to be brought up to the quarterdeck and himself placed in it so that he could continue to watch the enemy and direct the battle. He had the added humiliation of watching the French ships coolly cluster round their damaged countryman and tow it away, while the English ships let them get on with it virtually unmolested. Roused to fury, Benbow sent a message by hand to his captains, ordering them to behave "like Englishmen". Far from having the effect he hoped for, it brought on board the flagship one of them, Richard Kirby (or Kirkby) of the *Defiance*, 64 guns, to protest that any further attempt to engage the French would be disastrous for the English ships which did not possess the strength to overcome such dangerous opposition.

This rejoinder must have come near to finishing Benbow off, agonized as he was from his wound and mortified by what he had witnessed during the past six days. He straightway called his other captains aboard the flagship for consultation, only to see, to his added chagrin, Kirby produce a document which every captain signed, even including Vincent, who had fought his *Falmouth* resolutely, and Fogg, captain of Benbow's own flagship. The paper ran:

At a consultation held on board her Ma^tys^. ship *Bredah*, 24 August 1702, off Cartagena on the Maine Continent of America, it is the opinion of us, who's names are undermention'd, vizt:

First — Of the great want of men, in Number, Quality and the Weakness of those they have.

21y — The Generall want of Ammunition of most Sorts.

31y — Each Ships Masts, Yards, Sailes, Rigging and Guns being all in a great measure disabled.

41y — The Winds are so small and variable that the Ships cannot be Governed by any Strength each Ship has.

5thly — Having experienced the Enemyes force in Six dayes Battle following. The Squadron consisting of Five Men of Warr and a Fireship under the Command of Moun:^r^ du Cass, their Equipage consisting in Gunns from Sixty to Eighty and having a great Number of Seamen and Soldiers on board for the Service of Spaine.

For which reasons abovementioned Wee think it not fitt to Ingage the Enemye at this time; but to keep them Company this night and observe their motion, and if a fair oppertunity shall happen (of Wind and Weather) once more to trye our Strength with them

Richard Kirkby

Sam:^ell^ Vincent

John Constable

Chr. ffogge

Coop:^r Wade
Thos:^s Hudson

At best, it was an echo of Torrington's defence, based on the value of a "Fleet in Being" — or, if one prefers it in rhyme, of Goldsmith's

For he who fights and runs away
May live to fight another day;
But he who is in battle slain
Can never rise and fight again.

a sentiment which, we can rejoice, has held no appeal for the majority of those who have served in our Navy down its history.

At worst the declaration was an admission of cowardice, for it was simply not true that the French force was stronger than the English or that the English had suffered the greater damage and, in any case, the captains' reluctance to fight dated from the very outset of the engagement, before a single shot had been fired at them.

Benbow warned them that the paper would spell their ruin. They disregarded the threat. Faced with their determination to fight no more, he was compelled to break off contact with the enemy and turn away towards Jamaica.

Benbow's leg was amputated soon after his arrival in Jamaica. After several weeks' suffering, during which he nearly died of fever, he was thought strong enough for a court martial to be convened to try five of his captains for their conduct. They were Kirby and Wade, accused of cowardice and other crimes; Constable, charged with breach of orders and neglect of duty; and Vincent and Fogg, who, though they had done their duty, had nevertheless signed the paper advocating the

231

abandonment of the action and had to answer for it. The only captains not tried were Walton, who had fought his *Ruby* so bravely and had retired to Jamaica before the incident of the paper, and Hudson of the *Pendennis* who had signed, but had died from an illness after returning to port.

Public feeling ran high at the trial, and, for all his unpopularity in the islands, Benbow had everyone's sympathy, so markedly did his personal conduct and courage contrast with the apparent cowardice of his captains.

To a packed courtroom, Kirby seemed to be almost off his head. His defence, though insistent, was confused, at times almost hysterical, and his witnesses were unconvincing. The one argument by which he might have persuaded the court that there were some grounds for the action to be broken off as he had urged, that is, the lack of a fair wind, was demolished quite simply by Benbow who showed that no more favourable conditions could ever have obtained:

> for we then had the wether gage, a fine gale of wind, six ships to four, and one of them quite disabled, all our ships in as good a posture for fighting as could be expected and not 8 men killed in all our ships (except the *Bredah*) and to defer this to a fitter oppertunity to the Adm:[ll] seemed a perfect deniall who having seen the cowardly behaviour of some of them before had reason to believe that either they had a designe against him, or to be traytors to their country if an oppertunity happen'd that the French could have destroyed the Admirall.

Evidence was also brought that Kirby had behaved with personal cowardice during the action, ducking into cover whenever a shot was heard. He was found guilty and sentenced to death by shooting. The same verdict and sentence were passed on Wade who was shown to have kept his *Greenwich* deliberately out of range, but had fired from time to time with the remark that the Admiral must be led to believe that he was in the fight.

Constable, who was said by some witnesses to have been drunk while the action was on and had made no effort to engage, was dismissed from the Service. Fogg and Vincent, on both of whose behalf Benbow testified, declared that they had signed Kirby's paper only because they suspected some form of treachery by their colleagues which would lead to the capture or destruction of the English ships if the action were not broken off. They were found guilty of signing, but were not punished.

The mystery of the Benbow affair lies in the motives of Kirby, Wade, and perhaps one or two others. Either they were cowards or they acted as they did out of personal spite against their Admiral: in which case they must surely have realized that they were running their heads into a noose. Benbow seems to have been convinced that they held a grudge against him or hoped he might be killed so that they could surrender their ships. It is known that he had had trouble with them earlier and had not spared his language, yet it seems incredible that naval officers, in time of war especially, should hazard their ships, their country's honour, and their own lives simply to pay a man back for an insult.

The answer to the enigma, which no one has ever found for certain, may lie in the difference between "tarpaulin" and "gentleman". Benbow had heaped abuse on his inferiors in rank and superiors by birth. They sailed burning with resentment, and found in this an excuse for indulging their natural cowardice. That Kirby at least was a superior sort of being there is little doubt. Someone approached Queen Anne on his, Wade's and Constable's behalf, but she coldly refused to interfere with their sentences.

Cooper and Wade were shot on board HMS *Bristol* at Plymouth on 16 April, 1703. But they outlived the man they had set out to ruin. He had died on 4 November of the previous year, only three weeks after the court martial of the cowardly captains had immortalized his name.

> *So here's to John Benbow, who loved the salt sea,*
> *Was never a seadog more merry than he.*
> *So gallantly fought he, so roundly he swore,*
> *The like of John Benbow we'll never see more.*

22: LOST ATLANTIS

Of all the legends of the sea the most persistent is that of Atlantis, the lost continent. The thought of that land-under-the-waves has fascinated map-makers and historians from the earliest times, as though, submerged, it still calls to men and bids them dive for its treasures.

The legend was first recorded by the Greek philosopher Plato, who was born about the year 428 B.C. In one of his Dialogues, the *Timaeus*, he described a great land — "a country larger than Asia Minor with Libya, situated just beyond the Pillars of Hercules". If it existed at all, modern geography places it opposite the present Strait of Gibraltar. It was said to have been a highly civilized land with great cities, noble buildings, flourishing arts, organized industries, fabulous riches. Its women were beautiful and its men brave and strong. On the whole, the Atlanteans were a peace-loving race, but occasionally they invaded other countries, as when they overran the Mediterranean lands, and only Athens resisted them. All this is according to Plato.

In the *Critias*, the fragmentary Dialogue following the *Timaeus*, Plato describes the ideal commonwealth of Atlantis. It was a country that lived up to the highest principles, which he had set forth himself in his *Republic*, Its people existed in a climate of spiritual health. Philosophers, men of action, lovers of pleasure took equal part in its scheme of life; it was the ideal aristocracy, or "rule of the best".

The only weakness of the Atlanteans was spasmodic warmongering. Perhaps the disaster which overtook Atlantis was a divine judgment on this. Whatever the reason, calamity struck. "With great earthquakes and inundations in a single day and one fatal night", Atlantis was swallowed up and disappeared beneath the sea. Thereafter the waters above it became unnavigable, for the keels of vessels would strike the mountains of sand which covered the towers of the buried cities.

This happened, said Plato, about 9600 B.C. And in case his readers should think it a tall story, he added that it was not an invention, but in every respect a true account.

So much for Plato. How much is he to be believed? Some have thought that he told the story of Atlantis merely as a fable, to illustrate the principles of his *Republic*. It certainly resembles in detail the ideal states of other writers — More's *Utopia*, and William Morris's England as seen in *The Dream of John Ball*. But belief in Atlantis is too strong to have been born solely from a philosopher's dream. Even in the eighteenth century, the Age of Reason, such intellectuals as Montaigne, Buffon and Voltaire declared their faith in the story. Interest in the question has never flagged and many theories have been put forward about the location of Atlantis.

There is evidence that the sea covers something that was once dry land in the region of the Dogger Bank. When trawlers began to explore the seabed there they found tree-roots, bones, flints and other primitive tools, the remains of Pleistocene fauna and flora. Perhaps this was Atlantis. But if so it was inhabited millions of years ago, and could not possibly have been the civilized state of Plato's description. The same conclusion can be drawn from the findings concerning the Atlantic ridge, discovered in the nineteenth century. This ridge runs from the Arctic to the Antarctic, some 9,000 feet higher than the ocean bed; its peaks rise as islands, such as the Canary Isles and St. Helena. Sixty million years ago it was probably dry land. The "relics of primitive man" found on St. Helena proved to be only natural stones. No voyager or explorer in any century has found the slightest trace of a sunken country as late in date as the one Plato mentions.

Yet signs exist to indicate that the continents of America and Africa were not always divided by a waste of water. There are shared customs and rituals, shared varieties of animal and insect. The tombs of ancient Mayas contain ornaments made of green jade — but jade is not mined in Central or South America: and in both continents, among early peoples who had not read the works of Plato, the story of Atlantis was told.

Perhaps Atlantis was really a place, known to us by a different name, which still exists. It has been variously identified as Africa, discovered long ago by the Phoenicians, who then lost track of it again, as Spain, or Western Libya, or the North Frisian Islands. A group of the Cape Verde Islands, and three of the Canaries, have been named as part of it.

If indeed it existed, how was it submerged? Plato's version is not very likely. Possibly a volcanic eruption, followed by a tidal wave, was responsible, or a climatic upheaval caused by vapour from Venus, when the planet was unusually near Earth. If Atlantis was a volcanic island, it may have vanished as suddenly as did the Island of Sabrina in the Azores. The most likely explanation of the whole mystery is that Plato heard of the event — which must have taken place millions of years before his lifetime — and used it to illustrate his philosophy.

But Atlantis is not the only lost land to haunt the minds of men. In medieval times there were many circumstantial tales of other sunken islands in the western sea, such as the Isles of the Blest, or Fortunate Isles, which occur in Greek mythology. These are said to be peopled by mortals on whom the gods have conferred immortality, a legend often attached to such islands. The Isle of Avalon, or Avilion, is in Welsh folklore the Kingdom of the Dead, and thither, according to Tennyson, the body of King Arthur was borne after he received his fatal wound.

I am going a long way...
To the island-valley of Avilion;
Where falls not hail, or rain, or any snow,
Nor ever wind blows loudly; but it lies
Deep-meadow'd, happy, fair with orchard-lawns
And bowery hollows crown'd with summer sea,
Where I will heal me of my grievous wound.

Arthur was to enjoy immortal life in Avalon, the Isle of Apples. The same name is given to the Somersetshire ridge which culminates in Glastonbury Tor, but that has come about by a confusion between the Anglo-Saxon name for Glastonbury and the old Teutonic word Glasberg, Kingdom of the Dead.

In the Arthurian saga, too, is mentioned "that sweet land of Lyonesse". This was a tract of land supposed to stretch between Land's End and the Scilly Isles, now submerged "full forty fathoms deep", and said to have contained about a hundred and forty villages. It is described by Tennyson:

A land of old upheaven from the abyss
By fire, to sink into the abyss again;
Where fragments of forgotten peoples dwelt,
And the long mountains ended in a coast
Of ever-shifting sand, and far away
The phantom circle of a moaning sea.

In Ireland, they talked of St. Brendan's Isle, or the Promised Land of the Saints, discovered by the hero-saint during an

238

Atlantic voyage. Miraculously it appeared and disappeared, said the stories, though a rationalist traveller in 1759 dismissed this as the effect of mirage.

Scottish lore has Tir nan Og, the land of the ever-young. But the Lyonesse tradition is the closest to that of Atlantis. It was described in early English chronicles, such as the *Chronicon ex Chronicis* of Florence of Worcester, with a wealth of detail and no suggestion of tongue-in-cheek. Like Atlantis, it was a flourishing, highly civilized state which disappeared suddenly beneath the sea. Very similar was Antilia, or Antilla, a lost island firmly believed in by the Portuguese in mediaeval times. In the grand-ducal library at Weimar it can be seen marked in maps of 1435, 1436, 1455 and 1476, and on the famous globe made at Nuremburg in 1492. The mediaeval geographer Martin Behaim said that about the year 734, after the Moors had conquered Spain and Portugal, the Island of Antilia or Cepte Cidade was colonized by Christian refugees under the Archbishop of Oporto and that a Spanish ship had sighted it in 1414.

But who has seen it since? Did it vanish with the fifteenth century?

And what happened to the Island of Saxemburgh, between South Africa and South America, which was said to exist between 1670 and about 1820 — but has now disappeared? Or Thompson Island, 1,600 miles south-west of Cape Town, which vanished about the same time?

Then there was Lemuria, a tract of land that is supposed in prehistoric times to have connected Madagascar with India and Sumatra. It, too, has sunk without trace.

The truth may be that some of these places — perhaps all of them — did exist at some time, and vanished less dramatically than the folktales say. Every year the sea eats away at coastlines, claiming dry land for its own. Along the edge of the English coast are buried once-flourishing towns and villages, gardens and forests. Off Selsey Bill in Sussex is a stretch of water called by sailors "the Park" — an inappropriate name, one would think. But in the sixteenth century the deer of Henry VIII roamed there among the trees. In Cheshire, where Birkenhead Docks are, was once a great birch forest, as an old rhyme tells:

> *From Birchen Haven to Hilbre*
> *A squirrel might hop from tree to tree.*

In Yorkshire, a city mentioned by Shakespeare in *Richard II* is a city no more.

> *The banish'd Bolingbroke repeals himself,*
> *And with uplifted arms is safe arriv'd*
> *At Ravenspurgh*

Ravenspurgh, or Ravensburgh, was larger and more important than Hull. Edward IV landed there from Flanders in 1471 on his way to fight the battle of Barnet. Now it is beneath the waves.

Off the north-east point of the Norfolk coast, they say, the bells of long-drowned Cromer churches can be heard ringing as a warning of coming storm. At Bognor and Bosham in Sussex the same story is told. At Reculver in Kent the ancient church has survived, its twin towers still standing at the edge of the land — but the rest of Reculver town has gone, eaten away by the sea.

There is hardly a stretch of English coast that has not some such history of slow destruction. There is a morbid fascination about such drowned places: houses and churches, farms and civil buildings, gardens and cemeteries, once the scene of human life in all its bustle, now the playground of fishes. Perhaps this partly explains the lure of the Atlantean legend; this, and the fact that the unknown land is always the most attractive. Not to mention the eternal lure of hidden treasure — those coffers of gold, jewels, and the precious "orichalc" mentioned by Plato (some think it to have been ivory) that were the wealth of Atlantis. In search of this, the Dutch East India Company sent out an expedition in the late seventeenth century to St. Helena Nova, between St. Helena and Africa. But they found nothing.

Whatever the truth about Atlantis, however probable the explanation that Plato's Utopian dream was responsible for much of its lore, men have never ceased to believe in it, longing to reclaim what the sea stole. In the down-to-earth nineteenth century a Mrs. Elizabeth Blossom of Cleveland, Ohio, financed many voyages by her namesake, the schooner *Blossom*, in the hope of finding Atlantis. And in England, that complex character Mr. Gladstone urged the Government to send out a man-of-war to the waters where he was sure the lost island lay. We are not told whether the request ever reached the Queen herself, but if it did no doubt her disapproval of Gladstone increased substantially from that day. The Government vetoed his suggestion as being uneconomic.

Ideal country of wealth, beauty and enlightened rule, Atlantis represents mankind's dream of the perfect world spoilt only by war, a vision of eternal summer and plenty, even — in some of the legends — of immortality. The geographical and historical truths of it may always remain a mystery. But they really hardly matter at all.

241

23: CAPTAIN ROBERTON'S SECRET

The man was sitting on a rock, watching two half-naked youths skinning a seal. It was not a pretty sight, nor was the butchery of other seals that was still going on, farther along the shore. But it did not seem to put the man out in the least or spoil the flavour of the long cigar he was smoking. Captain William Smith, who was used to seeing all sorts of human riff-raff in these islands of the Bass Straits, between Tasmania and the south-eastern tip of Australia, was struck by the unusual appearance of this nonchalant character. Tall, dark and elegantly slim with a look of the swordsman about him, he was dressed in a dark blue jacket and breeches, gilt-buttoned and of good quality. The high stock that almost engulfed his chin was clean, and clean linen on Cape Barren Island was a rarity in the year 1826. On second thoughts, the man might be a naval officer. Smith decided to find out.

The man acknowledged his greeting unsmilingly, and accepted the offer of a swig from Smith's pocket-bottle of rum. Smith noted that his accent was curious — predominantly Scottish, but with a flavour of something else as well, suggestive of warmer countries — while his eyes were at the same time dark and cold, an unusual combination except in reptiles. Their gaze rested thoughtfully on the schooner *Caledonia*, rocking gently at anchor.

"Yours?" the man inquired.

"That's right." Smith was also a man of few words. "Been with her a good few years."

"She looks a tight enough craft."

"You're a good judge. Thought she was breaking up on me last year, though. Found myself in Westernport — over there." He nodded toward the Australian mainland. "Nearest thing to the end of the earth. Not a drop of tar and pitch to be had for her seams."

"How did you get her seaworthy, then?"

"Melted down the gum of the grass-trees. Worked like a charm."

The stranger said nothing, but his appraising look registered approval of Smith's resourcefulness.

"What's your trade?" he asked.

"Anything I can get. Sealskins from here. Wallaby skins over yonder. Wattle bark. Tusks. Stuff the locals carve."

The man smiled coldly. "A species of sea pedlar."

"Call it that. I've not much choice of goods."

His companion appeared to be about to say something, but changed his mind. His long, Scottish mouth shut in a thin line. Smith's curiosity was now thoroughly aroused. He was a sharp-witted, enterprising man with a nose for a bargain and he scented in this apparently casual conversation the possibility of something good coming his way. He sniffed the air exaggeratedly.

"Devil of a stink round here, with them skins. Care to step aboard and take a glass with me?"

The stranger contemplated his cigar which was almost smoked through. This appeared to make his mind up for him and he rose to his feet. He was even taller than Smith had judged at first and, glancing sideways at the impassive face as they walked towards the *Caledonia*, Smith thought involuntarily of the legendary Flying Dutchman. If the dreaded Vanderdecken ever existed, Smith thought, he might have looked very like this.

"Welcome aboard the *Caledonia*, Mr. — I didn't get the name."

"I didn't give it. Captain Roberton."

"Smith. William Smith." They shook hands formally and sat down at the table in Smith's cabin. A bottle of rough red wine was followed by another, and under their influence Roberton's dour aspect began to soften a little. Drink, shrewdly noted Smith, who himself had a head like teak, was the key to Roberton and to any useful information he might have.

Gradually details began to emerge. It was not clear where Roberton had earned his title of captain, but he had certainly been at sea. During the last few years he had served under the British admiral Lord Cochrane, first in the Chilean navy, fighting Spain, then in the fleet which in the previous year, 1825, had won the independence of Brazil. From fighting he had turned to whaling and had landed on Cape Barren Island a few days before from a whaler that had come down from the North Pacific. Smith sensed that these autobiographical details omitted a good deal. There was a strong Spanish flavour about Roberton's conversation, particularly in the oaths he dropped as the wine flowed more and more freely. Smith felt there might be a whiff of piracy about his new acquaintance, but he was not one to quarrel with that or with the offer that was forthcoming.

"Sick of peddling, aren't you, Smith? Stinking hides and bits of gimcrackery — that's a poor cargo for a good vessel."

"I told you, Captain, it's all I can get. Unless — unless you know of something better."

Roberton's face was inscrutable. "I might. You're a canny man, I take it?"

"I can keep my own counsel."

"Aye, but can you keep mine?"

"If it's worth my while, Captain."

Roberton leaned forward, elbows on the table. "Here you are, then. Will you let me charter the *Caledonia* for a private voyage?"

"Depends where, Captain."

"To the Ladrone Islands — north of New Guinea, south of Japan. Some call them the Marianas. Will you take me?"

"Depends how much, Captain."

"Fourteen thousand Mexican dollars."

Smith concealed his excitement. "It's a long way."

"It's a lot of money."

Smith appeared to deliberate. "Cash down?"

"I'd be a fool to carry that much cash in these parts, wouldn't I? But my word's my bond — you can rely on that."

Smith looked dubious. "I'd have to know what was at the end of it, Captain. An honest trading vessel can't afford to get mixed up in anything, you know."

"*Madre di Dios!* You've a lot of scruples for a poor man." Roberton pushed back his chair and rose. "There are plenty will take me if you won't."

Smith casually reached into the cupboard behind him and produced a brandy bottle, from which he poured two liberal measures.

"Sit down, Captain. You can trust me. Stands to reason, before I hire out my ship, I've got to know why — now don't it stand to reason?"

Roberton drained his glass of brandy. His face was no longer sallow, but had a purplish flush. He stared at Smith with a kind of triumphant defiance.

"All right, *mi amigo*, since you're so particular. I'm after treasure — gold, silver, jewels — lovely treasure, lying about in

Tom Tiddler's Land for the right man to pick up. Now are you interested?"

Smith was interested. He was no more immune to the beckoning sparkle of treasure than the next man, and in any case 14,000 dollars was a heap of money. Even without cash in hand, he agreed to Roberton's proposition. Roberton, who knew the North Pacific waters better than he did, should pilot the *Caledonia* while Smith was retained as master. The bargain was concluded over the rest of the brandy, after which Roberton collapsed sideways on to the cabin floor, unconscious and snoring.

But Smith was still perfectly sober.

Before they could embark, the *Caledonia* had to be fitted out for the long voyage. Smith went for this purpose to Launceston, in northern Tasmania, the nearest place of any size where he could get the supplies he needed. Roberton remained behind on Cape Barren Island, lazily smoking and saying little to anybody. There the *Caledonia* picked him up and set off on her long and pleasant voyage. Around the New Hebrides she wove, in and out of the Solomon Islands, in the languorous airs of those tropic seas. And first all was well aboard. There was plenty to drink, the vision of treasure glittered before Smith's eyes, Roberton was relaxed and good-tempered. He said things under the influence of rum, wine and brandy which suggested that they were after a splendid prize indeed. But what it was, and exactly where, even the most potent cup could not induce him to reveal and Smith's prodding questions usually provoked a flare-up of rage and a volley of polyglot oaths.

Smith's own temper did not improve either. After all, he had not yet seen a whisker of his 14,000 dollars — which was not all that good pay for such an expensive voyage, when he came to think of it. He had had to take on extra crew, more provisions: where did Roberton think the money was coming from? They began to quarrel openly.

Then Smith saw Roberton in what looked like a conspiratorial conversation with one of the crew. The few words he could overhear confirmed his suspicions. He had the man in and questioned him fiercely. Yes, Roberton had been talking — about treasure; about how he would lead them to it if they would agree to ditch Smith. Closely pressed, the man admitted that this was to be done by the old-time method of knocking Smith out and throwing him over the side.

Smith's face was thunderous. Shoving the man violently to one side, he strode past him out of the cabin and up on to the deck where Roberton was lounging in the sun. Smith marched up to him.

"So you'd plot against me with my own men, would you? Steal my ship and grab the loot yourself?"

Roberton smiled contemptuously.

"Don't believe everything you hear, Skipper."

"I've heard enough! Why, you slimy scum, I'll knock you from here to —"

As he approached Roberton, flailing his fists, the other man jumped nimbly to his feet and closed with him. The noise brought the crew up on deck. They were wise enough to stand back and let the fighting cocks alone. It was a short battle, for Roberton was younger and tougher. A cracking blow to Smith's jaw from his iron knuckles sent the captain reeling backwards. His clawing hands could not catch at solidity. Over the rail he went, and into the sea with a tremendous splash.

Roberton advanced triumphantly towards the watching men.

"Well? Now he's out of the way, you'll find you've a better captain, lads. Let's have a drink all round to celebrate!"

But the crew were not, as he had thought, unanimously anti-Smith, and they did not trust Roberton's ability as a pilot. A boat was lowered and the floundering Smith retrieved. The evening was not a cordial one, but, much as he would have liked, Smith cared too much about the treasure to have Roberton ditched. Over a bottle, the two agreed hypocritically to forgive and forget.

"But you'd be well advised to tell me where we're making for," Smith said. "Suppose you were to be taken with one of them tropic fevers? Why, you'd be dead in a matter of hours, and we'd have made the voyage for sweet Fanny Adams."

"You'd be inconsolable, I'm sure," smiled Roberton. "All the same, I'll keep my own counsel till we get there."

No amount of sly prodding, outright questioning or alcohol would change his mind. *Caledonia* sailed smoothly on. She was very near her objective now. The island of Guam, southernmost of the Ladrones, was little more than a day's sailing away. Captain Smith's spirits rose — only to be severely dashed one morning when he awoke to find his best boat gone, together with Roberton and the pick of the crew.

What he said is best left to the imagination. Then, without wasting time, he steered straight for Guam. The Ladrones were under Spanish rule, and from what Roberton had let slip in his cups about his activities when fighting the Spaniards under Cochrane, Smith guessed that they might be more than willing to catch and punish him.

Landing in Guam, he reported to the Governor, Don Francisco Villalobos. Don Francisco was charming. Of course he sympathized with Smith. He had no personal knowledge of Roberton's part in the Chilean naval war, but obviously the man was a villain. He, Don Francisco, would organize his

248

pursuit and capture. A Spanish brig would give chase, under the able command of Don Francisco Miranda.

"I'd like to go with him," hastily interrupted Smith. "I want to see justice done."

"Of course, of course. There is just a small difficulty..."

Don Francisco's interpreter then explained that Señor Smith had, quite innocently, broken the law. No foreign vessel was allowed to put into Guam without a licence from the King of Spain. Señor Smith did not have such a licence? No? Then, regrettably, *Caledonia* and her skipper would have to remain in Guam until official permission had been obtained.

"But the treasure — if Roberton gets his hands on it..." Smith spluttered.

"I think you may leave that to us, Señor." Don Francisco handed the frustrated Englishman a particularly fine cigar.

So Smith did not have the satisfaction of seeing Roberton taken — and taken by an old enemy. For in the war years Roberton and Miranda had met when Roberton was a sailor of fortune and had thrown in his lot with Chilean independence, and Miranda was a much-respected Spanish naval officer. Roberton had captured him in a skirmish between their two vessels, had taken him aboard and had him mercilessly flogged. It had been a peculiarly embittering experience for the proud Spaniard. Now the hour of his revenge had come. Captured at sea before he could reach his goal, Roberton had been brought before Miranda for judgment.

They faced each other on the deck of the brig. Both faces were impassive.

Miranda spoke first.

"This treasure. You will tell us where it is."

Roberton sneered. "Find it."

"You British talk much about fair play. I will give you another chance. Tell us the location and your punishment will be lighter."

Roberton's reply, in Spanish, was unprintable. Miranda turned to the men beside him.

"Tie him up."

They lashed Roberton to the mast. Two large, strong men, each armed with a cat-o'-nine-tails, took up positions on each side of him while another stripped him of jacket and shirt.

"Is the treasure on Guam?" asked Miranda. Roberton stared back at him defiantly, lips set. The cat fell — once.

"Is it on Agana?" Another terrible stroke. The man with his face to the mast did not cry out. Only an involuntary quiver showed that he had felt anything.

"Is it on Rota? On Tinian? On Saipan? On Anatahan? Pagan? Asuncion? Uruacas?"

When Miranda had run out of islands, the strokes continued relentlessly. Altogether three hundred fell, until Roberton's back was an angry mass of raw meat. Then they rubbed salt into it and threw him into the hold.

Next morning the questioning went on.

"Were you, perhaps, misleading, *el Capitan* Smith? It is not on the Ladrones at all, but in Japanese territory. On Marcus Island, perhaps?"

Roberton's sufferings were dreadful, but he neither spoke nor cried out for the first twenty-nine strokes of the cat. At the thirtieth he broke.

"I'll tell! Let me go and I'll tell — blast your eyes, you…" He was sobbing and cursing incoherently as they cut him free. A cup of wine was offered him, but he jerked his head aside.

"Very well. You will take us to the treasure personally."

Roberton nodded.

"Is it far from here? Near enough to reach by boat?"

He nodded again, and Miranda gave orders for a boat to be lowered. Roberton seemed too enfeebled to get into it unaided. A man at each side, they lifted him in. But with one spring he slipped out of their hands like a flash and leapt over the side into the sea.

Consternation followed. Miranda shouted orders from the brig: a Manilan diver who was in the boat must go after the escaping man. This was easy enough, for Roberton was too badly injured to swim powerfully and the lithe native soon brought him to the boat's side. They had him alive! Then, with one desperate twist, he was free. He plunged downward into the green depths and all the diver's skill could not find him again. Captain Roberton, mystery man, was gone, and his secret with him.

But perhaps luck was with Spain. For when his belongings were searched a map was found — yellowed, dog-eared, but undoubtedly a map indicating treasure. Here was the shape of an island — here a palm tree, a rough drawing of a chest, a cross and some figures. This was the clue they wanted; they had only to find the island.

Northward they sailed, towards Japan, pausing at and scouring every island. Miranda was a thorough man, and had an excellent working knowledge of the Ladrones. But not a trace did he find of anything resembling the island represented on Roberton's map, nor a single dollar of treasure. Defeated, he returned to Guam and confessed failure.

Now it was Smith's turn for interrogation. Because Don Francisco Villalobos in his wisdom sensed that the Englishman was too stupid not to reveal any knowledge he might have, only verbal questioning was used, and it was clear that Smith knew nothing. Courteously waiving regulations, Don Francisco allowed him to reclaim the *Caledonia* and bade him a polite farewell.

Back to Australia went Smith, the poorer for the cost of his long voyage, back to run-of-the-mill trading, a sadder and a wiser man. Roberton's story of treasure had been a pack of lies, he decided, and it would be a long time before he listened to any more such tales from the riff-raff of the islands.

In the Governor's residence on Guam, Villalobos considered evidence to the contrary. Close inquiries had revealed that years ago Roberton's varied career had placed him on a Manila-bound vessel laden with treasure — among it 90,000 dollars in gold. She had left Callao, but had never made the port of Manila. Just another ship lost at sea, it was thought at the time. But there were strong indications that Roberton, at some point in the voyage, had taken charge, gained the support of some of the crew and disposed of the others, then, after sinking the ship, had buried the treasure.

But where? Even the guile of Spain could not extract that information. Perhaps the map left behind by Roberton was deliberately misleading — it was the sort of joke that would have appealed to him. And to this day the Callao treasure may still lie buried beneath golden sand on one of the Ladrones, or somewhere else. Only Roberton knew — and they could not make him tell.

24: MEN WHO DISAPPEARED

Many men and women have disappeared at sea. Some have gone quietly, deliberately, slipping unobserved over the rail at dead of night to drop gladly into the obliterating embrace of the sea, rather than carry on living lives that had become insupportable. More have gone against their will, swept overboard by a sudden wave or after losing balance; or, in a few cases, because someone else intended them to go, and saw to it that they did.

In just a few instances, though, ships' passengers have vanished in circumstances owing nothing to any of these causes; and at least two have left behind them mysteries which to this day have never been completely solved.

One of them was Francis Gasparini, a dignified, forty-year-old man of Italian birth who contrived, in August, 1888, to escape from a police escort aboard the trans-Tasman steamer *Wakatipu*, between Wellington and Sydney, and to disappear in a manner which brought about a diplomatic storm and accusations against a Cabinet Minister of complicity in a carefully planned scheme.

Gasparini had first come to the notice of the New Zealand public in April of that year when Detective John Walker's sharp eyes had seen a movement in an unoccupied house at Kingland, near Auckland. Tiptoeing stealthily in, he was able to creep up behind the crouching figure of a powerfully built man with cropped hair. As a board creaked under the detective's feet the man whirled round, revealing a bearded face and an expression more of despondency than menace. Slowly he stood up, stiffening into an erect, military stance and spreading his arms wide to signify that he would not resist.

In a thick accent he gave his name as Francis Gasparini and went on to admit that he was an escaped convict. He and a companion, he said, had managed to steal a boat and get away from the hellish French penal settlement on the Pacific island of Nou, New Caledonia, one thousand miles north-west of New Zealand. They had succeeded in reaching Auckland and slipping ashore unobserved a few days ago. While his companion remained in hiding, Gasparini had searched in vain for work and accommodation, sheltering in the empty house meanwhile.

The detective was sympathetic: New Caledonia's reputation was well known to New Zealanders. Convinced that Gasparini was telling the truth, he told him he might stay in the house for the rest of the night, but must report to the police station next day, more for his own good than as an offender. Gasparini obeyed and, on arriving at the police station, was painfully astonished to be placed under arrest.

It transpired that his fellow escaper had given himself up to the police the previous evening and had told all, slanting his story in a way damaging to Gasparini, whom he described scornfully as an embezzler, defrauder and receiver of stolen goods, while he himself, Remi Philibert Lamfrey Cury, aged fifty, was simply an unfortunate bankrupt, unjustly sentenced to a penal settlement where he was compelled to mix with common criminals. Twice he had tried to get away and twice been betrayed. In desperation, he had swallowed his natural revulsion for a man of Gasparini's type and teamed up with him for one more attempt.

Together, they had broken away from the prison settlement and hidden on the island for nearly a month before seeing their chance to wade out to a 16-foot yacht.

Plenty of hazards awaited them. Time after time they tried to take their small craft through the reef encircling the island and at every attempt had to veer away sharply as the thin hull scraped the coral. They then returned the yacht to its mooring, waded back to land and climbed a small mountain from where, when daylight came, they could look down on the reef and see clearly the opening they had missed. Without waiting for dark, they returned to the yacht and sailed successfully out into the open Pacific — to be greeted almost at once by a sudden south-westerly storm which carried away the rigging and jib, smashed the rudder, soaked their scanty provisions into useless pulp and upset their water container.

The storm continued for three days, leaving them too exhausted from hunger and the battering they had suffered even to bail out their nearly swamped craft. Then, as she delights in doing, the Pacific suddenly tired of raging and went to sleep. Day after day, as the sea slumbered, a dead flat calm held the maimed little craft motionless and by the seventh day the two emaciated men were almost wishing they had stayed to endure the brutalities of convict life.

Then, before starvation and exposure killed them or sent them mad enough to jump overboard, a breeze sprang up. Hastily rigging a makeshift sail, they ran before the freshening wind and soon had the good fortune to be sighted by the sailing ship *Howard* of Melbourne. Her captain took in their situation at a glance. He had heard all the stories of the "Devil's Islands" of the French penal system and had no doubt that the two gaunt figures who stared beseechingly up at him from their small craft were not sailing about the Pacific for the good of their health. He took them aboard, ordered the yacht to be sunk, and resumed his passage to New Zealand. The crew shared his sentiments. By the time the *Howard* reached Auckland, seventeen days later, the two escapers had regained their strength and everyone looked the other way when they slipped ashore and vanished.

This was the story told by Cury, whose weedy frame, grizzled whiskers and doleful countenance contrasted markedly with Gasparini's manly, almost noble, bearing. But the Auckland police had no alternative but hold them both in custody while the French authorities were notified. As soon as this was done, the French Consul, the Vicomte Alexandre Louis Ferdinand Joffrey d'Abbans, demanded the return of the two prisoners to New Caledonia. They, not unnaturally, begged for asylum in New Zealand, Gasparini pointing out that his return to the penal settlement would mean remaining there for the rest of his days. He had been sentenced in 1883 to eight years, but by attempting to escape four times had earned additional sentences totalling forty years. For this final escape that figure would be doubled and added to the forty, making an accumulated sentence of 120 years in all. Italian settlers in New Zealand heard of the monstrous fate awaiting one of their fellow countrymen and opened a fund to engage counsel to fight for permission for Gasparini, if not for both men, to be allowed to stay.

Despite French protests, the Acting Governor-General of New Zealand, Sir James Prendergast, decided to give the escapers a chance to argue their case before him at Government House on 20 July. A leading barrister, E. G. Jellicoe, attended on the instructions of the Italian community, who were also represented by the Hon. George Fisher, five times mayor of Wellington, who, perhaps not altogether properly, was both a Minister in the New Zealand Government and Consul for Italy. The Vicomte d'Abbans was present for the French Government and several other lawyers were also in attendance at what Sir James Prendergast had determined should be an entirely impartial and fair hearing. Its almost inevitable outcome, however, was that the two men were informed by the Acting Governor-General that, as escapers from penal servitude in French territory, he had no alternative but to order their deportation. He left them one loophole: they would be held in custody for fifteen days, to give them time, if they wished, to apply for writs of *habeas corpus*. When Gasparini asked how he should go about doing this, the Hon. George Fisher intervened to tell him to leave it to him.

In due course the two men appeared in the Supreme Court to hear their plea argued once again. To Cury's delight — not shared by the French Consul — the court ruled that no case for his extradition had been made out. By breaking the French bankruptcy laws he had committed no crime under New Zealand law and could therefore scarcely be deported. On this nice technicality he was set free.

It was clear, in the light of this, that Gasparini's application must fail. The crimes which had earned him his original sentence would have been crimes if committed in New Zealand, too. In vain he described the brutalities he would face if he were returned to New Caledonia and the lingering death which must be his fate. He would, he declared, prefer to be executed on the spot. There were few present who remained unmoved by the court's inescapable decision that he be returned to the penal settlement by the first available ship.

The steamer *Wakatipu* was due to sail on 11 August for Sydney, from where Gasparini would be transferred to a smaller vessel bound for New Caledonia and living death. The detective who had found him in the empty house four months earlier went as his escort. A big crowd saw them embark, amongst whom stood the bearded figure of the Hon. George Fisher. If any of those around him could have read the thoughts in the Cabinet Minister's mind as he watched quietly with them they would almost certainly have been in for a considerable shock.

The triumphant French Consul, Vicomte d'Abbans, was determined that the desperate Gasparini should not avoid the grim future awaiting him and approached Detective Walker on the quayside, urging him to have his prisoner put in handcuffs and leg-irons while the ship was in sight of the New Zealand and Australian coasts. Walker politely told him he considered it unnecessary.

Six days later a frenzied Vicomte d'Abbans was in a position to say, "I told you so!" A cabled report from Sydney, prominent in all the New Zealand newspapers, gave the news that the *Wakatipu* had arrived in Australian waters — without Gasparini.

Detective Walker, the report went on, had seen the Italian safely into bed the night before the ship was due to berth. When he looked in later to check, Gasparini's bed was empty. The purser was able to tell the detective that he had seen his prisoner walking the deck not long before.

With the ship's carpenter, who knew every smallest place in which a desperate man might find concealment, Walker searched the ship from stem to stern: no Gasparini. On arrival at Sydney, every disembarking passenger and crew member was scrutinized, and a watch kept to make sure that no one sneaked on to the wharf after dark: no Gasparini. When the ship sailed on round the coast to Newcastle, Detective Walker was still aboard her to carry out yet another complete search:

still no Gasparini. It seemed there could be no doubt that rather than face convict life again he had slipped overboard that night before the ship reached Sydney and drowned in the Tasman Sea.

Vicomte d'Abbans' fury was monumental. He made the affair into a full-scale diplomatic fracas by complaining to the New Zealand Government that the Consul for Italy, the Hon. George Fisher, had used his influence as a Cabinet Minister to ensure that Gasparini would be inefficiently guarded during the voyage, thus enabling him to take the way out he had chosen for himself.

Fisher retaliated vigorously, accusing the Frenchman of making trumped-up accusations. The Vicomte replied with equal spirit; and so the correspondence, vituperative yet diplomatically phrased, swung back and forth, until Fisher had the shrewd idea of sending his opponent nearly into hysteria by publishing all their letters in the Press.

The Vicomte was replaced by M. Lostalot de Bachoue; the Acting Governor-General was relieved by a Governor-General proper, Lord Onslow. One of the latter's earliest acts was to assure the new French Consul of Her Majesty's Government's regret that the Consul for Italy in one of Her Majesty's colonies should have seen fit to make public an exchange of diplomatic correspondence. He trusted that the Frenchman's undoubted tact and feeling for the diplomatic niceties would move him to consider the dispute at an end. M. de Bachoue, not a little relieved, signified that he considered the matter closed.

The case had a double sequel. Years after Gasparini's disappearance, a letter bearing his signature reached the Hon. George Fisher, informing him that the writer was living happily in the United States where he had gone soon after being smuggled ashore from the *Wakatipu* at Sydney in a crate made specially for him by the carpenter who had helped the detective search every hole and corner for the vanished man.

Just how genuine the letter and the details in it were is uncertain. Just how much Detective John Walker had known of, or co-operated in, an escape plan he never revealed. Just how much the Hon. George Fisher was involved never emerged either. But the Italian Government created him a Chevalier of the Order of the Crown of Italy — for his devoted work on behalf of Italian nationals living in, or passing through, New Zealand.

A more recent disappearance from a ship, and a mystery which, after more than a quarter of a century, remains unsolved, also has Auckland for its setting.

If the man who disappeared from the liner *Dominion Monarch*, then a troopship anchored in Auckland Harbour, is alive today — and there is no evidence to suggest that he is not — then he is middle-aged and probably named something other than Dick Humphrys. We hope life has gone well for him, for as Dick Humphrys he was more a victim of circumstances than a criminal.

He was born in England in 1919, the son of an Army officer and his New Zealand wife. Soon after, the family went to New Zealand to settle on a farm and wait for a large inheritance.

As a boy, Dick Humphrys showed abundant signs of the restlessness that was to land him in so much trouble as a man, also revealing an early taste for disappearing. He played truant often and would sometimes leave home for several days at a time. Surprisingly, boarding school succeeded in taming him temporarily and turning him into a keen pupil and head prefect until the end of his schooling coincided with the long-awaited arrival of the inheritance. His parents took him back to

England, but a brief taste of circumscribed English life made him persuade them to let him return to New Zealand. He had not been back long, working on a number of farms, before war broke out. Unable to get home to enlist, he volunteered for the New Zealand Army.

Hanging around a depot in New Zealand with little to do proved too much for his restless nature and he absented himself without leave, living as a casual farm worker and travelling from place to place on an old motorcycle, until friends persuaded him, for his own good, to give himself up. He did, but found a cell at Trentham Camp so claustrophobic that he picked the lock and escaped within forty-eight hours. Arrested at Auckland, he was placed in the guard-room of Freeman's Bay camp. The wooden building stood on a jetty. When he saw a moment's chance, Humphrys made the first of his sea escapes by clambering down a jetty pile and swimming to the shore. He was free for only a few days, but in that time committed his first civil crime. At an Auckland magistrates' court he was savagely sentenced to two years' reformative detention for stealing an old lumber jacket, valued at £2, from a wash-house.

The journey to the detention centre was by train. Just before they were due to arrive, Humphrys asked his guards' permission to go to the lavatory. They stood up, preparing to accompany him, when Humphrys leaped through the carriage door, slammed it in their faces, and swung himself out and up on to the roof. He worked his way along the carriage tops to the rear of the train, ready to jump off as it slowed down to run into Te Awamutu. Then, while searchers back-tracked along the lines looking for a mangled corpse, he snuggled down between sheep in a railway wagon, and a few days later was in Tauranga, innocently regarding yachts at their moorings.

He selected one named *Jeanette*. Without troubling to conceal what he was doing, he went around buying stores and fuel for a sea voyage, ferrying them out to the yacht of his choice by night. There was no challenge, except from the sea: he had never sailed a boat in his life. With police and aircraft searching for him over the land, he set sail and soon found that, wherever he thought he might be heading, he was not going to get there. Inexperience and the buffeting of a rough sea forced him into Ruatoria, where he was arrested on sight.

At his trial in the Supreme Court at Auckland on 27 March, 1941, Dick Humphrys heard his counsel say of him: "There is no question of any moral weakness in this man. He has no vices in the ordinary sense of the word... I suggest this is a form of claustrophobia. All the escapes have tied up with his desire to be out of confinement or discipline." Mr. Justice Blair agreed with this view. Sentencing Humphrys to a total of eighteen months' imprisonment for three charges of theft and one of escaping, he endorsed counsel's opinion that inquiry should be made into the two years' sentence for stealing an old jacket. Public sympathy, too, was with Humphrys, but after he had served five months of his sentence in Mount Eden jail, Auckland, he heard that a petition for his release had been rejected. He decided to grant his own remission, put on a pair of dungarees he found in a shed in a warder's garden where he was working, and simply walked away to freedom.

During the next six months he worked his way almost the length of New Zealand, from Auckland, near the top of the North Island, to Invercargill, near the bottom of South Island. At Invercargill he chose the sea once more, this time with astonishing success. Selecting a 27-foot auxiliary launch, he openly loaded it with stores and fuel, sometimes assisted by unwitting onlookers. Then, with a book on navigation to show him how, he achieved the staggering feat for a single-handed novice of crossing the Tasman, one of the world's most treacherous seas, arriving at a beach on Tasmania on 14 February, 1942. He had covered some 1,500 miles in nineteen days.

He was arrested by the first policeman he met.

With wartime delays in finding transportation back to New Zealand, a strong movement arose among the Tasmanian public on Dick Humphrys' behalf. A lawyer was retained to urge that instead of being extradited he should be allowed to enlist in the armed forces in Tasmania. The owner of the stolen launch would be compensated by public subscription. The Tasmanian Government could not, of course, accede to any such request, but a recommendation to the New Zealand Government to show mercy to Humphrys was signed by no less than Tasmania's Lieutenant-Governor, Premier, Leader of the Opposition, and the Mayor and Archdeacon of the island's capital, Hobart, as well as many others. It read, in part:

> ...Reports published in the Press have convinced us that the extreme severity of this punishment (*for stealing the lumber jacket*) has been a contributing cause to all subsequent offences.
>
> Your petitioners and the people of Tasmania generally have been deeply stirred to admiration of the accused by the remarkable feat of courage and endurance performed by him in crossing the Tasman Sea alone in a small yacht and they venture to suggest that if generous pardon could be given the accused for past offences the course of his life may be diverted from one of crime into a useful channel.

The *Dominion Monarch*, on a trooping run, carried Dick Humphrys and his escorting detective to Auckland, arriving early on the morning of 13 June, 1942. Then Humphrys learned that the Tasmanian petition had failed to persuade the New Zealand Government not to take action against him. He did not wait to be taken ashore. At 2.15 a.m., wearing only a white singlet and blue trousers, he sprang from his escort's side, dashed across the deck and took a flying leap over the rail to plunge seventy feet to the cold, dark waters of the Waitemata. The detective, running to peer over the rail, could see nothing.

From that day Dick Humphreys has never been seen — or, at least, not officially. A few people claim to have met him at various times. One of them, a journalist, asserted in a book that he had talked with Humphrys who had told how he had swum to safety that night, after which he had found work on a remote New Zealand farm while planning to make yet another Tasman crossing.

Did he make the crossing? Did he endeavour to do so, and fall a victim this time to the Tasman's treacherous wiles? Did he drown that night in Auckland Harbour?

Or is he still alive to read this account?

A more romantic story, worthy of an operatic libretto to itself, is that of "John Orth". Those who want a full account of this remarkable man can find it, in German, in the British Museum. He was born a member of one of the most famous of Royal families, the Habsburgs.

His father was Leopold II, Grand Duke of Tuscany, his mother Maria Antonia of Sicily. The child born to them in 1852 was given the resounding names of Johann Nepomuck Salvator; Archduke by title. Leopold was a mild ruler, given to appeasement and the peaceful development of the state rather than to warmongering, which was probably the reason why he found himself deposed when Johann was seven. There were three older boys, Ferdinand, Louis and Charles.

From sunny Tuscany Johann was translated to the cooler and more stimulating climate of Vienna. It suited him. Vienna in the reign of the Emperor Franz Josef resembled the London of Doctor Johnson — it held everything that life could afford, especially if you were young, romantic, gifted and the Emperor's cousin. The sleepy Alt-Wien of earlier days was giving way to the splendid, lushly romantic city that has inspired so many musical comedies. Great buildings were going up, classical statuary abounded, beautiful gardens were laid out. Archduke Johann enjoyed it all, particularly the nights he spent at the Opera House and the Burgtheater. His gift for music (plus his influential connections) enabled him to have an opera performed and a waltz played for the delight of Viennese society. Neither piece rivalled the works of Strauss and neither has survived.

Johann was not solely a drawing-room type. Strong and manly, he enjoyed soldiering as much as theatre-going. By the age of twenty-nine he was a general, resplendent in brilliant uniform.

One of his best friends was his cousin Rudolf, the Emperor's son, a strange young man of fitful talents and unconventional ideas, whose tragic death in the hunting-lodge of Mayerling was to shock Europe.

Perhaps it was the influence of Rudolf which led Johann into the paths of non-conformism. At any rate, he got himself into the Emperor's bad books by publishing a sharp criticism of the Austrian Army's brass-hats. Less and less was Johann welcome at court. This did not dismay him, however. He now preferred to spend his time at the theatre. Following the Emperor's own example with the actress Katharine Schratt, Johann himself acquired a mistress from the theatre — the beautiful and fascinating Ludmilla Streubel.

Now he gave up soldiering and turned his thoughts to the sea. Whatever he did, he did thoroughly. Soon he knew all a man needed to know to sail a ship; in fact, he gained a master's licence. This was the life, he felt. He abandoned the Habsburg name and all connection with the court, and rechristened himself John Orth: the Orth was the name of a château in Switzerland belonging to his mother's family. He fitted out a ship, the *Sainte Marguerite*, and in 1889, with Ludmilla Streubel aboard, sailed to London. Next year, alone, he engaged Captain Sodich to act as master to the *Sainte Marguerite* on a voyage to South America. This time Ludmilla was not to go with him — she would follow.

Their reunion took place at Buenos Aires. From here they were to sail to Valparaiso. Valparaiso and Buenos Aires are almost exactly opposite each other, on the west and east coasts of South America, not a great distance apart by land, but widely separated by sea. People who were with him in Buenos Aires said that he made some very odd remarks before he sailed. "I shall die, yet live. Don't think I'm dead, just because you don't see me any more." His crew, hearing these wild statements, were no doubt relieved to find themselves discharged. With new men and no trained officers he embarked on the voyage. As they sailed from Buenos Aires Ludmilla stood beside him on the deck. They were a handsome pair, with something exalted and strange about them.

The *Sainte Marguerite* never reached Valparaiso, nor was anything seen of her or anybody aboard her again.

Had "John Orth" a mystic premonition of disaster? Did he see himself as a new Flying Dutchman? What lure drew him to sea at all, from a background so far removed from it?

The most likely explanation, in the view of the present authors, is that Archduke Johann shared the morbid romanticism of his friend Rudolf. To Rudolf, a death shared by his forbidden beloved, Marie Vetsera, proved preferable to life without her. The Mayerling tragedy had happened in 1889, the year "John Orth" had bought the *Sainte Marguerite*. He may well have done so with the deliberate intention of scuttling her and enjoying a highly romantic double suicide with Ludmilla. Not that there was any reason why he should not marry her, as he had renounced his royal connections; in fact there were rumours that they had been married in London. But the Habsburg mind was a strange one, and "John Orth" one of the strangest Habsburgs who ever lived.

That he ever died was never proved. For many years claimants came forward saying that they were the lost Archduke. None of them put forward a very convincing case.

Perhaps a ghostly three-master still rounds the Horn on misty nights, and the dark eyes of a beautiful actress still look out to sea, as unfathomable as the ocean itself.

25: A GHASTLY CREW

The tale of the *Mary Celeste* is famous. Less well known, but more macabre, is that of the *Marlborough*, a merchant vessel of Glasgow, occurring eighteen years later.

For all her fine military name, the *Marlborough* carried a mild enough cargo — sheep — and a number of passengers. She sailed from Lyttelton in the South Island of New Zealand on a pleasant day in January, 1890, under Captain Hird. She was manned by a competent crew: there was no reason why she should not reach England in the scheduled time. She was sighted off the Straits of Magellan on the date when she was expected to arrive there. At home, relatives waited. But no further news came of the *Marlborough* and from the day she steamed out of sight of Chile she was neither seen nor heard of again.

A year and three months passed. At home, hope had been given up for her crew and passengers. A special inquiry was set up, but in spite of the telegraphic and other communications which were in wide use by this time, no more could be discovered of her. The *Marlborough* was officially written off as "lost with all hands". In many a church a tablet with no grave commemorated someone who had sailed with her. It is always more harrowing not to know the fate of a missing person than to have sure and certain evidence of it. That evidence was to come to light at length, but not until many of the relatives themselves were dead. For the *Marlborough* was eventually found — twenty-three years after her disappearance — and all those who had sailed in her were still aboard.

It was on 3 November, 1913, that off Tierra del Fuego, at the southernmost tip of South America, the British sailing-ship *Johnston* saw what appeared to be a large three-masted vessel in trouble. Signals produced no reply from her and the skipper gave orders to approach. As they drew nearer, the crew began to mutter with surprise. For she was a green ship — mast, rigging and woodwork were all green. Some of the superstitious among the sailors crossed themselves, nor were their fears lessened when they were near enough to see that the over-all colour was caused by seaweed and mould.

The master and some of the crew lowered a boat and rowed to the ship which was rocking gently and steadily. Details became clear — rotting ropes, a salt-corroded boat: every sign that she was a long-abandoned derelict. As they rowed under her stem the master looked up. Beneath the smothering crust of green could be read the words: MARLBOROUGH GLASGOW. He had found the ship that so many had searched for during nearly a quarter of a century.

With difficulty, for her woodwork was slippery and rotten, the men climbed aboard, only to recoil with cries of horror. The spongy, decaying decks were covered with skeletons. One lay under the wheel, as if his hands had held it to the last. A heap of bones on the poop proved to be the remains of three people, and seventeen more were found in the wardroom and fo'c'sle. A smaller skeleton lay on a cabin floor among the tattered remnants of a dress, a coil of long dark hair spread underneath the skull. It was all that remained of the *Marlborough*'s one woman passenger. The bones of many sheep littered the hold like dried twigs in a forest.

The captain ordered a thorough search of the vessel for clues to the mystery. But though the ship's log was found, it was rotted and indecipherable and all other papers had been destroyed. Not a single piece of evidence remained to show where the ship had been during those twenty-three years, how she had weathered heavy seas, winds, storms and currents without a crew in waters which needed fine seamanship and a high degree of control. Nor could it ever be discovered how crew and passengers had come to lie where they had fallen, like the stricken inhabitants of the Sleeping Beauty's palace. Had they died of some virulent epidemic, or of poison? Had they, even, been murdered by pirates for what valuables they carried? Nobody will ever know what terrible stroke of Fate turned the strong, confident *Marlborough* into a floating graveyard.

Less gruesome, but no less strange, is the story of the *Everest Webster*. An American schooner, she had been wrecked early in 1907 and had become one of those floating derelicts which menace living ships.

She had almost foundered, but not quite. A bit of her stern could be seen sticking out of the water — a useful guide to the vessels which went out to sink her, except that for some reason they never succeeded.

It was in March of the same year that the four-master *Quevilly* sighted her. Recognizing her, the master sent a boat to investigate. With some difficulty an officer boarded the wreck, followed by a handful of the crew. They waded through water on deck as far as the after-cabin, of which the door had jammed, swollen with damp. With combine pressure they managed to force it.

They fell back at what they saw inside. On bunks lay a number of corpses, ghastly-faced and open-eyed. The officer approached one — and it moved! One after another, the dead-looking forms began to stir, tried to speak. It was a terrible moment for the men from the *Quevilly*, for how could they believe that these were living creatures, after the derelict had been afloat for so long?

But that was the case. With fantastic power of survival they had kept alive on hope. Now, starved, cold-racked and half-crazed, they were as overcome to see their rescuers as their rescuers were to see them. When they had partly recovered from their dreadful state, the *Quevilly*'s captain asked them what had happened to the *Everest Webster*. But neither then nor subsequently could any of them tell a coherent tale, and to this day nobody knows what their experiences had been.

The case of the *Zebrina*, a small cargo-vessel, was a curious and sinister mystery in the same category as the *Mary Celeste*.

On the face of it, no mystery existed. The *Zebrina* was found drifting off Cherbourg in 1917. She had all sail set, but no living thing was aboard her. Tables were laid for the crew's meal, said the newspaper report of her finding, and it added that the men who had been aboard her were presumed to have fallen victim to the Germans. A memorial was raised to them at Trinity House, London.

But fourteen years later, David Masters, an indefatigable searcher after the sea's secrets, put in some detective work which threw rather a different light on the matter and published his findings in his book, *When Ships Go Down*. He began by proving that the *Zebrina* had been found as described. There, sure enough, was the official Admiralty report. But he could not find her name in the list of war casualties. Finally it came to light in a subsidiary list, which, Masters learnt, was because her case had been a doubtful one.

Finding that she was still afloat, he traced her owners, who were in no doubt that she had been a war casualty. Then another contact added a few details to the original newspaper notice. This man, who had known both the ship and her master, said that he was not sure whether a meal had been partly prepared when she was found. But the table had been laid, and the galley fire was burning, from which it was certain that the crew had not long left the ship. To the question "Were all sails set?" Masters' informant replied vaguely that she was "just flapping about" in a mirror-like sea.

Then a new piece of evidence turned up. It was the log of the *Zebrina*, which had been found aboard her. Masters studied it: the names of the crew, the little ship's calls at Appledore in Devon, and Swansea in South Wales. He eliminated the possibility of her having sailed in cargo as she made for the port of St. Brieuc, where she was to unload, from Falmouth, her last port of call.

Here he came to a stop — until a new thought struck him, and he investigated the incidence of damage done by German submarines between the northern coast of France and the southern coast of England around the time of the *Zebrina*'s disappearance. The results were interesting. Seven vessels, including a trawler, had been sunk in two days. This meant that the *Zebrina* had been sailing dangerous waters, where U-boats lurked like sharks. She might very easily have fallen a prey to one of them.

But if so, why did they not sink her? Why take the crew off and leave the ship and her valuable log, which would prove their claim to have captured her, untouched? Perhaps the crew *had* been taken prisoner. But a submarine has little room for extra men and there was no report of the *Zebrina*'s crew ever having reached Germany. Possibly the submarine had been sunk by the British. But there was no report of any such happening around the time when the *Zebrina* was found.

Masters was again baffled, but his detective instinct would not let him rest. Turning again to the *Zebrina*'s log and to the account he had received of her "flapping about" in a calm sea, he compared this with meteorological records which told of continuous bad weather about the time she was leaving Falmouth — heavy rain and wind blowing up to a gale. The ship was fully loaded and would have been hard put to it to fight such seas. Perhaps the crew had been swept overboard.

At the same time, he discovered that the ship's lifeboat had remained aboard her — and this was the only means by which the crew could have been conveyed to a submarine; also that her register, which like the log was highly desirable to captors, had not been missing. It was all further evidence against the submarine theory.

Masters now felt fairly certain that a storm, and not enemy action, had disposed of the missing men. A great gale and a wall of water must have swept them from the deck, torn the helmsman from the wheel, the captain from the bridge, washed the hands overboard as they fought uselessly with the elements.

In his own words: "Struggling all day under these conditions saps the strength of the strongest; men grow utterly worn out, cold, wet, wretched... I can imagine a great wave with irresistible force sweeping the man from the wheel into eternity; another brave fellow rushing to steady the schooner, being caught and knocked senseless by tons of water which drove him on and over in a moment; the others, shocked by the tragedy, releasing their grip of the rigging to attempt to get to the wheel; the sails cracking like gunshots, the wind howling, the seas boiling over the deck. I see a wall of water curl over on a struggling man, a bigger wave thundering down to engulf the survivors, the ship healing under, then shaking herself free — and the tragedy is complete."

It is the only satisfactory explanation. As to the set tables and the burning galley fire, we shall not stay for an answer.

26: "MY LIFE FROM CORRUPTION": THE ORDEAL OF JONAH

Once upon a time God summoned the prophet Jonah to go and prophesy against the great, wicked city of Nineveh. But Jonah was afraid and instead took ship to Tarshish. As he lay asleep below hatches, a great storm sprang up. To lighten the ship, the terrified crew cast overboard everything they could lay hold of, praying fervently as they did so. Then the master stumbled across Jonah and called on him to awake and pray with them.

Jonah awoke and the men questioned him, where he came from and who he was. When they heard that he was flying from the Lord's Command, they were full of fear and cried that he had brought the storm upon them. Calmly, Jonah told them to sacrifice him by throwing him overboard. But they would not do this before they had first tried to reach land by rowing their hardest. At last, begging God to forgive them, they did as Jonah had asked and threw him into the sea. And at once the sea ceased from raging.

> *Now the Lord had prepared a great fish to swallow up Jonah. And Jonah was in the belly of the fish three days and three nights.*
>
> *Inside the fish Jonah prayed and praised God for having saved him from the deep waters.*
>
> *"For thou hadst cast me into the deep, in the midst of the seas; and the floods compassed me about; all thy billows and thy waves passed over me...*
>
> *I went down to the bottoms of the mountains; the earth with her bars was about me for ever; yet hast thou brought up my life from corruption, O Lord my God."*

And the Lord spake unto the fish, and it vomited out Jonah upon the dry land.

The terrible ordeal and deliverance of Jonah has been dismissed by some Biblical commentators as symbolism, Jonah standing for Israel and the fish for her enemies. Others have seen it as Hebrew folklore. The obscure term "great fish" is usually taken to mean a whale, though it could also apply to a sea serpent — the Leviathan referred to in the Book of Isaiah and the Book of Job. Either interpretation makes the episode appear to be one of the Old Testament's taller stories.

But is it? Some Biblical "miracles" that were laughed at in the past have been duplicated since. And at least two happenings recorded in more recent times indicate that Jonah's adventure was not impossible, however fantastic it may seem.

Edward Rowe Snow, recorder of so many strange stories of the sea, found at Cape Cod, Massachusetts, one of the strangest. It was in March, 1863, that Peleg Nye, a whaler, leant too far over the side of a longboat — and dropped, like a plum from a tree, into the jaws of a great sperm whale. The whale was not waiting for Peleg. It is the habit of the species to swim along with open mouth to catch plankton. No doubt it was surprised to find that it had caught something more substantial than the tiny marine animals and plants that were its normal fare. Automatically it closed its jaws, catching Peleg somewhere above the ankles, and took him, struggling frantically, down through the waves.

It is not clear whether Peleg's shipmates saw this happen. But after his disappearance over the side they stayed around to retrieve him, or his body. A few anxious moments passed, then a shout went up. He had surfaced and was floating limply, apparently dead. The longboatmen rowed alongside and hauled him in. To their relief he was not drowned, but unconscious.

When he recovered he told his mates what had happened, so far as he could understand it himself. Shock and the effect of being pulled suddenly under the water had made him unconscious. Only great good luck had sent him upwards when the whale released him, instead of down like a stone to the bottom.

The most curious feature of the whole episode was that not long after Peleg had been rescued another body appeared on the surface. It was the whale — quite dead. The tale does not say that the whalers had attacked it previously, so what had killed it? Peleg, watching the great lifeless body bobbing on the waves, must have thought himself a fantastically lucky person, though it is unlikely that an echo of Goldsmith's famous lines crossed his mind:

> *The man recovered from the bite*
> *The whale it was that died.*

A more gruesome story, almost incredible, is told of another whaler, in 1891. The French newspaper which published an account of it five years later checked it again and again for accuracy, and the American twentieth-century magazine *Stag* regarded it as a true event.

The whaling ship *Star of the East* was combing equatorial waters in search of victims. The intensive slaughter of the sperm whale had gone on for so long that the species was dying out. In 1844, the United States alone was using 315 whaling ships to track down the creature that yields precious sperm oil and ambergris. The harmless monster — its diet is mainly plankton and cuttlefish — does not attack humans, has no weapons of defence, and is hampered from the start by its unwieldy size, the male animal often being as much as sixty-three feet long and enormous in circumference. The old hand-

277

harpoon had, by 1891, been supplemented by the use of the harpoon gun, so that the whale's attackers could pierce its hide from a distance, no longer in danger of being capsized by the agonized threshing of the creature's tail. For all his puny size, Man has the advantage over Whale every time, and each whaling expedition is virtually a Massacre of the Innocents. The nineteenth-century whaling man, revelling in the bloody killing and dissection of his prey, then going home to spend his profits in drunken orgies before returning joyously to the hunt, is possibly the least attractive of all seamen. He turned a trade into a blood sport, and liked to combine whaling with sealing — the ruthless murder of the mothers and babies of the gentlest of all sea creatures. We have never heard the jolly chant of the men who have killed, squandered, wenched, and now

> *To Greenland go for more, brave boys,*
> *To Greenland go for more!*

without reflecting that sometimes, by the law of averages, the poor whale must have his revenge.

And so it was in the case of James Bartley.

He was probably a brave man, no worse than anybody else aboard the *Star of the East*. Unlike Jonah, he does not seem to have personally provoked Divine wrath. He was coxswain of one of the *Star*'s boats on the day she sighted a sperm whale. Out went the boats, racing each other to reach the creature already wounded by a harpoon-gun. Bartley, standing up in the boat, poised his hand-harpoon, and the whale, "insane with pain", says the account, made blindly towards him. It charged the boat, and Bartley fell — into the whale's open mouth. The immense jaws closed, and a shocked boatload watched as whale and man vanished beneath the water, as whale and man had vanished when Peleg Nye met a kinder fate. The crew were too horrified and disheartened to pursue the hunt. A whale's death was sport, but a man's was a different matter. As Jonah's shipmates had probably hastened from the scene, they rowed rapidly back to their ship.

Refreshed, no doubt, by rum all round, they resumed whaling later in the day. It was the next morning when the body of a whale was seen boating near the vessel. He was a huge, well-developed male and his blubber would be a rich prize — it is said that he weighed about 100 tons. The horrible business of removing the blubber took two days. At the end of it the stripped corpse was left, of no further interest to anybody: except to one man — or boy, for accounts differ. Thinking back two days, he suggested that this might be the swallower of James Bartley. There was a harpoon wound at the point where the whale had been struck. It seemed a wild idea, but just in case there might be some substance to it the dissecting team once more set to work with their reeking knives. Theirs was not a pleasant or easy job. But at last they had cut through flesh and muscle to the stomach of the whale. Within it was a great mass of shrimps which poured out when the incision was made — and something else — the shape of a man.

With indescribable feelings, they worked like fiends to remove it in a dreadful parody of a gigantic Caesarean operation. Soon they could reach and drag it free. Yes, it was their comrade Bartley. But at first he was unrecognizable, for he was steeped from head to foot in the whale's blood and "purple", as the account graphically states. His face was a mask of horror.

But, unbelievably, he was alive. They worked on him for five hours. When his eyes opened at last, they were blank — then grew wild. His limbs began to thresh and he struck out with his fists at the men around him, raving incoherently. There was nothing for it but to tie him to the bunk he lay on. There he remained, babbling of a burning fiery furnace, of flames that consumed him. A whale's body is hotter than a man's, for it is a warm-blooded mammal, not a fish, and the temperature within its stomach, to one confined there, would be that of an oven.

At last Bartley regained his senses. He was washed, given restoratives and was able to talk. This is his own account of what had happened.

> I remember very well from the moment that I jumped from the boat and felt my feet strike some soft substance. I looked up and saw a big-ribbed canopy of light pink and white descending over me, and the next moment I felt myself drawn downward, feet first, and I realized that I was being swallowed by a whale. I was drawn lower and lower; a wall of flesh surrounded me and hemmed me in on every side, yet the pressure was not painful, and the flesh easily gave way like soft india-rubber before my slightest movement.
>
> Suddenly I found myself in a sack much larger than my body, but completely dark. I felt about me; and my hand came in contact with several fishes, some of which seemed to be still alive, for they squirmed in my fingers, and slipped back to my feet. Soon I felt a great pain in my head, and my breathing became more and more difficult. At the same time I felt a terrible heat; it seemed to consume me, growing hotter and hotter. My eyes became coals of fire in my head, and I believed every moment that I was condemned to perish in the belly of a whale. It tormented me beyond all endurance, while at the same time the awful silence of the terrible prison weighed me down. I tried to rise, to move my arms and legs, to cry out. All action was now impossible, but my brain

seemed abnormally clear; and with a full comprehension of my awful fate, I finally lost all consciousness.

It is hardly surprising that after this, the apotheosis of all solitary confinement, Bartley could not bear to be left alone. When he got back on shore he refused ever to go aboard again or to look seawards. He had had one of the most awful traumatic experiences it is possible to imagine.

Or had he? Was it all a very good horror story, to add to the shore income of the crew in between expeditions? They made sworn testimonials to its truth, but many oaths have been taken with crossed fingers. One may accept that Bartley may have remained alive because the whale's digestion could not cope with him and because it died before its body heat could stifle him altogether. But how his lungs functioned with no air at all going into them is something scientists have not been able to explain. It is a suspicious coincidence that his imprisonment was about the same length as Jonah's. If his mind was strong — and it must have been so for him to have remained sane — the body that went with it can only have been superhuman.

There is a more recent story of another terrible captivity, that of Hans Engellandt, master of the schooner *Erndte* of Hamburg, who in 1910 survived twelve days of being trapped in the hold of his capsized ship while she floated helplessly off the coast of Prussia. He was in none too good a state when a Norwegian ship rescued him — and he had had a certain amount of oxygen, some food, brandy and a keg of water, not to mention a lamp. The permanent claustrophobia with which those twelve days left him can have been nothing to the hell that haunted the mind of James Bartley.

If...

27: THE MYSTERY OF THE MISSING CREW

When the American schooner *Sarah W. Hunt* sailed cautiously into Lyttelton, New Zealand, on 8 December, 1883, port officials who went down to greet her got the shock of their lives. The 88-foot, 116-ton vessel was manned by only two men — her captain and her steward.

After they had heard the captain's explanation of how a normal complement of more than a dozen had become reduced to two, they were even more astonished. The entries in the *Sarah W. Hunt*'s log told a tale that seemed almost too remarkable to be true — and before long many were contending that it wasn't.

The *Sarah W. Hunt* had left New Bedford, Massachusetts, six months before with a crew of thirteen, excluding the captain. Most of the sailors were not seamen at all, but young Americans and Germans who felt it wise to leave the United States for a time until personal difficulties of one kind and another had been overcome. They included a stove moulder, a railwayman, an iron founder, a clerk and a chemist's assistant. The master was Captain Sanford Stoddard Miner, a tyrant of the first water, whom one American writer suggested later could be classed with Jack London's ruthless sealing skipper, Captain Larsen, of the *Sea Wolf*.

The original sailing plan was to touch at the Azores and then sail round the Horn and across the Pacific to Campbell Island, several hundred miles south of New Zealand. Instead, the vessel sailed south along the west coast of Africa and around the Cape of Good Hope, then around the south of Australia to Campbell Island.

There were several incidents on the way, recorded in the sometimes quaint English of the German First Mate, Charles Strichert:

> Wednesday, 29 August: First part of this day strong gale, with squally weather, wind hauled round — at 2 p.m. the Second Mate watch hauled to S.W. got all sails aback, parted the main boom tackel and sheet and unshipped the main boom, sum of the men got hurted.

A more serious mishap occurred another day:

> …Stronger squalls and strong breeze. At 8 a.m. Louis Scharffenorth was lost overboard, had to go about but could not find him, went about again and then went on our course.

On 3 October, after they had rounded the Cape, another tragedy occurred:

> At 8 a.m. I sent a man aloft and he fell overboard and by the time we got the boat over he sunk — his name was Julius Jager.

Gale after gale tested the schooner's strength as she beat towards the sealing grounds. They "sited land" on 3 November, and dropped anchor off Macquarie Island later that day. Bad weather delayed them there, but by 20 November they were within sight of Campbell Island.

> Monday, 26 of Novbr.: This day light wind from the north — in the morning sent Boat out and scrubbed out hold, after dat histed Fore and Main sails and Topsails for to dry — in the afternoon Kaptain me and second Mate mended sails — sah a

Seal long side the Vessel, in the evening I went with my boat to look for him sah him and shot him but sank like a stone — after waiten till 9 p.m. went on Board, histed Boat in and dat ended this day. Pumps attended to.

That was the last entry Charles Strichert ever made in the log of the *Sarah W. Hunt.* He prepared the heading for the next day's entry, but never got a chance to write it. From 27 November on, the mystery of the *Sarah W. Hunt* was recorded in the hand of Captain Miner himself.

While lying at anchor, the Port and Starboard boats left the vessel with orders to search inshore for seals, a light breeze then blowing from the N.W., the Port Boat being in charge of the first Mate and five Seamen and the Starboard boat of the second Mate and five Seamen. Taking no provisions but with the intention of returning to the vessel for dinner or shortly thereafter, leaving the Steward and Captain in charge of the vessel.

During the day no fear was felt for their safety although the weather became more squally towards afternoon and a succession of heavy squalls came down during the night...

There being plenty of creeks and inlets around the island it was naturally supposed that they had put into one of them to wait till morning when they could have made for the vessel where they could have arrived during the day.

28th. Not having returned by noon of the second day great anxiety was felt for their safety and preparation was made to go in search of them but being only two men on board it was difficult and exceedingly dangerous to undertake anything ... but in the evening we concluded to make the attempt and in the evening reefed the foresail and made everything ready to start at break of day.

They were unable to move until 30 November, and after seeing nothing of the missing boats they set the flying jib and headed for New Zealand on 2 December. They were lucky to strike good weather for those treacherous southern waters, and reached Lyttelton without trouble, a remarkably good feat of seamanship for one sailor and a steward.

In port the steward refused to work any more, abused the captain roundly and stamped off on shore. When he returned he was drunk, in which condition he remained for most of the Christmas period. On 28 December Captain Miner handed him over to the police for absenting himself without leave.

An inquiry into the loss of the *Sarah W. Hunt*'s crew, at which the captain repeated the account appearing in his logbook, failed to satisfy some members of the public. Two days later the Christchurch Chamber of Commerce held a meeting to urge the Government to send a vessel in search of the missing men and offered to subscribe the cost of hiring a suitable ship.

The Government steamer *Stella* was sent and within a few days was back at Port Chalmers with the second mate of the *Sarah W. Hunt* and five members of her crew.

When found, only two of them had been able to stand; the rest were almost dead from privation. Nothing had been seen of the second boat.

The second mate reported that a gale had sprung up after the two boats left the schooner, blowing them apart and well away from land. For two days his boat was almost out of sight of land, then it drifted offshore for another five days. There was nothing to eat except 1½lb of bread between six men. A bucket, holding one gallon of fresh water, was knocked over. Reaching the island after a week, they replenished their water, then set off to find the schooner. It had disappeared.

A more sinister note was sounded by a report in the *Lyttelton Times* that the rescued men of the *Sarah W. Hunt* had refused under any circumstances to rejoin their ship.

Then followed a statement by their spokesmen, Tierney and Hertwig, who had an incredible version to give of what had really happened to them at Campbell Island. Captain Miner, they pointed out, had told the authorities that when the two boats were sent ashore he told the men not to hunt seals, as it was the closed season.

In that case, why had he sent them ashore anyway, and why had he ordered sealing gear to be taken?

If the captain and his steward had managed to sail the *Sarah W. Hunt* all the way to New Zealand, why had they not been able to tack about the mouth of the inlet for a few days longer, to give the boats more time to get back?

On the day the schooner left for New Zealand, the second mate's boat had been in sight of the island all day and there could be no justification for concluding that it had disappeared to sea. Their suggestion was plain — they had been deliberately marooned, to fend for themselves on bleak, uninhabited Campbell Island.

The most likely reason for this inhuman action was the failure of the sealing expedition. Rather than face the embarrassment of being unable to pay the crew their overdue wages, Captain Miner had chosen to get rid of them and spin the yarn that they had been lost in a storm.

When Tierney and Hertwig added an account of their captain's vicious character, it did not seem too fantastic after all to believe that he had tried to maroon them.

In his rages he had often laid about him with iron bolts and other weapons. Men injured in storms were forced to continue working and when the second mate dislocated his arm he was allowed no rest.

Once a wooden bucket was lost overboard and the captain put the ship about and searched for two hours until it was found. Yet when Julius Jaeger fell from the rigging into the sea, Captain Miner would not even stop the ship!

In a desperate hurry to save the drowning man, the mate had tried to cut the tackle to save time in launching a boat. The captain had furiously ordered him to launch the boat in the normal way, which delayed the chances of rescue. After ten minutes' searching, Captain Miner recalled the boat and sailed on.

The rescued seamen's claim against the master and owners of the *Sarah W. Hunt* for overdue wages and breach of contract was heard in Christchurch, but it was resolved that the American owners were beyond the jurisdiction of the court and that the captain and the owners were indivisible as defendants.

The crew of the *Sarah W. Hunt* were provided with passages home by the American Consul at Auckland, and their old ship, with Captain Miner still in command and a new crew, sailed on 4 July, 1883, from Auckland for the Horn.

It was not until September, 1886, that she ended her cruise at New London, after sailing right round the world, with three separate crews to work her — and not a sealskin in her holds to show for it all.

The last thing recorded of Captain Miner is that he walked off the ship at Barby wharf, New London.

The affair remains a mystery. Did Captain Miner deliberately try to maroon his crew — or did they see in their misfortune a chance to gain revenge for his tyranny. No inquiry was ever held in America, but the United States Government sent inscribed gold watches to the masters of the New Zealand ships *Kekeno* and *Stella*, associated with the rescue of the castaways.

28: UNLUCKY SHIPS

Some people are accident-prone. If there is a paving stone slightly out of alignment they fall over it and sustain a compound fracture of the tibia. If they are doing some home decorating, they are sure to fall backwards from the ladder instead of descending in the more usual way. If there is a man with smallpox on a bus, they will find themselves sitting next to him.

So it is with ships, the most human of man's creations. From the day her keel is laid a ship develops a marked personality and mysterious tendencies to either good or bad fortune.

Nelson's great ship the *Victory* was lucky — perhaps because she was built in the same year as Nelson's Good Angel, Emma, Lady Hamilton, was born. *Victory* carried famous captains' flags before she became Nelson's flagship in 1803 — those of Hood, Hotham and St. Vincent.

Even today her luck holds — she is the only one of the magnificent British Fleet which fought at Trafalgar to survive. Others became prison hulks and were broken up, their splendid past forgotten. But *Victory* queens it still in dry dock at Portsmouth, the most beautiful of all historic relics

She must have had many companions who were obviously not launched by the right godmothers — like the *Elephant*, which could not be induced to go in the proper direction however skilled its commander and crew, but was more often to be seen lumbering helplessly round and round, like a harassed shopper at sale-time. Nelson among others found this habit of hers perfectly infuriating.

What perverse marine gods rule such ships? And how have such gods been offended? One has only to look at a few records of disasters to be convinced that the naval equivalent of a gremlin is a very active creature.

Many of these incidents belong to the last quarter of the nineteenth century — a vintage period not only for sailing ships, but for sensations of all kinds, besides classic murders. The annals of late-Victorian salvage companies provide fascinating reading. There was the very strange affair of the SS *Newburn*, for instance.

Steaming harmlessly along in the Thames estuary, *Newburn* found herself enveloped in fog. She reduced her speed, and prepared to go carefully. But before anyone aboard knew what was happening there was a nerve-shaking crash. She had rammed another ship. The *Winston*, her victim, promptly rolled over and sank. *Newburn*, badly damaged by the violence of the collision, was beached for safety near the wreck of the *Winston*, while a small guard-boat stood by to warn other shipping.

Towards them, slowly and cautiously in the thick fog, steamed the large, powerful *Erasmus Wilson*. What happened then is not clear. Perhaps the *Erasmus Wilson* heard the guard-boat's warning siren but misjudged her distance from it — perhaps she did not hear the siren at all. At any rate, she crashed straight into the *Newburn* at right angles, bisecting her as cleanly as a carving knife. All three ships — *Winston*, *Newburn* and *Erasmus Wilson* — lay in a heap, totally wrecked.

A case of triple bad luck, perhaps. But *Newburn*, the Jonah of the episode, came off worst. The *Erasmus Wilson* was repaired, at great cost, the *Winston* was sold for £900. The *Newburn* went straight to the "knacker", or ship-breaker, and her two halves fetched £15 and £79 respectively, a humiliating finale, the marine equivalent of a pauper's funeral.

Then there was SS *Daphne*, launched on the north-east coast of England, a tight and trim steamship to all appearances. Like Mary, Queen of Scots, another unfortunate lady, "in her end was her beginning", for at the end of the launching ramp she capsized, drowning 124 workmen who were aboard her.

In spite of the tragedy it was decided to refloat her, and the East Coast Salvage Company got her up by a combination of pumps and pontoons. She was put into the shipyard for repairs, emerged from it as good as new, and was renamed the *Rose*. Sailors do not care for a ship with a bad name: change the name and you change the luck — sometimes. Not in this case.

They got her as far as Londonderry. Barely out of the harbour, she suddenly and unaccountably filled with water. The crew saved themselves, and the *Rose* was once again in the hands of the ship-doctors. They pumped her out and she set off once more on her travels. At Millport the *Rose* broke down yet again: further repairs needed. But this time the owners were too nervous to risk more trouble and money. They sold her.

The new owners re-christened her *Ianthe*, a charming name suggestive of one of the merry nymphs of ancient Greece. They would have done better to have called her Cassandra, for she was no sooner afloat again than she started off on a further career of disasters. Quickly, they too got rid of her.

A Greek firm bought her next — perhaps attracted by the name — but superstition was too strong for them to retain it. They called her the *Eleni*. When last heard of she was giving trouble near Smyrna, and her final fate is unrecorded. Perhaps it is better so.

More sensational was the affair of the *Micronesia*. Steaming innocently off the Kent coast, near the South Foreland, with a cargo of nitrate, she suddenly, terrifyingly, burst into flames. Her crew escaped, but their ship was utterly consumed. No doubt the fire had started by spontaneous combustion and run along the bags of nitrate in the hold, acting like a torch to ignite them. Every scrap of woodwork in her was burnt away, leaving only a steel skeleton. Her charred bones were taken in tow by a tug and hauled on to the shingle beach of Deal, fire-hardened nitrate clinging to her remains like lava to the corpses of Pompeii. The only luck in this case was that of *Micronesia*'s owner, who had providentially insured her for £13,000, though she was only worth £6,000.

A very curious thing happened to the Norwegian ship *Turiste* as she lay in Barry Dock, Cardiff, on 6 October, 1896, doing no harm to anybody. It did not seem possible, in that peaceful spot, that any accident could happen to her. Around her, in the water, large baulks of timber were idly floating. One of them got caught under her keel and by some mysterious agency heaved her partially out of the water, heeled her over, and left her derelict.

Then there was the barge *Edward*, another example of bad luck befalling the innocent well-doer. She had brought supplies to a great ship which lay in dock, and was moored alongside. As the tide fell, the monster lazily rolled slightly to one side, like a basking whale, and crushed to matchsticks the unfortunate *Edward*, the quay wall acting as the other arm of the nutcracker.

History does not tell us, in the case of older ships, what figureheads they bore. It may be that their good or evil fortune was in the keeping of those beautiful carvings, with their air of power and resolution. To walk through the Hall of Neptune at Greenwich, the Victory Museum, Portsmouth, or the figurehead collection on the *Cutty Sark* is to find oneself in the presence of superhuman personalities strong enough to have survived their ships and generations of crews. It is difficult not to believe that they had an influence on the vessels whose names they bore.

What malignant nymph was that lovely figurehead who was found floating in the sea on 4 November, 1861, among the bodies of those who had been aboard the *Maritana*, a square-rigger approaching Boston from Liverpool? In a pitch-black night and a snowstorm she ran on to the terrible Shag Rocks, and was destroyed. The keeper of the Boston Light thought he had spotted another corpse, and a boat went out and brought the body aboard. But it was a pretty, smiling female figurehead, woman-size — so charming that it was not chopped up for firewood, as too often happened to figureheads that would be priceless today. Besides, she had a certain patriotic significance in Boston: she had been part of a French warship, *Le Berceau*, captured by an American vessel. They kept the figurehead for her beauty and fine carving, and built her into a new craft. The ship went down on her maiden voyage.

Once again the figurehead was rescued, and transferred to a ship which promptly sank, with heavy loss of life. The wooden maiden came up smiling sweetly as ever, and beguiled her rescuers into keeping her. By 1857 they had forgotten all about her previous bad record. She was given command of the *Maritana* — with fatal results four years later.

After this she was kept on land. The Bostonians must have been extraordinarily trusting people. They put her up on Lincoln Wharf as a decoration, and there she stayed, like Patience on a monument, smiling at Grief, until fire swept through the wharf and destroyed it. But not, of course, the figurehead.

Pleased to have their relic still intact, they put her in the Old State House for safety. It caught fire; the figurehead was saved.

Many people by this time would have reached for the axe, but the Bostonians were more tolerant. They restored the enchantress to a position of honour, and accidents and disasters continued to occur in her vicinity with monotonous regularity. It was even said in the early 1880s that a white figure resembling her was seen strolling by night on the quay: surely the only ghost of a figurehead to be seen without its ship in the whole history of the sea.

Perhaps the whole thing was the revenge of a determined Frenchwoman on the enemies of her country who had captured *Le Berceau*.

Another lady who led her ship to destruction was seven feet high, crowned with laurel and wearing a dress patterned with green stripes. Found floating in the Atlantic in 1854, she was thought by many to have been the figurehead of the ill-fated *City of Glasgow*, the emigrant vessel which vanished without trace between Liverpool and the New World. Others said she belonged to the *Shandon*, another total loss. Whatever her ship, she had been the very opposite of a mascot to it.

It is surely small wonder that sailors are a splendid market for good-luck charms, or that superstition means more to them than to landsmen. Perhaps this is not so much the case in these enlightened, mechanized days. But at one time it was thought desperately unlucky to have a corpse on board — or, even farther back, a woman. Cats were lucky: to kill one meant endless misfortune. The same rule applied to stormy petrels and albatrosses, though Coleridge is supposed by some people to have invented the legend on which *The Rime of the Ancient Mariner* is based.

There is the true tale of a "growler" — what would be called today a chip-carrier — on a ship homeward bound from Portland, Oregon. He had something to complain of in all his shipmates — even the ship's friendly, playful black cat. One day, incensed by having seen a young sailor playing a game with the cat and a ball of twine, he called the cat down from the rigging and threw it into the sea. Next day, at dawn, a gale blew up — and from almost the position where the cat had been, the "growler" fell to his death. And serve him right, said most of the crew.

Even in the radar age, perhaps one may still note that:

> ...*sailors eye their mates and catch their breath,*
> *And talk with fear of hatches overturned,*
> *Knives stuck in masts, and low blue lights that burned*
> *But yestereve about the weather-vane;*
> *Of many foundered ships that tried in vain*
> *To run a Friday's voyage; of drowned cats,*
> *And vessels out of which the auguring rats*
> *Decamped when last in port; of sneezes done*
> *To left — night-squealing pigs, and whistling on*
> *The bow by thoughtless lads ... and other things*
> *Which fill the sailor's mind with murmurings,*
> *And speak to him of wrecks.*

One of history's unluckiest ships was the steamer *Triumph*, which, on a calm, clear night in 1883, rammed an island virtually at the foot of New Zealand's most powerful lighthouse. Admittedly, her master and crew were described as "a set of thorough-paced lubbers"; but is the rest of her appalling record due only to coincidence? She was: run ashore in China; grounded off New Zealand again; sunk and refloated in the Tyne; sunk and refloated in the Clyde; wrecked and abandoned on the Norwegian coast; salvaged, then sunk and refloated in a Florida port. She lies at the bottom of the Mediterranean, where, as the trooper *Hilonian*, she was sent by a U-boat in 1918.

BIBLIOGRAPHY

Contemporary periodicals and volumes of The Annual Register for the appropriate years.

Armstrong, Warren, *Last Voyage*, Frederick Muller, 1956

Benwell G. and Waugh, A., *Sea Enchantress*, Hutchinson, 1961

Bradford, Ernie, *Drake*, Hodder & Stoughton, 1965

Bridges, T. C., *The Book of the Sea*, Harrap, 1927

Bridges, T. C., *Romances and Mysteries of the Sea*, Newnes, 1940

Bywater, Hector C., *Their Secret Purposes*, Constable, 1932

Crocker, Sir William Charles, *Far from Humdrum*, Hutchinson, 1967

De la Croix, Robert, *Mysteries of the North Pole*, Frederick Muller, 1954

De la Croix, Robert, *Ships That Did Not Return*, Frederick Muller, 1959

De la Croix, Robert, *Mysteries of the Sea*, Frederick Muller, 1956

Dunbabin, Thomas, *Slavers of the South Seas*, 1935

Elias, E. L., *The Book of Polar Exploration*, Harrap, 1928

Gould, Charles, *Mythical Monsters*, W. H. Allen, 1886

Hadfield, Robert L., *The Phantom Ship*, Bles, 1937

Hampshire, A. Cecil, *They Called it Accident*, William Kimber, 1961

Hutton, J. Bernard, *Frogman Extraordinary*, Neville Spearman, 1960

Kirby, Percival R., *The True Story of the "Grosvenor" East Indiaman*, O.U.P., 1960

Masters, David, *When Ships Go Down*, Eyre & Spottiswoode, 1934

Maugham, Robin, *The "Joyita" Mystery*, Max Parrish, 1962

Peter Freuchen's Book of the Seven Seas, Cape, 1958

Roden, Hans, *Treasure Seekers*, Harrap, 1966

Snow, Edward Rowe, *Sea Mysteries and Adventures*, Alvin Redman, 1964

Taylor, Joseph, *Remarkable Providences*, Hatchard, 1821

Uncle Hardy, *Notable Shipwrecks*, Cassell, Petter & Galpin, *c.* 1875

Valentine, L., *Heroes of the British Navy*, Warne, *c.* 1900

Villiers, Alan, *Of Ships and Men*, Newnes, 1962

Whymper, F., *The Sea* (4 vols.), Cassell, *c.* 1885

The authors wish to thank Rear-Admiral P. V. McLaughlin, CB, DSO, for his assistance with the chapter on the Tobermory treasure; and Mr. J. Bernard Hutton, for permission to extract material from his book *Frogman Extraordinary* regarding Commander Crabb.

A NOTE TO THE READER

If you have enjoyed this book enough to leave a review on **Amazon** and **Goodreads**, then we would be truly grateful.
The Estate of Michael and Mollie Hardwick

Sapere Books is an exciting new publisher of brilliant fiction and popular history.

To find out more about our latest releases and our monthly bargain books visit our website: **saperebooks.com**

Made in the USA
Columbia, SC
08 March 2024

32739058R00163